Adolescent Vulnerability

a sympathetic look at the frailties and limitations of youth

John J. Mitchell

Detselig Enterprises Ltd.

Calgary, Alberta, Canada

Canadian Cataloguing in Publication Data

Mitchell, John J., 1941-
    Adolescent vulnerability

Includes bibliographic references.
ISBN 1-55059-128-2

1.   Adolescent psychology.   I.   Title.
BF724.M57   1995   155.5   C95-911079-8

Detselig Enterprises Ltd.
210-1220 Kensington Rd. N.W.
Calgary, Alberta, T2N 3P5

Detselig Enterprises Ltd. appreciates the financial assistance received for its 1995 publishing program from the Department of Canadian Heritage and the Alberta Foundation for the Arts, a beneficiary of
the Lottery Fund of the Government of Alberta.

COMMITTED TO THE DEVELOPMENT OF CULTURE AND THE ARTS

Cover Design by Bill Matheson

Printed in Canada   SAN 115-0324

ISBN 1-55059-128-2

Contents

Acknowledgments

My indebtedness to friends and colleagues who helped me with this book is far greater than I can express in this short space.

Much of this book was written while I was the recipient of the University of Alberta's McCalla Research Professorship. The time I was able to devote to research during the year of this award made this book possible.

My father, Robert Vincent Mitchell, contributed helpful editorial assistance, as he has to all of my books over the past three decades. Several colleagues at the University of Alberta, especially David Wangler and Bruce Bain, offered solid assistance with several of the chapters. Joanne Tessier was instrumental in shaping the ideas presented in the chapters on narcissism and the narcissistic attitude. Her research on the Narcissus myth helped me to better organize my ideas on this topic.

Last, and most important, I gratefully acknowledge the 150 young people who shared their feelings, their thoughts, and their secrets with me over the past three years. From my interviews with these young people I have come to a deeper understanding of adolescent vulnerability.

J. J. Mitchell
University of Alberta
December, 1995

Preface

This book explores vulnerability among the young. Lacking a better phrase, I refer to these ideas and their connections as "the inherent corruptibility of youth." This book also explores our responsibility to provide youth with productive involvement and meaningful participation in the important machinery of society; and, equally, our need to help them to recognize their social responsibilities and to assume their rightful obligations within the shared community in which they live and grow.

At this moment in time we desperately need a more realistic assessment of young people's need for assistance in the growing-up process. This means that we need an open-eyed examination of their self-destructive habits and a straightforward recognition of their limited ability to prevent pregnancy and the physical and emotional pathology associated with it. We would also benefit, I believe, from a deeper appreciation of the legitimate rights of youth, and, simultaneously, from higher expectations concerning their obligations to their parent society. In sum, we need a more enlightened vision of how youth can lead richer, more productive lives.

The lessons we have learned so well, and have taken to heart, about the other great developmental stages (infancy, toddlerhood, preschool, middle childhood) seem to elude us when our children reach adolescence. The first rule of human survival, that parents provide for the best interests of their children, is strangely abandoned when our children turn 14, 15, or 16. A parent who carries her sick child through a freezing winter storm to obtain the medical treatment she needs, will, thirteen years later, stand idly by while this same daughter risks pregnancy, school expulsion, and drug addiction, all of which, by every impartial standard, are more severe in their consequence (at least in North America) than most childhood illnesses.

We see the features which inch budding youth into young adults as beacons proving they no longer need the advice, the direction, and the love they needed as children. Nothing could be further from the truth, for it is during adolescence that pitfalls take their most tragic toll. And, in this regard, we are distinct from all previous generations. Today we have mastered many of the tragedies which befall children but no such progress inoculates against the tragedies which plague adolescents.

I do not count myself among those who argue that adolescents are immature juveniles to be sheltered from responsibilities or obligations. Quite the contrary. I am among those who champion the strength, the vitality, and the resilience of youth, but who, at the same time, recognize that youth have responsibilities to their parent society. In *The Adolescent Predicament* (1975), I documented how our culture unfairly trivializes the adolescent experience, and why adolescents require meaningful, tangible work, (beneficial not only to them but to the entire society) to build decent, legitimate self-esteem. Throughout the '80s I worked with The National Commission on Resources for Youth, an organization dedicated to the proposition that teens benefit immeasurably from volunteer work, from serving as tutors to younger kids, and working on construction projects such as renovating low-income housing. As well, I have served as a consultant, and a resource person for the National Center for Service Learning in Early Adolescence. In my role as Professor of Adolescent Psychology at the University of Alberta, I have been an advocate of the Carnegie Council on Adolescent Development's Task Force on Education of Young Adolescents.

From these experiences I have learned something about the skills and talents, the vulnerabilities and the frailties of youth. But I have also learned that no improvement in the destiny of our youth will be made until we leave behind the graveyard of banalities we presently call "adolescent psychology" and begin to honestly acknowledge the risks our children face in their everyday lives. Perhaps more than ever before in our history, the young need the guidance, the wisdom, and the compassion which only adults can provide.

J.J. Mitchell
University of Alberta

Introduction

the inherent corruptibility of youth

"It is dangerous to show man too often that he is equal to beasts, without showing him his greatness. It is also dangerous to show him too frequently his greatness without his baseness. But, it is very desirable to show him the two together."   Blaise Pascal

My concern in this book is not so much with corruption as with corruptibility. The differences between the two may appear slight, but at least in my estimation, they are significant. Corruption has to do with the outside forces and influences which have a corrupting effect, whereas corruptibility has to do with characteristics inherent to what (or who) is being corrupted. The language of corruption is troublesome for most educators and youth professionals because implicit to it are images of that which is spoiled, tainted, infected; images which do not fit comfortably with the real, living, breathing people with whom they are so deeply concerned. These distressing images of corruptibility, however, are not inappropriate when one is attempting to understand the adolescent experience as it is lived in North America. In this book I will try to explain why I believe this is so.

Corruptibility, we should recognize from the start, does not mean evil, or wickedness, or depravity; it means *vulnerability* to corruption. The idea is more Rousseauvian than Hobbesian, which is only to say that it is not based on any concept of innate wickedness. As Rousseau expressed it in his classic essay on the origin of inequality: "let us not conclude that because man has no idea of goodness, he must naturally be wicked; that he is vicious because he does not know virtue." And, as far as adolescents are concerned, Rousseau gives us good advice.

What we are dealing with are the differences between innate corruption and the vulnerability to corruption. These are two ideas of completely different merit. The first idea, that youth (or children) are innately corrupt implies an inevitable condition, and brings to mind something akin to hereditary determinism, and therefore, in my opinion, deserves to be discarded. This, I believe, is what Ashley Montagu was getting at when he claimed:

> The view that the child is born . . . evil, in 'sin' is widely held, and it is nothing more than a projection upon the child of our own conditioning . . . in evil, in 'sin'. The alleged innate depravity of the child is not supported by the facts (1966, p. 89).

The latter idea, that youth are *vulnerable to corruption*, is, as I see it, a demonstrable fact. Indeed, much of this book is dedicated to demonstrating the "what, where, when, and why" of adolescent vulnerability.[1]

I do not assume that youth are inherently virtuous, nor do I assume that they are inherently wicked; but I *do* assume that many of their good habits are susceptible to erosion and deterioration, and that they easily shift from good to bad in morals, manners, and actions. I also assume that, because of these predispositions, it is the moral responsibility of adults to assist youth in negotiating the minefield adolescence has become in the past few decades.

My starting point in this investigation of adolescent vulnerability is the thought process itself.

The adolescent thought process

"All rising to a great place is by a winding stair."	Francis Bacon

The vulnerability of youth, in great measure, is the result of their limited success with clear, coherent thinking. In chapters one through four I discuss the strengths and weaknesses, the peaks and valleys, of the adolescent thought process. Chapters one and two are rather straightforward reviews of the academic theories and psychological research which have transported us to our present understanding of how adolescents think and reason. Chapters three and four have a different slant, they spotlight some of the forces within the thought process which narrow, becloud, and contaminate thinking.

The starting point for most investigations of the adolescent thought process since Jean Piaget splashed his signature across developmental psychology, is "formal thought" – the cluster of mental attributes which give adolescent intellectualism its defining qualities. These defining qualities of adolescent thought include:

- the capacity to deal with both realities and possibilities;

- the capacity to utilize hypotheses, verification, experimental control, and other subsets of scientific reasoning; and,

- the capacity to hold several ideas in mind at once and combine them in logical ways.

Adolescents, quite obviously, do not always use formal thought to its maximum potential. Sometimes they rely upon more primitive thought forms ("concrete" thought), and sometimes they, bewilderingly, prefer not to think at all. To further complicate things, formal thought does not answer to only one master: it serves both the rational demands of objective reason *and* the emotional needs of the self. Therefore, in its everyday expression, formal thought is sometimes objective and well-reasoned, but sometimes it is used merely to protect self-interests, even to deceive or falsify. Finally, as all educators know, formal thought does not spring forth in full blossom; considerable practice, coaching, and patience are required before it is utilized.

Egocentrism exerts such a powerful influence on adolescent thought that it is impossible to discuss one without the other. To be egocentric is to be insensitive to the concerns of others; it is a mixture of imperviousness to, and unawareness of, issues beyond the circumference of self. Its "pure" form is expressed in the characteristic self-centredness of children who, seemingly, reduce all experiences to their point of view and thereby distort without realizing it. Such extreme egocentrism also typifies, although to a lesser degree, the thought of adolescents.

To say that thought improves evenly and uniformly during adolescence involves certain violations of the true picture. In fact, adolescent thought is darkened by a series of "beclouding tendencies" (discussed in chapter four), including:

- The tendency to regress to concrete thought; that is, the tendency to use thought which focuses on the real rather than on the ideal, which emphasizes the present rather than the future, which fixates on small segments rather than comprehensive wholes, which promotes specific conclusions without checking out the methods by which the conclusions were derived.

- The tendency to be persuaded by affective logic (a narcissistically imbued form of thinking in which connections are forged on the basis of their emotional significance).

- The tendency to reason from a premise of entitlement.

- The tendency to distort arguments through emotionalizing and egocentrification.

- The tendency to use reason only to further one's personal interests or to justify one's actions.

Selfishness and self-ish-ness[2]

Of the three domains to which I have directed this investigation (the domain of thought, the domain of self, and the domain of relationships) the domain of the self presents the most serious theoretical complications and the gravest practical contradictions. For these reasons, and a few others, it is also the most exciting.

I want to make clear that my emphasis on egocentrism and narcissism is not merely a return to selfism, nor a plea to reduce morality to selfish ethics. (Ayn Rand enthusiasts will find no fodder here.) Rather, it is an attempt to ascribe to adolescent motivation the rightful importance of selfishness and self-interest. And while this approach may provide us with certain insights not forthcoming in other analyses, it poses fresh difficulties as well.

Part of the problem is that we simply don't understand in any dignified way self-importance during adolescence; we are far too little concerned with *what the adolescent feels important about*. And, quite frankly, social workers, probation officers, high school teachers, and, of course, parents, are exhausted from dealing with youngsters whose sense of importance has been corrupted by consumerism, by violence, and, in the case of teen pregnancy, by fables and fantasies about having a baby.

Worthy self-importance, in contrast to the mere self-inflation which so often passes for it, flows from two primary sources: the esteem and respect one *earns*; and, the constructive, worthwhile things one actually does. In the adolescent community, however, little opportunity arises either to build useful products or to assert oneself affirmatively. As a society we, in the words of Beatrix Hamburg, President of the William T. Grant Foundation, simply do not provide youth with opportunities "to act adult in positive ways." As a consequence of our failure to provide meaningful work and meaningful participation, consumer goods, peer approval, and primitive intimacy are avenues to self-inflation which youth travel. As much as anything, the lack of legitimate self-importance contributes to the vulnerability of youth in modern society.

Friendships and relationships

In chapters eight through twelve, day-to-day survival in the social world of teens is investigated. My observations on this topic are not comprehensive, but they do touch upon dimensions of the adolescent experience overlooked in most traditional approaches. The main thrust of these chapters has to do with the search for approval, friendship, and intimacy. But with a few twists:

Pertaining to friendship selection: In chapter eight we are concerned with how frustration and tension influence the alliances which are formed during adolescence; and, with how friendship choices are influenced by flattering mirrors, reciprocal rationalization, and particularization.

Pertaining to the young person's quest for approval: (chapter nine). This chapter investigates how consumerism shapes the adolescent's search for approval, and how work-for-pay shapes the psycho-economics of teen approval.

Pertaining to irrational attractions: (chapters eleven and twelve). In these chapters we explore the idea that the magnet in adolescent bondings is not always the human qualities of the person with whom the bond is made, but, rather, with the emotional and erotic energy excited by the bonding.

Pertaining to intimacy and love: (chapter ten). Here we investigate the assumption that *shared* intimacy and *reciprocal* love evolve from the coherence of two combined identities. We also advance the hypothesis that primitive identity tends to produce primitive intimacy, while mature identity tends to produce genuine intimacy.

Here is the heart of the matter. The forces which bring young people together, whether in casual, "buddy" connections or profound intimacy bondings, are not always the forces of light and radiance; sometimes the forces which attract youth to one another are the same forces which eventually erode them.

Our image of youth

Our image of adolescence is amiss today just as our image of children was amiss a century ago. We mistakenly assume that youth will master certain tasks on their own which consistently they do not; and, at the opposite extreme, we assume that our youngsters will avoid self-destructive habits when, consistently, they do not. These misperceptions are not caused merely by devaluation (or over-valuation) of youth's abilities. Rather, they are caused by a pervasive ignorance of how teens think and reason, how they form and dissolve relationships, how they evaluate themselves, how they react to drugs, sex, love, and violence.

Adolescents are a population which, for their own health, require consistent, constructive, decent intervention; the problem is that no one really knows how, or where, or when, or for how long, to intervene. The predicament facing us is that the nature of the intervention cannot be determined until the nature of the client is determined, and it is precisely with the nature of the client that we have our most serious problems. J.S. Musick, in her excellent work on the psychology of teenage motherhood, summarized the situation quite nicely.

> The current solutions have proved to be largely ineffective in bringing about positive change because they are seldom connected to the motivational roots of the problem. *Without a better understanding of the people for whom interventions are designed – a developmental and psychological*

understanding of them as people – there can be no useful understanding of the problems and no basis for solving them (1993, p. 6).

The moratorium

One of Erik Erikson's many contributions to our understanding of human development was his belief that adolescence should be a time of sanctioned freedom and open exploration. He coined the term "moratorium" to mean a period of permissiveness between the juvenile incompetencies of childhood and the full responsibilities of adulthood.

> By psychological moratorium, then, we mean a delay of adult commitments, and yet it is not only a delay. It is a period that is characterized by a selective permissiveness on the part of society and of provocative playfulness on the part of youth, and yet it often leads to deep, if often transitory, commitment on the part of youth, and ends in a more or less ceremonial configuration of commitment on the part of society (cited in Fuhrmann, 1990, p. 359).

The moratorium provides a protected period of experimentation to help young people gain practical experience so that they will be better able to assume personal obligations and to make meaningful commitments to their loved ones, and to their society. Moratorium, then, refers to the "in-between" world in which teens grow, mature, and prepare to meet the world.[3]

> Adolescence is a period in which society takes a relatively hands-off posture, allowing the adolescent to experiment behaviorally and attempt to find himself and his place. The hands-off posture refers to the laxness of society in enforcing rules on adolescents that apply to adults, as well as a general attitude that diminishes responsibility of adolescents relative to adults. The functional reason society takes this stance is to give adolescents time to mature and experience so that when it is time for them to enter the adult world, especially the occupational world, they will be ready, emotionally and educationally (Manaster, 1989, p. 163).

The *written* laws of our culture require the parent society to provide basic health care, to educate, and to protect the young from abuse and neglect. This historical bargain, like Rousseau's social contract, is an agreement in which some personal liberties are surrendered by all parties in return for the benefits of a well-ordered society.[4]

The adolescent wasteland

David Hamburg, president of the Carnegie Foundation, in his Keynote Speech to the Society for Research and Adolescence (1994) spoke of the pervasiveness of youth corruption in modern society. He told a spellbound audience about "the fateful choices" which shape the adolescent years; about "the easy access to life-threatening substances" and how frightening numbers of youth are enticed into behavior which "makes them a lifelong liability to their parent society." He also told his audience that these conditions, taken in their totality, require massive "generic interventions" if we are to avoid further "rotten outcomes."

Hamburg described the failure of youth to comprehend what is involved in mastering the adult roles they will shortly inherit, and their tendency to believe that someone will assume the roles for them if they are too difficult; further, he described the tendency for many young people to think that it simply won't matter if they do not carry out their future roles effectively. In today's society, Hamburg concluded, *the primary obligation of adults is the preventing of youth casualties.* Fateful choices, shared destinies. Here is a man who knows first-hand the vulnerability, and the corruptibility, of youth in modern culture.[5]

The Carnegie Foundation, over the past decade, has been investigating a wide range of behavioral disturbances among the millions of youngsters who inhabit the moratorium. Here, for illustrative purposes, I will highlight a few of the findings they reported in "The burden of illness, ignorance and wasted potentiality" (1986).

In North America about one in four adolescents does not graduate from high school. Statistically, the one dropout is far more likely to receive public assistance and to engage in crime than the three who graduate. One in ten girls becomes pregnant during adolescence. Again, this one girl is more likely to experience long periods of unemployment, to drop out of school, and to require hospitalization than the nine teen-age girls who do not become pregnant. "The pregnancy rate for white American adolescents is more than twice that for teenagers in any other industrialized country. The rate for black girls is almost twice that for white girls" (p. 7). The Center for Population Options estimated that *adolescent child-bearing* cost the United States $16 billion in 1985; current projections (1995) are closer to $24 billion.

Illicit drug use is thought by most experts to be greater in the United States than in any other "moratorium" country in the world. Estimates indicate that about 20 percent of American teens smoke cigarettes daily and about 6 percent consume alcohol *daily.*

Adolescents, because of their need (and desire) for experimentation, are vulnerable to a host of risks. In the short-term they are susceptible to sexually-transmitted diseases and accidents related to alcohol; delayed consequences include cancer and cardiovascular disease in adult life, both of which are encouraged by their high-calorie, high-fat, junk-food diet.

Add all these developmental causalities together, and we see that a substantial fraction of the age cohort is visibly damaged. Adolescent boys are at particular risk, having twice the death rate of adolescent girls. Indeed, until recently, teenagers were the only age group in the society for whom death rates were increasing (p. 7).

The research conducted by the Carnegie Council on Adolescent Development was among the first to document the massive numbers of young people doomed to the worst of the wasteland before they have attained the thinking powers to realize that the wasteland is their destiny. In "Turning Points: Preparing American Youth for the 21st Century," they claimed that the United States faces a youth crisis of greater magnitude than at any time since the Great Depression.

By age 16 substantial numbers of youth show signs they will reach adulthood unable to meet the requirements of the work place, the commitments of relationships in families, and the responsibilities of participation in a democratic society. These youth are among the estimated 7 million young people – one in four adolescents – who are extremely vulnerable to multiple high-risk behaviors and school failure. Another 7 million may be at moderate risk, and they remain a cause for serious concern.

Bad news comes so rapidly when describing the adolescent wasteland that it is instructive to repeat a few of the major points. Approximately one of out every four American adolescents approaches adulthood:

- without the occupational skills to obtain and hold a job;
- without the interpersonal skills to maintain a family;
- without the social skills to carry out the duties of a citizen in a democracy;
- without the confidence to overcome these limitations.

With a predictable consistency these kids hate school, achieve poorly, and do not acquire the literacy skills required for economic advancement. The bottom line is that they lose whatever natural zest for learning humans usually possess during the wonder years, they become alienated from virtually everything that healthy youth are attached to, including their parents, their schools, their community, and their churches. They are lured to drugs by other damaged peers, by the glory of intoxication, or simply the desire to retreat from an environment that the vast majority of people reading this book would never allow their own children to enter even for a day. About 70% of them drop out of school, sealing their economic fate.

The evidence is undeniable that many of our youth are moratorium casualties. Also undeniable is that many youngsters cannot negotiate the demands of life without tremendous assistance from many quarters.

Postscript

While it is true that adolescents share important commonalities with adults, it is also true that they are, in vital ways, profoundly different.[6] All young people are "in-process," which is to say, growing, changing, idling, and improving all at once. And, like children, they cannot be honestly understood except within the developmental structures which shape their humanity. Growth, change, and *improvement* are the defining features of adolescence. In the midst of this swirl young people learn about themselves and their world; however, what they learn, and how they learn, is influenced greatly by the swirl itself. Underlying my thinking on this topic is the assumption that adolescents, like children, are driven by a cluster of developmentally-based needs which shape their personhood.

Taking all this into account, what, then, do we mean when we speak of "the corruptibility of youth"? Essentially, we mean that:

- young people all too easily become less than what they could be, and that their great potential is easily eroded and diminished.

- their natural zest for life can shift into indifference and scorn, that their eagerness to contribute to their family and to their society can be suffocated by the impulse to negate and to destroy.

- their capacity for clear thought is easily contaminated by beclouded, egocentrified thought.

- their natural and wholesome self-ish-ness can deteriorate into chronic, narcissistic selfishness.

- they have, without active assistance from adults and peers, a limited ability to prevent pregnancy.

- especially during early- and middle adolescence, their ability to accurately envision long-term consequences is weak and underdeveloped.

- In sum, that without positive, constructive, and loving intervention they are easily transported into a downward spiral in their behavior and their sociability.

One might reply that these are not new observations, that youth have always defied society and trumpeted themselves, and that they have always been impulsive and driven by short-term concerns. This reply, while thoughtful, is only partly correct. What it lacks is *explanation*. Explanation for defiance, explanation for placing oneself above one's own family and one's own society, explanation for making, in the words of David Hamburg, "selfish, impulsive and ignorant choices."

Explanation for choosing fantasy over fact, for bonding with partners who degrade decency, for taking one's inspiration from fables and fictions. And perhaps most importantly, explanation for the willingness to commit oneself to something less than oneself.

In this book I attempt to provide explanations for these mysterious twists and turns by peering through three windows. The first is the adolescent thought process: how youth think, and how their thinking is vulnerable to misperception and to miscalculation. The second is the adolescent self, especially the growing person's need to establish and protect himself (herself). The third window through which we look into adolescent life is companionship and friendship: how teens make their human connections, whether casual or serious, matter-of-fact or passionate, superficial or intimate.

I have worked diligently to insure that this book is grounded in the factual conditions of youth, and not merely in a Pollyanna vision of their most glorious moments.[7] A very large part of the labor involved in writing this book has been expended on the contradictions which infect our understanding of youth, on our failure to see them as they are. Of special concern to this investigation are the forces which push young people toward an obsessive self-investment, toward an exaggerated preoccupation with their own private interests, and away from the shared cooperation that Alfred Adler called "social interest." For, when all is said and done, these are the critical youth issues not only of our era, but of every era.

Endnotes

[1]   There is no need to overview the theories of human depravity which claim that we humans are driven by genetic (or evolutionary) forces which, somehow, can cause us to be criminals and corruptors of each other's humanity. As near as I can surmise, there is no real benefit to reducing the less worthy in our nature to genetic and biological forces; not merely because to do so contradicts our capacity to govern our lives as self-directing agents, but, more importantly, because the scientific evidence which supports such a determinism is paltry and unconvincing. There is no one-way street between behavior and biology, and everyone, even the sensationalizers, knows it. Robert Ornstein, in *Roots of the Self*, summarized it succinctly:

> whenever the news trumpets some version of "biology affects behavior," it obscures the fact that biology and behavior form a two-way street. Hormones affect sexual drive, for instance, but sexual activity affects hormone levels. An active brain seeks a stimulating environment, but living in a stimulating environment literally changes and enriches the brain. Fatigue and boredom cause poor performance on the job, but stultifying job conditions produce fatigue and boredom.

Scientists and writers who reduce our personalities, problems, and abilities to biology thereby tell only half the story, and miss half the miracle of how human biology works (1992, p. 55).

[2] The term "**self-ish-ness**" takes a bit of getting used to. I find it useful when trying to distinguish between the self-concerns natural to adolescence and the selfishness of selfish people. A complete delineation of these terms is undertaken in chapter seven.

[3] The underlying premise of the moratorium is that experimentation and exploration help a young person to cultivate self-knowledge and self-direction, and, hopefully to become more competent and dignified. When either party fails to live up to its end of the bargain (the adolescent fails to mature in the expected direction, or when the society fails to provide the means to dignified identity) problems arise. Society calls these "youth problems" but youth know them as "society problems."

[4] **Youth's obligation to the parent society**: The collective agreement which serves as the legal core of the moratorium makes several demands on the young. First and foremost, it requires them to attend school. Most demands, however, are of exclusion. For example, youth cannot intern or apprentice for meaningful employment in any systematic way. Historically, young people's work had direct continuity with the work they would perform as adults; this is not true today.

Secondly, youth cannot leave their home without parental permission before the age of 16. We no longer tolerate what Edgar Friedenberg called "therapeutic runaways" – youth who leave what they consider to be the deplorable conditions of their household to pursue what they consider greater opportunities.

Third, youth cannot join trade unions. Nor can they, in any legitimate manner, access well-paying jobs before they graduate from high school.

[5] Even though Hamburg directly faces the responsibility of adults to help overcome the young person's vulnerability to corruption, everyone does not. In some circles, to presume to know what is best (or worst) for youth is thought to be "paternalistic"; to assume that adolescents do not solve problems effectively is said to "stigmatize"; to tabulate the medical costs of rescuing their premature babies is thought to "view them as a societal problem rather than a resource."

M. J. Quadrel, et al. (1994) concluded their overview of adolescent vulnerability with a summary which tells us a good deal about the prevailing attitudes among psychologists.

> claims about the incompetence of adolescents... threaten to disenfranchise and stigmatize adolescents. They encourage denying teens the right to govern their own actions, as well as viewing them as a societal problem rather than a resource.... They make teens rather than society responsible for teens' problems. *They place adults in the flattering position of knowing what is right* (1993, p. 114).

Their intent, I presume, was to caution against the unfair trivialization of adolescents and to warn us against holding too narrow a vision of their talents and abilities. Such chivalry brings to mind what in the '60s we called "body wisdom," a concept borrowed from biology which claimed that an organism, left on its own, would grow straight and tall. Perhaps primitive creatures living in a pristine environment honor such unfailing ground plans, but in today's human world this view is nothing more than idealized negligence. The self-destructive options are too bountiful and too available for everyone, including teens. And while it may be true, as Quadrel, et al. suggest, that pointing out the corruptibility of the young is a form of "paternalism" which threatens to "disenfranchise and stigmatize" them, and that such accuracy of reporting may deny teens "the right to govern their own actions," we must, in the name of honesty and compassion, report that many of our children do not fare very well when left to their own resources. We can deny indignantly that our youth need guidance and direction, but we cannot deny the daily evidence which proves that they are hurting.

[6]   **Identity beyond adolescence.** Researchers investigating what is variously called "maturity," "psychological health," or "competence" recognize adolescence as a starting rather than a finishing point. Abraham Maslow, an influential early investigator, claimed he would not even look at adolescents if he were selecting mature, self-actualized persons to study. His reasoning was that they are simply too immature to serve as acceptable subjects.

Throughout adulthood we tend to increase in our potential for symbolization, that is, for putting our experiences into symbolic form, whether words, music, art, dance, or gesture. During adulthood the personality tends to become more allocentric, more attuned to issues beyond itself. As a result, adults seem better able to focus long term energy on a valued goal. In essence, becoming more allocentric entails the increasing ability to take a multiplicity of perspectives toward a problem, the humanization of values, and the development of cooperative relationships (Heath, 1977).

Attaining increased maturity also means becoming more integrated. Coherence and synthesis become more integral to our nature, and as well a certain internal logic to personal values, ambitions and actions begins to manifest itself. Closely allied is the adult tendency to become more stable and autonomous. Stability enhances self regulation and releases energy for other life demands, rendering the person more able to effectively deal with the problems of life, love and work. In sum, a great deal of social growth and emotional maturity occurs *after* adolescence.

[7]   The '50s image of teen-agers as innocent youth toying with emotional bewilderment is ancient history, even though, like all history, its lessons are instructive. The age of teen innocence was cancelled at some unknown moment in our recent history when the adult community excluded youth from important work and from community relevance, and when the adolescent community, in turn, dropped duty and responsibility from its agenda and replaced them with demands for greater entitlements and broader rights.

Section I

some prefatory comments

At the heart of the issue we find a mystery which, loosely presented, reads something like this: Are the limitations of the human thought process – its fables and fictions, its denials and oversights, its selective spotlighting – generic to all humans? Or, are important differences to be found among different groups of people?

The answer to this mystery is easy if one chooses the right groups for comparison. The most convincing differences are between children and adults. On this score the evidence is undeniably compelling: adults are more adept than children at reasoning, more gifted at propositional thinking, and more adroit at all forms of abstract thinking. The mystery becomes murkier, however, when we substitute adolescents for children. Here the controversy heats up because the mental gap between teens and their parents is much narrower, everyone agrees, than between young children and their parents.

In Section I a good deal of time and effort is invested in this mystery. The underlying assumption which guides our investigation is that adolescents *are inclined to* (not the same as rigidly locked into) mental and perceptual habits which increase the probability that they will make inappropriate (even destructive) choices when more appropriate alternatives are readily available.

However, simply because adolescents are inclined to faulty thinking does not mean that their thinking, in general, is flawed. Quite the contrary, *in general terms*, the thinking abilities of adolescents are excellent. The irony is that the richness and the poverty of their thought co-exist in the same intellectual reservoir, intermingling in an enchanting rhythm, alternatively enriching and impoverishing the other. The point to seize is that when we focus on one part of this ecological rhythm we must not deny the existence, or the power, of the other.

To me it is self-evident that certain intellectual strengths and weaknesses are best explained in developmental terms, that is, in terms of qualities inherent to age and maturity. In chapters one though four I suggest that the thought process itself places adolescents at a disadvantage in dealing with the hard realities of daily life. In these chapters I do not suggest that teens are incapable of thinking effectively because, quite obviously, they *are* capable. Rather, I try to describe some of the mental habits which get in the way of clear, effective thought.

This book is one part of a larger trend among contemporary researchers to investigate an issue which Jean Jacques Rousseau made much of two hundred years ago: the relative importance of intellect and character in human conduct. We are now beginning to re-examine this old issue with a fresh urgency because from many quarters we are hearing that, in the young, intellect without character is far worse than character without intellect. As we shall see, this is an idea worthy of our consideration.

Chapter One

the thought process during childhood and adolescence

"When I approach a child, he inspires two sentiments; tenderness for
what he is and respect for what he may become."   Louis Pasteur

---

Although it may not be customary to begin with a confession, I
would like to do so just to set the record straight: it is my belief that
anyone who claims to know exactly how children think, or, for that
matter, exactly how anyone thinks, is an imposter. To report what
children say or do, or to describe the mistakes they typically produce,
is not too difficult; but to know exactly *how* they think is another thing
altogether.

On the other hand, it is only fair to report that we do know a good
deal about how children think, especially with regard to the patterns
they prefer and the problem solving strategies they employ at different
ages. All professionals in the discipline of child psychology accept that
we cannot avoid the inherent complexity of this topic simply because
we cannot fathom it in its entirety. We must work with what we know
if we are to better understand the inner workings of children. But one
thing we do know with certainty: the thought process of the adolescent
cannot be grasped without first understanding the thinking of children.

In my attempt to describe these processes I do not promote exclusively any particular "school," or cling to any single theory; as a result,
I have more trouble than many (far too many) with the "how" and
"why" of children's thinking. And while it is true that the themes in this
chapter reflect my respect for the vital ideas pioneered by Jean Piaget,
the tenor is decidedly more descriptive than theoretical, and more
eclectic than monolithic.

*   *   *   *

As near as we are able to surmise, young children (four- to eight-
year-olds, for example) are essentially unaware of the process which
directs their mental lives; this "unawareness" of their own thought is
one of the defining features of their intellectualism, their personality,
their innocence, their charming candor. It seems clear, at least at this
moment, that children have only limited awareness of how they solve
mental problems, how solutions are triggered, and how to assess the
effectiveness of their thought by any measure other than consequences.
As Robert Ornstein (1993) expressed it: "There is a great deal of psycho-

logical research that shows that children don't grow up directly knowing what they are thinking" (p. 3). Neither, it appears, are children particularly good at beckoning a mental strategy when there is no compelling reason to do so. These are not ground-breaking observations; if you are patient, in the right setting with cooperative children, they will let you know, in one way or another, that this is how they operate.

In this chapter children's thinking is not an end in itself. My hope is that by describing the thinking of children I will be better able to describe the thinking of adolescents. With these all too brief prefatory comments behind us, let us see what we can learn from a general overview of children's thinking.

Concrete thought: A profile of the thinking process in children 6 or 7 through 11 or 12 years

The thought that characterizes children of the age we are concerned with here is known, in certain circles, as *concrete thought*. This term, coined by Jean Piaget, was intended to convey thought dominated by real objects processed through a fairly rigid mental apparatus. Concrete thought, though primitive when compared with adolescent thought, nevertheless represents a considerable advance over previous thinking; during the period of concrete thought children acquire mental rules which allow them to make better sense of the physical world; importantly, they begin to grasp classes, relations, quantities, and mental representations.[1]

In previous stages younger children learn to operate physically on the environment, and to internally represent static states. When they acquire concrete thought they are better able to manipulate mentally their internal representations, much as they earlier had become better able to manipulate physical objects. These internalized actions make thinking more powerful and more precise. Two features of operations are that they are reversible and that they are organized with other operations into larger systems. When we say that an operation is reversible we mean that its steps can be executed in reverse order and, therefore, the original situation can be recreated. When we say that operations are organized into larger systems we mean that the child is able to combine several different ways of looking at a problem and recognize their implications for each other.

With regard to *classes*, concrete thinkers learn to deal with the whole and parts of the whole at the same time. For example, if a boy not yet at the stage of concrete thought is asked, "Are there more boys or more children in the theatre?" he may answer that there are more boys, more girls, or more children. His answer is unpredictable because he has difficulty thinking about a class and its subclasses (that is, the whole and the parts) at the same time. With the advent of concrete thinking, the boy recognizes that children must outnumber boys because boys are only one of two subclasses (the other being girls) that compose the class known as "children."

With regard to *relations* the child comes to understand, for example, that brightness is a relative phenomenon. A 60-watt light bulb is bright in relation to a 40-watt bulb but not in relation to a 1000-watt bulb, and the same 60-watt bulb could be the brightest in a group of three bulbs. This recognition makes relative comparisons more effective, and absolutes less necessary. The concrete thinker becomes aware that the world is filled with phenomena related to one another comparatively. This mental promotion is why very few 10-year-olds believe that Dad is the strongest person in town while most 5-year-olds do!

During the stage of concrete thought children accept that quantity remains the same even when its shape is altered. For example, the nursery-school child usually believes that if the liquid in a short, wide jug is poured into a tall, thin jug, the latter actually contains more liquid. Because the liquid assumes a different shape, the child infers that the quantity also has been changed. During mid-childhood children learn that quantities remain the same regardless of the shape they assume. Piaget, and virtually everyone since, refers to this as "conservation."

Youngsters who grasp conservation find humor in this ditty:
Susy and her friend went into the restaurant and ordered a pizza. The waiter asked "Shall I slice it into four pieces or six pieces?" Susy replied: "Four pieces, please. We're not hungry enough to eat six pieces."

Pre-concrete thinkers (four- and five-year-olds) don't understand. They might laugh if they suspect it really is a joke, but they usually think it's about pizza. They fail completely to recognize that the sum of the parts (at least when pizza is the topic) cannot be greater than the whole.

In sum, during the stage of concrete thought three important acquisitions advance the intellect of the child:

- the ability to think about a whole entity and parts of the entity simultaneously;
- the ability to understand that some realities acquire their qualities only in relation to the qualities of another reality (that is, for a light to be brighter, it must be "more bright" than another light);
- the ability to understand that quantity does not change simply because its appearance has been changed.

Why children are primitive thinkers

"A child of five would understand this. Send somebody to fetch a child
of five."   Groucho Marx

"Primitive" is a loaded term. Especially in today's intellectual
climate where every term with hierarchical implications is fervently
criticized. I use this term because it has a long history in developmental
psychology. Primitive infers the beginning of a developmental progression, a condition which, by its nature, will advance, mature, grow, and
develop beyond itself. Therefore, we say the embryo is more primitive
than the fetus, the newborn more primitive than the one-year-old, that
"toddling" is a primitive form of walking, that holophrasis is a primitive
form of speech, that trial and error is a primitive form of problem-solving. The primitive form stands in contrast to the sophisticated form;
during childhood *every* form is primitive when compared with advances to follow. So long as we direct our attention to the growth and
development in store, primitive loses its negative tone. The concrete
thinker will eventually mature to a more advanced status; until that
promotion, however, thought is primitive when compared with formal
thinkers, yet sophisticated when compared with pre-concrete thinkers.

We really do not know with unfailing certainty what concrete
thinkers are *capable* of achieving. We do know, however, that concrete
thought focuses primarily on the real, the physical, and the observable;
its strength lies in organizing facts as they are presented rather than in
evaluating how the facts were established. Seven- and eight-year-olds
tend to be practical, here-and-now, and to concentrate on what "is" and
on how to engineer it to immediate ends. A child's intelligence, in most
regards, is a practical intelligence; the wings which will allow it to soar
beyond immediacy and practicality are still sprouting.

Good journalists must report to their readers the "who, what,
when, where, why and how" of a story. Concrete thinkers cannot handle
this entire mandate because their thinking is monopolized by "who,
what, where, and when," but it is poorly equipped to negotiate "why"
and "how." They are not yet fluent with origins, causes, means, degrees,
method, purpose, motives – the very stuff of how and why.

Concrete thinkers rarely approach complex questions by analyzing all of the possible solutions inherent to the question; rather, they
respond to the first or second conclusion derived from piecing together
the available clues. Because of this predisposition to hastily choose one
solution, rather than to investigate more of the total possibilities, concrete thinkers are easily lured into viewing only one side of an issue or
basing their conclusions on only a small particle of the total evidence.
Hence, *concrete thought lacks comprehensiveness.* Because of this lack they
rarely attain the depth of perception which comes from exhaustively

investigating a problem in totality. This limitation within their thought process, ironically, allows them to offer solutions to highly complex problems which baffle adults or adolescents who recognize that before a solution can be offered all relevant variables must be considered. Having no obligation to thoroughness, concrete thinkers find complex problems easy.

Abstract meanings may escape the concrete thinker.[2] For example, if you ask a six- or seven-year-old to interpret the proverb "You can lead a horse to water, but you can't make it drink," the responses might make you cringe. The child may say that you shouldn't force animals to drink, that horses naturally locate water, or some such literal response. Hypothetical problems also confuse concrete thinkers. "If horses had six legs could they run faster?" Many kids draw a blank to this kind of question because it requires them to hypothesize something they know is false. They might reply "Horses don't have six legs." Contrary-to-fact propositions are especially difficult. ("If you lived one hundred years ago would you be happier than you are now?"). Concrete thinkers are not much good at making their own thought the object of investigation, hence they do not think very systematically about their own thoughts. Introspection is not a trademark of their mental lives.

Even though concrete thinkers reason from general to specific (deductive reasoning), and from specific to general (inductive reasoning), their deployment of logic is deficient because they *do not assemble evidence impartially.* When data support their hypotheses, concrete thinkers show a good deal of "objectivity" – or so it may appear to an outside observer. As soon as the evidence goes against them, however, concrete thinkers may simply reject it. Not until the advent of formal thought does the young person recognize that *evidence* determines whether one accepts or rejects an hypothesis.

In their arguments concrete thinkers are restricted by several limitations. First, they are limited to arguing for things they believe in or against things they oppose; they have only a budding capacity to test one thought against another, or to test their ideas against facts. Unlike adolescents, they cannot argue persuasively against their own belief system. They usually do not recognize the inner logic which validates a coherent argument, and for this reason they usually are surprised when they hear from a teacher or a parent that they have made a good point in an argument.

Children are so obsessed with finding answers to every question that they easily succumb to ridiculous explanations. Superstitious beliefs are epidemic. Nine-year-olds may understand molecular structures but also disapprove of opening an umbrella inside the house because of the tragedy that befalls people who do it. Lack of an explanation for the superstition does not dampen their conviction that the superstition is true.

Youngsters carry a planet of false information gleaned from misinformed peers. A bright eight-year-old may cling to the belief that Chinese are able to live for months without eating or that some horses can fly, if this information was provided by an apparently smart friend. Ten-year-olds somehow believe that vacant houses are inhabited by eccentric old-timers who stalk about after midnight. Curiosity generally triumphs over apprehension (as was also true in toddlerhood) and eventually a gang will investigate the house, bringing back intellectually disappointing but emotionally consoling information.

Though more advanced than during the preschool years, logic remains crude, hit-and-miss, and only marginally effective. Eight-year-olds stumble into just about every kind of logical inconsistency imaginable. Aristotle must have winced in chagrin at their total misuse of syllogism; children are able to draw a conclusion from a premise, but frequently it makes no sense to an adult. Middle-years children also use their intellect to protect their own feelings (a skill which attains state-of-the-art proficiency during early-adolescence). They use others as scapegoats and *invent reasons* to prove that a disliked classmate is really an unworthy person. Not until late-adolescence do many youth fully accept that the powers of the mind *should not* be used to deny the rights of others.

From what we have said thus far it will come as no surprise that children are not gifted at theorizing, that they are not system builders. As with so many other more advanced mental operations, assembling ideas and concepts into a coherent structure awaits formal thought. On this matter, Piaget noted:

> The child does not build systems. His spontaneous thinking may be more or less systematic (at first to a small degree, later much more so); but it is the observer who sees the system from outside, while the child is not aware of it since he never thinks about his own thoughts. . . . In contrast, the adolescent is able to analyze his own thinking and construct theories. The fact that these theories are oversimplified, awkward, and usually contain very little originality is beside the point (Piaget & Inhelder, 1958).

Despite the advances ushered in by concrete thought, the middle child's thinking is constrained by the following shortcomings:

- thought is primarily directed toward the real and, as a result, tends to overlook the ideal;

- thought is primarily directed toward the present; as a result, the long term implications of ideas are not given thorough consideration;

- thought is directed more toward organizing facts than toward discerning where facts come from; as a result, little mental energy is spent validating the origin of information.

- thought is greatly influenced by authority, and it authenticates information through the proclamations of accepted authority figures.

- thought lacks comprehensiveness; as a result, concrete thinkers are not skilled at seeing "the larger picture"; and

- thought is rigid; as a result, concrete thinkers tend not to double check the process by which their conclusions were derived.

Assimilation and accommodation

Before moving to our discussion of adolescent thought, I would like to make an important side trip to discuss two mental processes which, since Piaget, are known as assimilation and accommodation.

Assimilation is the process of applying established thoughts to a new object or event; blending new perceptions into what one already knows, interpreting new experiences so that they fit within the frame of past experiences. Assimilation is basic to everyone's thought regardless of age; every encounter with a new experience calls it into play. Wadsworth (1989) claims that one might compare our accumulated knowledge to a balloon and assimilation to putting more air in the balloon; when we do this the balloon gets larger, but does not change its fundamental shape. Assimilation, since it is essentially expansionistic, results in the growth of preexisting ideas and concepts.[3]

"Each new mental ability starts off by incorporating the world in a process of egocentric assimilation."   Jean Piaget

However, some new experiences do not fit pre-established categories. Time and again children confront information that cannot be processed within their narrow categories of understanding; such confrontations produce a temporary *disequilibrium* which is resolved only when boundaries expand. For example, when preschoolers discover that other children will take away their toys without permission they are perplexed because these actions do not fit their previous experience. They have trouble assimilating this new experience, and a state of disequilibrium is created; in time they *accommodate*, learning to hide favorite possessions or to anticipate attempts at their expropriation.[3a]

The conflict between past experiences and present realities forces mental expansion for the simple reason that data which do not fit can be processed only when the child *adopts a broader perspective*. Stretching the intellect involves not only new, stimulating experiences but expanding one's mental structures in order to accommodate to them.

Assimilation is the mind's way of "taking in." Just as the body assimilates food through the digestive process, so the mind takes in information. As the body accepts certain nutrients and rejects others, so the mind can only "take in" a class of information which the cognitive system is capable of dealing with at that point. The child's thought process, however, is so fluid that it assimilates information and, at the same time, accommodates it. In essence, these processes of assimilation and accommodation are the means by which knowledge is constructed. And even though the products of this interaction are primitive in the beginning, as when a baby who called all male strangers "Daddy" eventually modifies the schema of "Daddy" so that it includes only one person, they form the structural basis for advanced intellectualism during adolescence.

> During assimilation a person imposes his or her available structure on the stimuli being processed. That is, the stimuli are "forced" to fit the person's structure. In accommodation, the reverse is true. The person is "forced" to change his or her schema to fit the new stimuli. Accommodation accounts for development (a qualitative change), and assimilation accounts for growth (a quantitative change); together they account for intellectual adaptation and the development of cognitive structures (Wadsworth, 1989, p. 15).

Developmentalists accept that cognitive growth proceeds in episodes of assimilation and accommodation throughout the life cycle.[4] In assimilation we fit information into preexisting schemata; in accommodation we change schemata in order to fit new information. Accommodation results in qualitative change in our intellectual structures; assimilation merely adds to the existing structures. And, as we shall see in later chapters, the skill with which one is able to accommodate new ideas, to discard obsolete mental habits, and to recognize the new for what it is, dictates the flow of intellectualism during adolescence. Some of the most painful moments of adolescence occur when the individual must expand and transform their thinking to better meet the changing "facts of life"; the basis for this transformation is accommodation in the thought process.

Formal thought: A profile of the thinking process in youth 12 through 20 years

The cognitive skills of adolescence apply to logic, to form, and for this reason they are known as formal thought. This "form" of thinking advances beyond concrete thought in three important ways.

- Formal thought addresses not only actual realities but theoretical possibilities.

- Formal thought utilizes hypotheses, verification, and other subsets of scientific reasoning.

- Formal thought combines ideas logically; hence, formal thinkers can hold several ideas in mind at once and arrange them in logical ways.

Formal thought resembles concrete thought in two important ways: both involve mental operations and both are reversible. However, in formal thought, operations are organized into more complex schemes; formal operations are really operations on operations. Therefore, thought becomes more intricate, more abstract – and the thinker likewise.[5]

When the young person begins to think logically about hypothetical events he (she) has begun formal operations; thought is no longer confined to as-is reality, it investigates an infinity of "reality possibilities." In Piaget's now classic expression, "reality becomes secondary to possibility." A brief example of the differing strategies employed by concrete thinkers and formal thinkers may help to clarify what we mean when we say that "reality becomes secondary to possibility."

> The child begins his experiments with little foresight and does not have a detailed plan for carrying them out. The concrete operational child does not consider all of the possibilities before he begins. Instead, he is limited to thought concerning empirical results – considering things that are available to immediate perception. He fails to make consistent use of the method of holding constant all factors but one. The part played by possibility is very small indeed; it is restricted to the simple extension of actions already in progress.

In contrast, formal thinkers employ more elaborate strategies and more disciplined deduction in their problem-solving strategies.

> For the adolescent, on the other hand, possibility dominates reality. Confronted with a scientific problem, he begins not by observing the empirical results, but by thinking of the possibilities inherent in the situation. He imagines that many things *might* occur, that many interpretations of the data *might* be feasible, and that what has actually occurred is but one of a number of possible alternatives. The adolescent deals with propositions, not objects. Only after performing a hypothetical analysis of this sort does the adolescent proceed to obtain empirical data which serve to confirm or refute the hypothesis. Furthermore, he bases experiments on deductions from the hypothetical and therefore is not bound solely by the observed (Ginsberg & Opper, 1979, p. 199).

Why adolescents are advanced thinkers

Five mental breakthroughs signal formal thought. But before I describe them I should point out, to avoid misunderstanding, that I am departing from standard convention and am here using the term "formal thought" to refer to the adolescent's *capacity* for intellectual investigation. What follows, therefore, is not a description of how teens think 24 hours per day, but how they perform when they are at their best.

The first feature of formal thought is that it is abstract.

Margaret Donaldson, in her splendid work, *Children's Minds*, which Jerome Bruner claimed was "One of the most powerful . . . books on the development of the child's mind to have appeared in twenty years," made an insightful observation on abstract thinking which is of special value to anyone trying to grasp the differences between "concrete" thinkers and "formal" thinkers. She says:

> It is when we are dealing with people and things in the context of fairly immediate goals and intentions and familiar patterns of events that we feel most at home. And when we are asked to reason about these things . . . we can often do it well. So long as our thinking is sustained by this kind of human sense, and so long as the conclusion to which the reasoning leads is not in conflict with something which we know or believe or want to believe, we tend to have no difficulty. Thus even pre-school children can frequently reason well about the events in the stories they hear. However, when we move beyond the bounds of human sense there is a dramatic difference. Thinking which does move beyond these bounds, so that it no longer operates within the supportive context of meaningful events, is often called 'formal' or 'abstract.'

In Donaldson's understanding of the topic, when the mind deals with familiar events, non-threatening patterns, or topics *which do not require much accommodation*, concrete thinkers get along fairly well. However, when the thinker must go outside the familiar the concrete thinker falters. This is the heart of the difference between the concrete and the abstract.

Moving beyond everyday experience to investigate ideas which have nothing to do with our own immediate lives is the challenge of abstract reasoning. If thinking about oneself can be thought of as "warm-blooded," abstract thinking can be thought of as "cold-blooded." Formal thought, at least in this narrow vein, is the metamorphosis from warm-blooded to cold-blooded thinking. Ultimately, there is a certain heartlessness to logic since one is bound to accept the direction in which one's premises, conclusions and observations take one. In abstract thought, one's loyalty is to defensibility, to coherence, not to sentimentality or desire. This is why calm reason stands in opposition to affective logic, to egocentrism and to narcissism; and, as well, why the adolescent vacillates between the affective and the reasoned.

The young person's increased facility for dealing with hypothetical ideas is the intellectual basis for relativism.

> Perhaps the most striking development during the formal operations period is that adolescents begin to see *the particular reality in which they live as one of only several imaginable realities.* This leads at least some of them to think about alternative organizations of the world and about deep questions concerning the nature of existence, truth, justice and morality (Siegler, 1986, p. 41).

The second feature of formal thought is that it is comprehensive.

When solving problems children do not usually recognize that an unexplored possibility may be as correct as the more obvious possibility. Adolescent thought is more comprehensive, less susceptible to errors of omission.

> Where possible, formal operational reasoners not only consider many possibilities, they consider all possibilities. This allows them to achieve a broad overview, to plan in considerable detail what they are going to do, and to interpret whatever they do within the total context. In contrast, concrete operational children tend to reason on a case-by-case basis and to plan less thoroughly. This sometimes leads them to misinterpret what they see and to leap to conclusions too quickly (Siegler, 1986, p. 41).

Comprehensiveness requires the ability to consider the effects of two, three, even four variables at the same time. This capacity is generally known as combinatorial thought.

> Combinatorial thinking is important in systematic hypothesis testing (versus trial and error) with regard to complex problems. This more sophisticated approach to problem-solving requires that the individual be able to consider all possible combinations of all factors of a problem and to test these in such a way as to permit only one factor to vary at a time; in other words, to observe the effects of one variable while holding all other factors constant (Lloyd, 1985, p. 75).

Whoever lacks comprehensiveness is forever a primitive thinker; without it the totality of possibilities cannot be assembled.

The third feature of formal thinking is that thought becomes the object of its own investigation.

> "I was thinking about my future, and then I began to think about why I was thinking about why I was thinking about my future." 16-year-old.

Adolescent thought is directed not only to the outside world but inward on the thought process itself. To children a thought is a thought is a thought; but adolescents discover that a thought may be born to rich or poor parentage, that it can be weakly constructed or strongly presented. Children, in most regards, are intellectually standardless; that is, they possess few standards by which they are able to judge whether one thought is more coherent than another.

When thought investigates itself it may create a self-doubt which rarely occurs during childhood. "Now that the adolescent can, so to speak, look at himself from the outside he becomes concerned about the reactions of others to himself" (Elkind, 1974, p. 102).

A fourth feature of formal thought is that it is propositional.

A proposition is any statement capable of being believed, doubted, or denied; propositional thought allows the thinker to investigate ideas beyond reality as it is presently understood.[6]

Hypothetical reasoning goes beyond everyday experience to things we have never directly known, things hypothetical. Formal thinkers can reason about hypothetical problems, and from this reasoning deduce logical conclusions. Wadsworth summarizes this process:

> Thus, when they are presented with a problem in a form "A is less than B, and B is less than C; is A less than C?" they can reason appropriately from the premise (A B and B C) and deduce that A is less than C (A C). When given the verbal problem "Bob is left of Sam, and Sam is left of Bill; is Bob left of Bill?" those with formal operations can make the correct deduction from the hypothesis or premises. Concrete operational children, lacking fully developed deductive reasoning about hypothetical situations, cannot solve problems in this form (1989, p. 118).

Hypothetical-deductive reasoning allows the adolescent to reason about hypotheses believed to be untrue and to draw logical conclusions from them. Here, again, Wadsworth helps us.

> If a logical argument is prefixed by the statement "Suppose coal is white," the concrete operational child, when asked to solve the problem, declares that coal is black and that the question cannot be answered. The child with formal operations readily accepts the assumption that coal is white and proceeds to reason about the logic of the argument. *The older child can submit to logical analysis the structure of the argument, independent of the truth or falseness of its content* (1989, p. 118).

In contrast, children focus on the perceptible elements of a problem; they speculate rarely about possibilities which do not bear directly on the matter at hand. They eagerly wade into a problem with no real strategy, no "game plan." When they solve a problem correctly they may not know how they solved it, or when faced with a similar problem, they may not be able to beckon the strategies that only a few minutes before were effective.

Political thought undergoes significant transformations during adolescence precisely because the formal thinker investigates hypothetical scenarios never before considered, and examines propositions inconceivable to the concrete thinker.

> Ordinarily the youngster begins adolescence incapable of complex political discourse. . . . By the time this period is at an end, a dramatic change is evident; the youngster's grasp of the political world is now recognizably adult. His mind moves with some agility within the terrain of political concepts; he has achieved abstractness, complexity, and even some delicacy in his sense of political textures; he is on the threshold of ideology, struggling to formulate a morally coherent view of how society is and might and should be arranged (Adelson, 1972, p. 106).

A fifth feature of formal thought is that it is future-oriented.

Children are not chained to the present, but neither are they free to take flight from it. Their concern is more with "here and now" than "there and then." Formal thinkers, on the other hand, are liberated from the clock, even the calendar; they glide through light years, infinity, timelessness in ways that concrete thinkers cannot even begin to contemplate. Immediate time is recognized as a flickering instant of eternal time; clock time is differentiated from experiential time. The adolescent's transformation to a future-oriented thinker is profound for many reasons, but most important is that thought is forever immediate until it can transcend present time.

The capacity to speculate about the future infuses new mystery into the identity project. "It must be clear that without the skills of hypothesis-raising, conceptualization of the future, logical problem solving, and the ability to anticipate consequences of an action, *work on identity formation could not really begin.*" Likewise:

> Without the capacities of formal thought, identity would be tied to the observable, the readily measurable or manipulable dimensions of experience. But with the door of abstract reasoning opened, *identity becomes a vision of what might be possible as well as of what has already been experienced.* Because of formal thought there is a chance to conceive of an identity that is a unique integration, a new combination of past, present, and future that takes a person along a new course (Newman & Newman, 1988, p. 366).

Formal thinking and "scientific" thought

The reasoning process used by scientists to arrive at generalizations or scientific laws is known as inductive reasoning – in simplest terms, reasoning from specific facts to general conclusions. Formal thinkers, when confronted with complex problems, are capable of reasoning in a way which resembles the reasoning of scientists. When we say this we mean that they form hypotheses, experiment with these hypotheses, control important variables, describe and record the outcomes of these experiments, and, from these steps, draw conclusions in a formal manner. This combination of mental qualities brings Santrock to observe: "the adolescent's thought is more like a scientist's than a child's . . . the adolescent often entertains many possibilities and tests many solutions in a planned way when having to solve a problem" (p. 130, 1990).

Scientific reasoning, since it compares differing effects with differing outcomes, requires one to think about several variables at the same time. Most adolescents (but very few children) can determine the effect of one, all, or some combination of a set of variables. Such mental bookkeeping, what Piaget called combinatorial reasoning, is beyond the grasp of children who reason most effectively when only one or two variables are investigated.

A similar thought promotion is observed in the domain of probability. To utilize probability the thinker must work with chance and proportion; consequently, it is rarely used with much proficiency before the stage of formal operations. Probability attains greater significance not only because it is a prerequisite to mathematical prediction but also because it is the basis to the common sense exercise of estimating the likely occurrence of specific events. Describing the functional prerequisites of effective probabilistic thought, Piaget claimed the thinker:

> must be able to apply a combinatorial system that enables him to take into consideration all the possible combinations of the given elements; and he must be able to calculate proportions, however elementary, so that he can grasp the fact (which eludes subjects on the previous level) that probabilities like three/nine and two/six are equivalent. It is not until the age of eleven or twelve that the child understands combinatorial probabilities (Piaget and Inhelder, 1958, p. 144).

In the end we come to see that the mental advances of formal thought, taken in their totality, expand and dignify human thought with these intellectual breakthroughs:

- Going beyond the real to investigate the ideal;
- Going beyond the physical to investigate the hypothetical;
- Going beyond fragments to investigate wholes;
- Going beyond "what is" to investigate "what if";
- Going beyond the present to investigate the future.

The thinker as person

One of the many challenges facing anyone who investigates the thought process is to do so without making young people appear incompetent or trivial, or conversely, unduly masterful and profound.[7]

Neither extreme is an accurate portrayal, yet both are correct some of the time. It is perhaps best to point out here that adolescents are genuinely capable of complex, sophisticated thought. My intent is not to make adolescents less than they are, rather, to demonstrate how certain components of their makeup undermine their common sense and contaminate their decision-making.

The point to be seized is that the thinking of children is locked into its own primitive mechanics. Children think transductively, which is to say that they infer a particular fact from another particular fact. Usually only an isolated part of a problem is seen. As Goldman explains: "What may be central in an incident to an adult may be relegated to an obscure and unimportant detail to the child, while what are obscure and unimportant details for the adult are often seen by the child as of the greatest importance" (p. 52). The child, for the most part, deals with only one problem at a time, and will oversimplify situations too complex for singularity of thought. All of which "leads to unsystematic and fragmentary thinking, which in turn leads to illogical and inconsistent conclusions because all the evidence has not been considered. But the major disability is the lack of reversibility of thought, the inability to work back from an inconsistency to check on the evidence in the light of conclusions reached" (Goldman, 1965, p. 52).

In practical terms, teens acquire mental abilities which allow them:

- to think about the possible as well as the real;
- to think about implications as well as facts;
- to think about alternatives as well as givens;
- to think about hypotheses as well as descriptions;
- to think about "what if" as well as "what is."

All in all, the probable, the possible, and the theoretical rival material reality as the object of thought. Thinking is no longer bound by what is, or what is not, real; it investigates possibilities beyond the limits of the concrete thinker.[8]

We also know that effective thinkers must be able to transfer what they know into effective decisions; in our culture, the challenge facing youth is not merely solid thinking but solid decision-making. Consider what David Hamburg has to say:

> Since all young adolescents . . . are ill-prepared to make fateful decisions with lifelong consequences and with powerful impact on others, it is valuable for them to learn how to make informed, deliberate decisions rather than ignorant and impulsive ones.

And, further:

Decision making has certain basic elements: Stop and think; get information; assess information, including consequences; consider options, or formulate options; try new behavior and get feedback. *These are fundamental elements of decision making that contribute to healthy adolescent development* (Hamburg 1992, p. 244).

We do well to remember that, as far as adolescent thinking is concerned, the real issue is not ability, but the effective exercise of ability; not potential, but the dignified expression of potential.

Postscript

"Everybody is ignorant, only on different topics."	Will Rogers

Formal thought is an ability teens do not always use; and when they do, there is no guarantee that they will use it efficiently. Formal thinking, as David Elkind observed: "*is a capacity which we possess but which we use in very special circumstances*" (p. 221, 1985). Individuals capable of formal reasoning may prefer to reason on a concrete level, or not to reason at all.

Formal thought may be used effectively in one area yet misused in another.

It is an additional mistake to presume that a person who is formally operational in one area is formally operational in another. The young person who thinks abstractly in areas of math or science may think in concrete terms in history and literature. Another young person may operate in an opposite way. Even within an area we may find ourselves using formal thought in one situation and reverting to concrete thought in another, depending on our mood, the complexity of the situation, or some other factors (Ingersoll, p. 148, 1989).

Teens are formal thinkers, but not exclusively; they alternate among formal thought, concrete thought, and affective logic. Adolescence is when we are first introduced to advanced thinking but, for most of us, it is not when this thinking is mastered.

Formal thought serves the rational demands of the intellect *and* the emotional desires of the self. In some youngsters it works far more aggressively in the service of one than the other. In fact, (as we shall see in chapter seven) some youth use their intellect almost exclusively for self-promotion and self-protection.

During adolescence (especially its early years) formal thought is deployed awkwardly and clumsily. Formal thought requires considerable practice, considerable coaching, and considerable patience before it is exercised with much proficiency.

Endnotes

[1]   When writing about "how children think" we repeatedly caution against over-generalization; but this is easier said than done since defensible generalizations are the very stuff of educated discourse. Be that as it may, I once again remind the reader that in the course of childhood all intellectual abilities change dramatically. In the stories and fantasies which engage children important differences exist between five-year-olds and the nine-year-olds. Five-year-olds, reports Kieran Egan: "readily accept magical or fantastic elements, being unperturbed by the processes by which Cinderella's Fairy Godmother turns mice into footmen and a pumpkin into a coach. Nor do they typically inquire where the Fairy Godmother comes from nor about her means of locomotion. By about age nine, however, while stories may obviously contain impossible elements, the impossible has to conform with a kind of realistic plausibility. Superman's powers, for example, cannot simply be asserted as are the Fairy Godmother's. We need to be told about his birth on the dying planet Krypton and his escape to Earth into the care of Mr. and Mrs. Kent. His great powers are explained . . . by the different molecular structure of our sun compared with that of his home planet Krypton" (1990, p. 87).

[2]   **Concrete thinkers and abstract reasoning**. Robert Seigler has some interesting observations on this topic. He claims:

> Although children in the concrete operations become capable of solving many problems, *certain types of abstract reasoning remain beyond them.* Some of the problems involve reasoning in sophisticated ways about contrary-to-fact propositions ("If people could know the future, would they be happier than they are now?"). Others involve treating their own thinking as something to be thought about. To quote one adolescent, "I was thinking about my future, and then I began to think about why I was thinking about why I was thinking about my future". Still others involve thinking about abstract scientific concepts such as force, inertia, torque, and acceleration. These types of ideas become possible in the formal operations period (1986, p. 40-41).

[3]   According to M. P. Driscoll, "**Assimilation occurs** when a child perceives new objects or events in terms of existing schemes or operations" (1994, p. 179).

[3a]   Again, according to M. P. Driscoll: "When existing schemes or operations must be modified to account for a new experience, **accommodation** has occurred" (1994, p. 179).

[4]   **Assimilation**. Kieran Egan (1990) forges these links between assimilation and accommodation: "We make sense of the world initially by seeing it in some degree in terms of the emotions and intentions which constitute our consciousness. We try, in Piaget's terms, to assimilate the world to these. As features of the world cannot be adequately assimilated, *so we accommodate to them*" (p. 108). The ability (and the willingness) to think "accommodatingly" is a precondition to thought liberation.

[5] **Formal operations differ from, yet are similar to, concrete operations**. Here is how B. J. Wadsworth explains it:

> Functionally, formal thought and concrete thought are similar. They both employ logical operations. The major difference between the two kinds of thought is the much greater range of application and type of logical operations available to the child with formal thought. Concrete thought is limited to solving tangible concrete problems known in the present. Concrete operational children cannot deal with complex verbal problems involving propositions, hypothetical problems, or the future. The reasoning of concrete operational children is 'content bound' – tied to available experience. To this extent, a concrete operational child is not completely free of past and present perceptions. In contrast, a child with fully developed formal operations can deal with all classes of problems. During this stage the child becomes capable of introspection and is able to think about his or her own thoughts and feelings as if they were objects (1989, p. 116).

[6] In Flavell's view, *propositional thinking* is the starting point of all advanced intellectualism:

> The important entities which the adolescent manipulates in his reasoning are no longer the raw reality data themselves, but assertions or statements – propositions – which "contain" these data. What is really achieved in the 7-11 year period is the organized cognition of concrete objects and events per se (i.e., putting them into classes, seriating them, setting them into correspondence, etc.). The adolescent performs these first order operations, too, but he does something else besides, a necessary something which is precisely what renders his thought formal rather than concrete. He takes the results of these concrete operations, casts them in the form of propositions, and then proceeds to operate further upon them, i.e., make various logical connections between them (1963, p. 205).

[7] M. J. Quadrel et al. (1993) remind us: "We do adolescents a disservice if we overestimate their decision-making competence (hence, deny them needed protections) or if we underestimate it (hence, deny them possible autonomy)." Much of the confusion in adolescent psychology is grounded in the tendency to sometimes overestimate and, at other times, to underestimate the abilities of teens.

[8] **Brain development**. Human thought derives from a brain which grows in rhythmic, time-bound progressions. Great advances in our knowledge of the human brain have taken place in the past several decades, including what we know about how it grows during the childhood years.

- *Increased lateralization*. The process by which one side of the brain takes control in organizing a particular mental process or behavior is known as *lateralization*. As children mature, one hemisphere attains dominance over the other which permits greater specialization and increased proficiency of psychological functions. Middle childhood is a time of increased brain lateralization, and it is also a time when more complex thought, and more effective coordination of action take place.

For example, complex behaviors such as writing with a pencil, and playing soccer are executed far more effectively in middle childhood. The skills we associate with mid-childhood owe their emergence, in great measure, to increased brain lateralization.

- *Brain size and activity.* The brain increases in size but also changes its patterns of electrical activity during middle childhood. Between ages 5 and 7 the rate of growth in the surface area of the frontal lobes increases rather sharply. The myelination of the cortex nears completion. The brain wave activity of *preschoolers* displays more *theta* activity, which typifies adult sleep patterns; between 5 and 7 years occurs an increase in *alpha* activity, which is characteristic of engaged attention in the adult. As middle childhood advances, alpha activity increases.

- *Brain complexity.* By middle childhood the brain has achieved a structural and neurological complexity almost equal to that of adults. The frontal lobes coordinate activity of other brain centres when the child is forming a systematic plan of action. Since middle children attain greater proficiency at systematic planning during the same time as these changes occur in the frontal lobes, some experts (most notably A. Luria) infer that brain development is responsible for this improvement. When we suffer damage to the frontal lobes our behavior is characterized by a weakened ability to maintain our goals, we become more easily distracted, and readily lose our concentration. In many regards, behavior and intellectual functioning resembles that of the *preschool* child who has not experienced frontal lobe maturity (Cole & Cole, 1989).

Near the end of middle childhood the brain has attained about 90% of its adult weight. Continued growth in the areas associated with foresightful activity permits more effective transaction of rule-bound games and projects. In addition, the right and left sides of the brain are bridged by neural connections in the corpus callosum, a linkage which brings language and thought into closer working units and, in general, engenders more effective classroom learning.

Chapter Two

egocentrism and thought: basic considerations

"Half our mistakes in life arise from feeling where we ought to think, and thinking where we ought to feel."   John Churton Collins

I have chosen the ideas of Jean Piaget to shape and direct these chapters; which is merely to say that I am using his formulations on the intellectual evolution of children and adolescents as my starting points. Piaget's work was primarily concerned with describing and explaining, in as precise a manner as possible, the growth of intellectual structures. His premise that all knowledge is "constructed" by the individual, while radical in his day, is widely accepted today. The theory of cognitive development associated with Jean Piaget is sometimes known as "genetic epistemology" ("genetic" meaning developmental, and "epistemology" meaning forms of knowing). But since this term adds little, reads clumsily, and in today's intellectual climate brings to mind the science of genetics, I tend to avoid it when discussing adolescent intellectualism.

As every student of Piaget will immediately recognize, these chapters make no attempt to delineate the totality of his elaborate, elegant theory. As all ideas in our fledgling discipline, his have been refined and streamlined; a few even have been abandoned when they failed to stand up to advances brought about by more precise, or better controlled, investigations. To recognize the importance of his contributions, and the brilliance of his insights does not, however, make one a hard-line Piagetian, and I certainly am not. But like all lesser contributors, I willingly, even thankfully, survey the intellectual landscape atop the shoulders of those who first charted the mysteries we, in our own humble ways, continue to investigate.

* * * *

The theory of egocentrism is concerned with the progressions through which we distinguish the workings of our own mental apparatus from the objects of that apparatus; that is, how we come to know the difference between our perception of an event and the event itself. And, as elementary as it may appear, the difference between thought and the object of thought is one of the most significant issues in adolescent intelligence.

41

To be "egocentric" is to be preoccupied with one's own concerns and relatively insensitive to the concerns of others. The term implies *imperviousness* and *unawareness*; egocentric behavior is governed by one's own needs and desires. Its "pure" form is expressed in the innocent and natural "self-ish-ness" of young children, but, most assuredly, it also colors the conduct of adolescents and adults. (In projective testing, for example, an "egocentric response" is one that refers to "me" or to "my" personal affairs).

As Piaget was fond of saying, egocentrism is an *embeddedness* in one's own point of view. In children this entrenchment exists without awareness, and this very lack of awareness contributes to its power; hence, the young child's thinks that what she saw at the parade is the same as what everyone else saw, and that the scenes in the movie that made her sad made everyone equally sad. The child reduces all experiences "to his point of view and *therefore distorts them without realizing it,* simply because he cannot yet distinguish his point of view from that of others through failure to coordinate or 'group' the points of view. Thus, both on the social and on the physical plane, *he is egocentric through ignorance of his own subjectivity*" (Looft, 1972, p. 75).[1]

Very young children believe that their personal point of view is identical to objective reality; they do not seem even to know that other perceptions of reality exist. Here is how Piaget expressed it:

> There is nothing in ego-centrism which tends to make thought conscious of itself (since this self-consciousness only arises through some shock with another mind), and this unconsciousness enables the objects of thought to succeed one another in an unrelated fashion. Juxtaposition is therefore the result of absence of direction in the successive images and ideas, *and this absence of direction is itself the outcome of that lack of self-consciousness which characterizes all egocentric thought* (S. Campbell, 1976, p. 29).

Margaret Donaldson adds to this a deceptively simple passage: "the child does not appreciate that what he sees is relative to his own position; he takes it to represent absolute truth or reality – *the world as it really is*" (p. 20).

Egocentrism makes children both victims and beneficiaries of single-mindedness. They are victims because they cannot stand back to evaluate their own thoughts; so, in a manner of speaking, they are at the mercy of them; beneficiaries because their egocentrism provides a clarity without which they would be lost in the buzz and swirl of infinite perceptual data.

No matter how cautiously we approach this topic we cannot escape what is known in psychological theory as the egocentric predicament: the impossibility of knowing things or persons *as they are* as distinguished from the way we know and experience them through our own personality. This predicament originates in an elementary starting point of human intelligence, namely, that each of us lives within the circle of our own private ideas, escape from which is impossible. The egocentric predicament haunts our investigation because the study of the thought process requires us to understand how children (and adolescents) perceive, understand, judge, and interpret, while the study of egocentrism, on the other hand, requires us to understand how children (and adolescents) *mis*perceive, *mis*understand, *mis*judge, or *mis*interpret.

Perspective-taking

"Neither the whole of truth nor the whole of good is revealed to any single observer, although each observer gains a partial superiority of insight from the peculiar position in which he stands."   William James

All children eventually attain the ability to think about an idea, an event, or an experience from the point of view of another person. This sounds easy to those of us who do it on a daily basis. However, it is a slow and deliberate procedure for young thinkers who are so thoroughly embedded in their own view that they fail to recognize that other thinkers operate from their own exclusive centres and that this exclusivity creates private, unique perspectives.

In so far as they are ego-centric, children always believe themselves to be in immediate agreement with everyone else. They believe that the other person always knows what they are thinking about and is acquainted with their reason for doing so; in a word, they always believe themselves to have been completely understood. This is why, in primitive arguments, each speaker confines himself to mere statements without motivation or with only such embryonic and rudimentary motivation as leaves the essentials of the matter unsaid (Piaget, 1928).

Going beyond one's natural self-immersion to imagine what another person is thinking or feeling is perspective-taking. This ability is a necessary building block for all human interaction which requires one person to take into account the frame of reference of another. Perspective-taking is an advance of heroic proportions in the human thought process; without it we are autistic.

R. L. Selman (1980), drawing upon the conceptual work of Lawrence Kohlberg and the structural blueprints of Jean Piaget, claimed that children attain perspective in five successive stages. He argued that each level of perspective-taking is qualitatively different from the preceding, that each level develops in sequence, and that most children mature through these progressive levels in approximately the same general manner.

Selman's ideas offer helpful instruction on the child's migration away from egocentrism since perspective-taking and egocentrism exist in a converse relationship, as one increases the other decreases – to know about one is to know, even if indirectly, about the other.

Level 0: Undifferentiated and egocentric perspective-taking (about 3-6 years)

The guiding principle of the most primitive form of egocentrism, the kind manifested among one-year-olds, for example, is "You see what I see, you think what I think." At age three, children recognize that other people disagree with them, but they have only minimal understanding of the basis for another person's point of view; they recognize the existence of their own thoughts, and the thoughts of others, but often they confuse one with the other. Even by age six, most kids don't think that another person could respond to the same situation differently than they did. Their understanding of others is blocked by a poorly differentiated understanding of themselves.

Level 1: Differentiated and subjective perspective-taking (about 5-9 years)

At this stage children understand that their interpretations of a social situation may be the same as, or different from, another person's interpretations of the same situation. They are aware that different people process information differently, and therefore, that they draw different conclusions, which is itself a considerable childhood achievement. In Level 1 children are able to think from another person's perspective in a very limited fashion. The most significant feature of Level 1 is the child's recognition that each of us formulates ideas through our own individual thought process. At this stage children still cannot judge their own actions from the frame of reference of another person if that frame is different from their own. Another feature of this level of perspective-taking is that children realize that others hold different perspectives, but they naively believe that everyone will agree once everyone is given the same information. Since they don't recognize the role of private thought in evaluating information, they mistakenly conclude that information itself molds conclusions. Hence, they have difficulty anticipating when disagreements will arise, and how disputes are resolved.

Level 2: Self-reflective or reciprocal perspective-taking (about 7-10 years)

A further advance in perspective-taking occurs when children attain the ability to see their own feelings and actions from another person's perspective. This allows them to anticipate other people's judgments of their actions more proficiently than in Level 1. Therefore, in addition to realizing that others have different perspectives, children now recognize that others can appreciate their perspective. Children now recognize that two people may disagree even though the same information is available to both. Most children at this stage still cannot think about their own point of view and the point of view of others simultaneously.

Level 3: Mutual perspective-taking (about 10-13 years)

This level witnesses the ability to step outside a two-person exchange and imagine how a third person might perceive the interaction. This extension of perspective-taking permits looking at an interaction from two perspectives simultaneously (my own and my parents', for example). In essence, Level 3 allows the child to think about how another person is thinking about him (or her). (It is a necessary precursor to the formation of the Imaginary Audience).

Level 4: In-depth and societal perspective-taking (about 14 years and older)

The distinguishing feature of this stage is that different values are respected. At this level, most youngsters recognize that perspectives are molded by systems of thought, and by larger societal values. For example, recognizing that a viewpoint is based upon "Judeo-Christian" concepts, or understanding that beliefs are influenced by unacknowledged chauvinisms, indicates in-depth perspective-taking. Recognizing that each of us is influenced by larger theoretical and conceptual forces and the realization that "no thinker is an island" are the advances of level 4.

This classification system helps us to understand the child's unfolding capacity to comprehend not only differing viewpoints, but different subsets of his (her) own viewpoints. The extended vision brought into existence by perspective-taking is the foundation for the first big strides toward empathy, diplomacy, and civility.

The developmental progression of egocentrism

"We do adolescents a disservice if we overestimate their decision-making competence (hence, deny them needed protections) or if we underestimate it (hence, deny them possible autonomy)."   M. J. Quadrel

Piaget recognized four stages of egocentrism (three during childhood and one during adolescence) each of which builds upon the advances of the previous stage, each of which contains its own unique modes of reality analysis, and, vital to our concerns, each of which *contains its own unique modes of reality distortion.*[2] As we would expect from even a cursory knowledge of childhood growth, each of these stages is associated with important advances in mental strategies; equally important, each stage is characterized by a particular differentiation failure which is not effectively overcome until the child progresses to the next stage.

<u>Sensorimotor Egocentrism</u> – "the conquest of the object" (birth to age 2)

In this, the first stage of cognitive development, thought is based primarily on action, by means-ends behavior, by trial and error problem solving, and by the repetition of actions which bring pleasure. The thoughts and actions of infants express radical egocentrism, the inability to differentiate self from the larger world. (An idea akin to, but not the same as, Freud's concept of primal narcissism). Egocentrism at this age is based upon the child's "belief" that sensory impressions are essential to the existence of the object. *Sensorimotor egocentrism begins to decline when the child recognizes that objects have their own existence independent of his (or her) perception of them.* This, in essence, is the child's first acknowledgment of the "as-is" world. Transcendence of this egocentrism arises from the emerging capacity for mental representation.

<u>Pre-Operational Egocentrism</u> – "the conquest of the symbol" (about 2-6 years)

The egocentrism of this age makes it difficult for the child to differentiate between the symbol and its referent. The child does not understand the relationship between the signifier and what is signified; symbols are viewed as identical to their referents.

> The egocentrism of this period is particularly evident in children's linguistic behavior. When explaining a piece of apparatus to another child, for example the youngster at this stage uses many indefinite terms and leaves out important information. . . . Although this observation is sometimes explained by saying that the child fails to take the other person's point of view, it can also be explained by saying that the child assumes words carry much more information than they actually do. This results from his belief that even the indefinite "thing" somehow conveys the properties of the object which it is used to represent. In short, the egocentrism of this period consists in a lack of clear differentiation between symbols and their referents (Elkind, 1967, p. 1027).

During this stage, when symbol and referent are confused, children's thinking about the world *is always in terms of their own position within it*. Children at this age are very likely to believe that their own perspective (the outcome of their thought) is shared by others, and that their particular understanding of things is, in fact, the only possible understanding. Transcendence of this egocentrism arises from the emerging capacity for concrete operations.

<u>Concrete Operational Egocentrism</u> – "the conquest of classes, relations, and quantities" (about 7-11 years)

At this age the child can perform elementary syllogistic reasoning, and propose concrete hypotheses. These advancing abilities transport the child from earlier, more primitive levels of comprehension, but, as well, they introduce new deficiencies predicated on these very advances. For example, children at this age think about reality but they do not understand that their hypotheses are "inventions" which need to be tested to determine if they are viable, probable. At this level "children too readily accept their own hypotheses as something factually given and believe that the facts must adapt to fit their hypotheses" (Muuss, 1988, p. 267).

During "concrete" operations children apply logic to specific, tangible problems. Their difficulty is that the egocentrism inherent to this stage makes it difficult for them to differentiate between perceptual events and mental constructions; hence, *they cannot think independently about their thoughts*. Hypotheses which require untrue assumptions ("snow is black") cannot be investigated with much proficiency. However, with the attainment of formal operations, especially the ability to negotiate propositions, this form of egocentrism diminishes.

Here again we see a deficiency: children cannot consistently differentiate their own mental constructions from objective reality. When they cannot solve a problem they may conclude that the problem is not solvable or that a trick is being played on them. They blame the situation rather than examining their own premises because they are blind to the realization that *errors take place within the thought process itself*. This "blindness" impedes their ability to solve problems efficiently, but, on the other hand, it is the basis for their supreme confidence in the rightness of their thinking, for their confident swagger in the face of infinite mystery.

In sum:

> Concrete operational egocentrism consists of the inability to differentiate with some degree of accuracy between the products of one's own mental reasoning and what is perceptually given . . . the inability to differentiate between what one thinks and what one perceives. *The inability to differentiate between an assumption and a fact is what constitutes concrete operational egocentrism* (Muuss, 1988, p. 267).

As we shall see in future chapters, the deficiencies inherent to this stage of egocentrism return to haunt the adolescent, especially when self-esteem, self-protection or self-promotion are at issue.

Formal Operational Egocentrism – "the conquest of thought" (12-20 years)

Since Piaget first described formal operations, the term "formal thought" has been widely used as a synonym for the thought process of adolescents; its arrival signals the beginning of a dramatically new, and higher, plane of intellectual functioning. Formal thought advances the intellect as profoundly as puberty advances the body.

Formal operations permit the young person to construct contrary-to-fact propositions and to reason objectively. "Formal operational thought not only enables the adolescent to conceptualize his thought, *it also permits him to conceptualize the thought of other people*. It is this capacity to take account of other people's thought, however, which is the crux of adolescent egocentrism" (Elkind, 1967, p. 1029, my italics).

Egocentrism is a mental operation, but its full fury cannot be grasped until one recognizes that egocentrism, in important ways, is akin to narcissism. As Nacke observed more than two decades before Freud's famous essay on the topic: *narcissism involves the pleasurable sensations and the emotional satisfactions which accompany self contemplation and self-preoccupation*. Indeed, all egocentric actions produce some narcissistic gratification. This relationship between egocentrism and narcissism, which we shall explore in later chapters, is absolutely necessary to understanding the psychology of the adolescent.

How egocentric are children?

In *Judgment and Reasoning of the Child* (1928), Jean Piaget set the stage for a lifetime of research and theoretical investigation when he, in one deceptively simple passage, set forth his understanding of the child's intellectual innocence. "Thought in the child is ego-centric . . . the child thinks for himself without troubling to make himself understood nor to place himself at the other person's point of view . . . these egocentric habits have a considerable effect upon the structure of thought itself. Thus it is chiefly because he feels no need to socialize his thought that the child is so little concerned . . . to prove his point." Seven decades later virtually all educators and psychologists accept that children are egocentric; that is, that the thoughts of children are embedded in their own processes, that they have trouble accommodating perspectives which conflict with their own, that their thought is sometimes impervious to relevant data, and that they are weak at locating and even weaker at correcting errors within their own mental apparatus. On these basic points not much disagreement exists.

This does not mean, however, there has not been dissatisfaction. Throughout the '70s several lines of research critical of Piaget's basic formulations spread through the academic community. Several researchers began to voice disagreement with Piaget's findings on *the degree to which* egocentrism dominates the thinking of children; they doubted that children are as egocentric as Piaget (or his followers) claimed. Jerome Bruner in *Actual Minds, Possible Worlds* put it this way:

> As we grow to adulthood . . . we become increasingly adept at seeing the same set of events from multiple perspectives or stances and at entertaining the results as, so to speak, alternative possible worlds. The child, we would all agree, is less adept at achieving such multiple perspectives – *although it is highly dubious . . . that children are as uniformly egocentric as formerly claimed* (1986, p. 109).

When psychologists claim that children are egocentric it is accepted that they are not unfailingly so. For example, even though 6-year-olds are egocentric in most situations they behave non-egocentrically in others; and even though 12-year-olds are less egocentric than 6-year-olds, when threatened or frightened, they behave even more egocentrically. Egocentrism attains its significance in both children and adolescents, not because of its consistent, predictable presence, but because of its fluctuating force and unanticipated arousal.

Partly because of this unpredictable quality, and partly because of the brewing discontent with some of Piaget's ideas mentioned above, researchers began to take more seriously the question "How egocentric are children?" In many regards their arguments were persuasive. Margaret Donaldson, another of the influential early critics, documented flaws in Piaget's data gathering strategies, some weaknesses in his assessment procedures, but most importantly, his underestimation of children's thought ceiling. The net effect of this broader critique of Piaget's pioneer work was twofold: (1) a tendency among professionals to believe that children are more capable of advanced reasoning than Piaget claimed; and, (2) a tendency among professionals to accept that children are less egocentric (hence more sociocentric) than had been previously assumed. The second point is of most concern to us, and we shall begin our look at it with a comment from Margaret Donaldson.

> Piaget would not disagree with the claim that egocentrism is never wholly overcome. The dispute with him is only about the extent – and the developmental significance – of egocentrism in early childhood. I want to argue that the difference between child and adult in this respect is less than he supposes; and then to argue further that the critical differences lie elsewhere (1978, p. 25).

She went on to surmise that children are not at any stage as egocentric as Piaget claimed; and that the gap between children and adults is not so great in this respect as the followers of Piaget would have us believe. She also concluded that children are not nearly so limited in their ability to reason deductively as Piaget claimed. In her studies on childhood egocentrism "we have seen that it reveals itself with great clarity in the comments they make while listening to stories. . . . At least from age four, then, we must again acknowledge that the supposed gap between children and adults is less than many people have claimed" (1978, pp. 58-59).

What does all this mean? For our purposes, not too much. The arguments are, for the most part, of degree not kind. Most developmentalists find it believable that children, especially under the right conditions, are less egocentric than Piaget thought they were. The main issue is that (even when one takes into account the impressive volumes of recent research) one cannot escape the realization that children, in the general contours of their thought, and in the general flow of their personality, *are convincingly and undeniably egocentric.* They are not universally, totally, and absolutely egocentric; that would, after all, make them autistic. However, egocentrism is clearly the defining quality of their thought, their social presence, and their interpersonal style. The more refined and sophisticated arguments brought forward by Margaret Donaldson, Jerome Bruner, and many others are legitimate, and they have probably have cast the thinking of children in a fairer light, but their contributions resemble fine tuning more than a major overhaul.

How is egocentrism lessened?

"When I was a boy of fourteen my father was so ignorant I could hardly stand to have the old man around. But when I got to be twenty-one, I was astonished at how much he had learned in seven years."

Mark Twain [3]

When all goes well egocentrism is overcome on two fronts: intellectually, when the child recognizes the differences between his (her) own thoughts and the thoughts of others; emotionally when the child reconciles the differences between his (her) feelings and the feelings of others. Egocentrism subsides even further when the thinker can effectively double-check the thoughts which present themselves to consciousness. "Present themselves" is critical. Younger children accept their conclusions without awareness that they are a function of the thought process itself. Children treat mental conclusions as, so to speak, facts of nature. They simply are. And what they are is. Thoughts are not double-checked because the child does not grasp the relationship between process and product. Which is to say that he or she really does not understand how conclusions work their way to the top of the thought chain.

Adolescents know better. They know conclusions derive from mental processes, and they also know that these processes are not error free. As a result of these insights into their own thought process they begin to double-check and to verify their own mental conclusions. From the moment of this insight, young people, for the first time in their lives, live simultaneously in harmony with, and in opposition to, their own thought process. The dialog which emerges creates standards for the thinking process, *and the quality of these standards*, in great measure, determines the balance of power between egocentrism and formal thought in the life of the adolescent.

The power of egocentrism resides in its ability to nudge the thinker into accepting inaccurate data, or to rejecting accurate data. Like the rest of us, adolescents make mental errors; no one is exempt from this human fact. Egocentrism, however, is not merely a random glitch in the information processing sequence; it persuades on the basis of whether the idea in question agrees with what "I" want, "I" need. This power to corrupt the thought chain is a significant obstacle in the young person's pursuit of objectivity and rationality.

Indicators that egocentrism is in decline

One may assume that egocentrism is losing its influence on thought and action when the following are in ascendance.

- When the adolescent increasingly recognizes that others have a private existence that parallels "my" existence and have rights which parallel "my" rights.

- When the adolescent begins to perceive adults as individuals who possess their own private individuality, their own unique history, and not merely as part of the generalized "other."

- When the adolescent accepts that it is impossible for another person to *completely* understand what it is like "to be me," and that to misperceive "me" does not derive only from defects within the perceiver. To recognize that it is natural for others to sometimes misread "my" actions and intentions.

- When the adolescent decreasingly demands that others always see things from "my" point of view.

- When the adolescent comes to realize that the listener shares parallel feelings and experiences that, while not perfect duplicates, are close enough to one's own feelings and experiences to be meaningfully shared.

- When the fable of one's unique singularity begins to share time with the belief that all people share important commonalities.

- When adolescents can accurately determine when their behavior is noticed by others and when it is not; when they accept that peers might joke about them, or make light of them, without being motivated by jealousy, envy, or malice.

- When the adolescent is able to join social gatherings without assuming that his or her arrival carries undue significance.

When I was 13, 14, and 15 I hated both of my parents, I hated their rules, and everything else about them. They didn't understand me at all. At around 16 or 17 my views started changing (I moved to college when I was 17). Near the end of my 17th year I got closer to my parents, and, now at 19, my parents are my best friends. I tell them almost everything, and even though they are three

In my experience over many years of working first-hand with
teens I have found that very few *early* adolescents attain much distance
from their egocentric nature; *middle*-adolescents, marching to a less
egocentric drummer, master several of the above indicators, but rarely
all of them. *Late*-adolescents exhibit a far greater facility with these traits,
and are thereby transported beyond more pronounced egocentric expressions of younger brothers and sisters.[4]

Early-adolescent vs. late-adolescent egocentrism

If we go back to the premises which guide this investigation we
will recall that mental growth naturally moves from an egocentric
orientation toward a sociocentric orientation, that thinking becomes
increasingly decentred, and that with increased maturity the individual
comes to recognize that other people have their own independent
existence. Most research supports our hypothesis that adolescence involves a gradual transformation away from egocentrism.

We infer that egocentrism is lessening as a force within the personality (and the intellect) when sociocentric tendencies take a stronger
position in day-to-day life. The decline of egocentrism is marked by the
ascendance of outside-the-self investments. About this there is not
much dispute since the issue is partly definitional, i.e., egocentrism is
in decline when opposite characteristics are on the increase. The *causes*
of egocentric decline, however, are not clear. It has been observed for
decades that the decline is correlated with increasing age, but age in
itself does not account for it. (As we shall see in our review of narcissism,
many young people become increasingly egocentric, increasingly narcissistic, and increasingly selfish during adolescence).

If we look closely at the psychological tendencies and the behavior
profiles of late-adolescents, we see trends which indicate that they are,
as a rule, less egocentric than younger teens. A brief look at these
age-based characteristics gives us a better feel for the decline of egocentrism during the adolescent years.

- During late-adolescence youth perceive more accurately the
  traits which define their personal uniqueness; as a result, their
  need for fables and fictions lessens.

- Late adolescents are developing their own standards of self-
  importance; therefore, they are less likely to think well of
  themselves only because they are highly regarded by their
  family or their peers.

- Late-adolescents become more accepting of the positive as well as the negative aspects of their nature; as a result, their sense of identity tends to be more consistent and freer from transient influences; hence, they are more inclined towards commitment.

- Late-adolescents are more adept than their younger brothers and sisters at *perceiving the unique personhood of others*, forcing them less frequently into predesigned patterns. They see more clearly the individuality of parents and relatives, and for this reason adults find them easier to get along with than younger adolescents who lack insight into the adult personality.

- During late-adolescence relationships with elders tend to undergo moderately predictable changes in the direction of comprehending the individuality, the eccentricity, and the privacy of older persons.

- During late-adolescence the trend is away from fleeting involvements and towards more continuous investments, partly in response to increased cultural demands for long-term decisions, such as job and marriage, and partly in response to a personal identity more secure with itself and more certain about what is meaningful in the long run. This deepening of interests precipitates greater interest in "larger" issues, and mapping out long range goals. Some psychologists claim that a general humanizing of values takes place at this age. Kimmel, for example, reports: "they are creating their value system out of their growing understanding and synthesis of their own feelings . . . with more empathy to the needs of others while at the same time they are creating their own unifying philosophy of life." All this accords with an *expansion of caring*, a growing empathy with others, and a greater concern for their feelings.

- During late adolescence there is a greater tendency to identify oneself in terms of beliefs, morals, and ideologies.

- During late-adolescence youth are less intrigued by the short-term calendar. A preoccupation with the future and its possibilities is possible only after hypothetical reasoning and a probabilistic view of future time are acquired, skills found in abundance among late-adolescents.[5]

Postscript

If a more pressing issue than egocentrism exists in adolescent psychology it has eluded me. Although I am not as extreme as Piaget, who, according to W. R. Looft, claimed that "egocentricity of thought . . . has perhaps been the central problem in the history of human existence," I am convinced that the consequences of egocentrism are pervasive among all strata of youth: in their private thinking, in their peer evaluations, in their confrontations with parents, and, most assuredly, in their fixation with pop culture, and in their valiant struggle to understand the world honestly and objectively while embedded in developmental narrowness. And, as we shall see in chapters six and seven, egocentrism is a vital connective link between the "developmental self-ish-ness" natural to youth and the "narcissistic selfishness" which corrupts them.

> *When I was 13 or 14 and my parents would not allow me to do something, I'd really be mad and try to stay mad for a long time (but it never worked). I could never see any reason in their decisions. Now that I'm older, late adolescence, when I'm told not to do something, I don't resent them for it.*
> 17-year-old university student's response to the question: "Did your attitude towards your parents change during adolescence?"

To assist those readers who seek a brief overview of the major ideas put forth in this chapter, the following summary is provided.

- Egocentrism is an *embeddedness* in one's own point of view. It implies that one is relatively unaware of, therefore insensitive to, the ideas and interests of others. Its "pure" form is expressed in the characteristic self-ish-ness of children, who, Piaget claimed, reduce all experiences to their own point of view and *therefore distort them without realizing it.*

- Perspective-taking is the ability to acknowledge the viewpoint of another person, to imagine what another person is thinking or feeling. Like egocentrism, it evolves in accord with a moderately predictable sequence of abilities and aptitudes. R. L. Selman, inspired by the work of Piaget, suggested that perspective-taking takes place on five fairly distinct levels, each more advanced than the previous, and each embracing a more complex whole. Selman's ideas interest us because they offer helpful instruction on the child's migration away from egocentrism. Perspective-taking and egocentrism exist in a converse relationship: as one increases the other decreases. As a result, to know about one is to know about the other.

- Egocentrism expresses itself in developmental progressions; in each stage of egocentrism the youngster overcomes certain limitations, transcends certain deficiencies, but encounters new handicaps.

- The "conquest" of egocentrism includes the ability to think in a less egocentric vein, and to perceive, in increasingly accurate terms, the thoughts, moods, and emotions of others. We recognize that egocentrism is in decline:

  - When the adolescent begins to perceive adults as individuals with their own private individuality.

  - When the teen is able to personalize, humanize (not the same as "idealize") someone he (she) does not know as a person.

  - When the adolescent recognizes that the rights of others exist on the same plane as "my" rights.

  - When the adolescent accepts that it is impossible for another person to completely understand what it is like "to be me."

  - When the adolescent ceases to demand that the others always accept his (her) point of view.

  - When the fable of total singularity begins to lose power.

- Late adolescents are less egocentric in thought and behavior than early adolescents.[6] Especially in the following ways:

  - Late adolescents perceive more accurately the traits which define their personal uniqueness; they acknowledge "the way I am" more evenly. They tend to be more accepting of both positive and negative aspects of their nature.

  - Late adolescents feel important when they have accomplished something important.

  - Late adolescents possess greater stabilization of ego identity; as a result, they are more inclined to make, and keep, commitments.

  - Late-adolescents see more clearly the individuality of parents and relatives, and for this reason adults generally find them easier to get along with.

  - Late adolescents tend to experience a deepening of interests, partly in response to increased cultural demands for long-term decisions, such as job and marriage, and partly in response to a personal identity which is more secure with itself and more certain about what is meaningful in the long run. Late adolescents are also more likely to possess greater insight into the feelings of others.

What we do not fully understand is *why* most youngsters become less egocentric during their adolescent tenure, while some become more; why most youngsters become increasingly clear in their thinking while others become increasingly beclouded; why most youngsters become more accurate in their social perceptions while others more distortional.

With these unknowns beckoning, we are now ready to embark upon a deeper look at egocentrism and its influence on the adolescent thought process.

Endnotes

[1]   According to Robert S. Siegler: "Piaget applied the term 'egocentric' to preschool-age children not to castigate them for being inconsiderate, but rather in a more literal sense. Their thinking about the external world is always in terms of their own perspective, their own position within it. Their use of language reflects this adherence to their own perspective, particularly their frequent use of idiosyncratic symbols that are meaningless to other people" (1986, p. 34).

[2]   **The concept of developmental "stage."** Everyone holds a general understanding of stages in human development, i.e., infancy, early childhood, adolescence. However, to developmentalists its meaning is more specific. *A stage is a level of development where traits emerge which did not exist in previous levels of development. Each stage is different from, and more mature than, its preceding stage; each stage is part of a sequence of stages.*
In biology the division of growth from an egg into a caterpillar into a butterfly is an example of clear-cut stage development. Humans are more complicated not only because their development is slower but also because it is less controlled by heredity and because in the culmination of their development humans attain a greater range of individual differences than any other species.
A stage is characterized:

- by *structure*; that is, within each stage abilities are linked by some kind of cohesive pattern.

- by *qualitative changes*. When growing through a developmental stage a child is not simply a bigger and better version of himself or herself than when he or she was in the previous stage, because a stage is characterized by traits qualitatively different from the previous stage.

- by *abruptness*. The transition from one stage to another should be rather brief (the most dramatic being the transition from fetus to newborn). The physical transformations of puberty, for example, fulfill this requirement.

- by *concurrence*. That is, the various achievements of a particular stage occur with a certain amount of harmony and concurrence. Development is, so to speak, orchestrated.

[3]   Here is how one university student described her changing relationship with her parents during adolescence:

> Yes, my attitude toward my parents did change during adolescence. As I became older, more mature, my thoughts and perceptions of them were more positive, much more positive. At a younger age, when friends were of extreme importance, and the attitude shared was that parents were more enemies, that were "old" and "didn't know anything." I considered my parents "uncool," at times embarrassed to be with them. I refused to see their side in an argument or suggestion, [I was] unhelpful, questioned things – why did I have to do this or that. As I became older, my parents were my best friends and still are. I took a complete turn – now I *want* to hear their advice or suggestions, I respect their advice as well as decisions, I help not only with perhaps physical labor but emotional support, I like talking with then, learning from them, etc.

[4]   **The Three Ages of Adolescence**. In previous works (*Human Growth and Development: The Early Adolescent Years*, 1973; *Adolescent Psychology*, 1980, and *The Nature of Adolescence*, 1989), I have documented the basic differences among early-, middle-, and late-adolescents. My efforts in this direction, of course, were not the first. Harry Stack Sullivan claimed that adolescent development unfolds in three segments: pre-adolescence, early adolescence, and late adolescence. Pre-adolescence, according to Sullivan, is characterized by the need for close personal relationships and friendships, usually with someone of the same sex and similar age. These relationships nurture the foundational skills for intimacy. During pre-adolescence the youngster first experiences peer loneliness because the need for social companionship is so forceful that its loss creates fearful feelings of emptiness. Early adolescence also witnesses a gradual shift from same-sex to opposite-sex companions. Learning to transact interpersonal relationships is a major preoccupation, perhaps even, in the language of Havighurst, the primary developmental task of this age. Sullivan believed that puberty nurtured "lust" (genital sexuality) which molds the desires, thoughts, and ambitions of young people. Although Sullivan overrated the urgency of early-adolescent "lust" (as did all male theoreticians in the first half of this century), he rightfully pointed out the numerous complications which arise when genital sexuality is blended with the need for interpersonal intimacy.

Peter Blos also accepted (although for reasons quite different from Sullivan) that adolescence spans three distinct periods – early adolescence, adolescence proper, and late adolescence. During early adolescence youth make the transition from same-sex friendships to heterosexual friendships. Adolescence proper is characterized by a reduction of emotional investment in people and objects which acquired their significance during earlier stages. This distancing from previous "investments" prompts a reassessment of fears, conflicts, and ambitions which came into being during earlier adolescent periods. As emotional attachment to these bonds weakens (or disappears) the adolescent reinvests this energy in new relationships with the real and ideal world. Thus, adolescence proper is a period of new attachments, new emotional investments, and new vulnerabilities. To Blos, the adolescent susceptibility to depression and nostalgia is an emotional reaction to bidding farewell to earlier attachments and love objects.

[5]   For those readers interested in a more thorough analysis of the adolescent's understanding of the social world I recommend Adrian Furnham's and Barrie Stacey's *Young People's Understanding of Society* (1991). This work, part of the superb "Adolescence and Society Series," edited by John C. Coleman, provides a thoughtful overview of the available data relevant to this topic. Special emphasis is placed on the young person's understanding of politics and government, economics and trade, work and employment, sex and gender, religion and spiritual matters, and law and justice. The prevailing themes of this chapter (especially how the younger adolescent's thinking is influenced by egocentric narrowness) are given solid coverage.

[6]   The following information, taken from *Young People's Understanding of Society*, by A. Furnham & B. Stacey, highlights several points relevant to the themes in this section.

> Using teenagers aged 14-19, Furth and McConville (1981) *examined adolescent understanding of compromise in political and social awareness.* Four aspects of political understanding were examined: the recognition of individual rights; articulation of other viewpoints; the need for reasonable compromise; and the separation of legal from conventional-moral regulations. *A clear progression in mature understanding of the conflictual issues was demonstrated with the 18-19-year-old group quite distinct from the 16-17 group, who were closer to the youngest age group.* They single out a number of specific aspects of political understanding that develop over this age range. The first is the adolescent's growing recognition of individual rights vis-à-vis those of society, and that awareness of the infringement of rights increased with age. *Secondly, older teenagers are able to articulate the viewpoint of other interested groups in society and to recognize and expect organized action on specific issues.* Thirdly, teenagers seem to acquire a much greater understanding of the concept of compromise over this period – the idea that to live in society the individual has to relinquish certain rights and others are legally protected by the government. Fourthly, older teenagers are able to distinguish between conventions and legal sanctions (p. 30).

Chapter Three

psychic theatre

"All the world's a stage, And all the men and women merely players, And one man in his time plays many parts." Wm. Shakespeare

Much of what gathers our interest in this book is the comparative ease with which the adolescent thought process is knocked off course; its susceptibility to unbeckoned intrusions and its vulnerability to unnecessary derailments. These entanglements are especially fascinating because adolescence is also a time of spectacular intellectual growth. The irony is that the power of objective thought is countered by an egocentricity which causes adolescents to mis-perceive the thoughts and intentions of others. "This may occur for a variety of reasons . . . most often, however, from egocentrism – a failure to distinguish sufficiently clearly between one's own point of view and that of others" (Conger & Peterson, 1984, p. 167). From this "failure to distinguish sufficiently clearly" much of the adolescent drama is scripted.

The previous chapter presented some features of egocentrism, and indicated how they map the thinking process. This understanding of egocentrism is certainly not the whole story. A case can be made that egocentrism influences a far wider spectrum than any of the pioneer psychologists recognized, and this influence spreads well beyond the structural thinking process. In this chapter, I shall try to make this case.

The early investigators were fully aware that egocentrism creates both perceptual and intellectual distortions.[1] Piaget, for example, claimed that the adolescent thought process sometimes operates as though the world should bend to it rather than it to the world; and furthermore, that: "Adolescent egocentricity is manifested by a belief that . . . the world should submit itself to idealistic schemes rather than to systems of reality" (1967, p. 63).

As we have already established, egocentrism is weakest when perceptions are determined by the characteristics of the object perceived rather than by the needs of the perceiver. This does not, of course, guarantee that one's thoughts are always accurate, but it is axiomatic that lessening private bias increases accuracy. Voltaire once suggested, with characteristic brevity, that truth is "a statement of facts as they are." It is a proposition of this chapter that facts "as they are" are problematic during adolescence because the young person's understanding of facts as they are is beclouded by the very processes which perceive them.

In this chapter I want to discuss the role of distorted perceptions in the adolescent's understanding of their interpersonal world. And, while doing so, I want to consider some of the consequences of these misperceptions. Consequently, four basic themes occupy the balance of this chapter:

- the tendency of adolescents to believe they are being closely observed when they are not;

- the tendency of adolescents to believe that they are so special and so unique that no one can understand them;

- the tendency of adolescents to try to reform the world so that it better fits their own needs and desires;

- the tendency of adolescents to infuse their speech with self-reference, and to shift the conversation topic to their own immediate interests and concerns.

* * * *

The roles we play and the dramas we act in our daily lives are a source of awe and perplexity to all of us, but to adolescents they are more than this because frequently they do not separate the roles they play from their own unfolding selves. In these settings, the stage is not a metaphor for life – it is life. And, without question, the task of coming to "know thyself," and the responsibility of formulating a coherent identity are complicated in the extreme when the subject does not know when it is being itself or when it is performing a role; or, equally perplexing, when the self cannot tell if it is performing before a real or an imagined audience.

Peers as spectators

"For, when they come together, each young person is an actor to himself or to herself and a spectator to everyone else."   David Elkind

The thinking of adolescents is stamped, quite incorrectly, with the presumption that everyone is attuned to, and concerned with, them. As a result, they believe mistakenly that other people are paying attention to them, are fascinated with them and are experiencing emotional reactions to them, when in fact they are not. This fundamental mis-perception shapes a good deal of their behavior, and therefore is of interest to all investigators of the adolescent experience.

In a sense, then, the adolescent is continually constructing, or reacting to, an imaginary audience. It is an audience because the adolescent believes that he will be the focus of attention; and it is imaginary because, in actual social situations, this is not usually the case. . . . The construction of imaginary audiences would seem to account, in part at least, for a wide variety of typical adolescent behaviors and experiences. . . . When the young person is feeling critical of himself, he anticipates that the audience . . . will be critical too. The adolescent's wish for privacy and his reluctance to reveal himself may, to some extent, be a reaction to the feelings of being under the constant, critical scrutiny of other people (Elkind, 1967, p. 1030).

The sense of being continuously evaluated produces an exaggerated self-awareness that resembles the hyper-self-consciousness adults experience during an important job interview. They mold every sentence, manicure every expression to elicit the desired impression; a keen eye is focussed on every reaction of the interviewer. Just as the adult is on stage, so the adolescent lives on a daily stage performing before an audience of peers, parents, and passers-by. One 20-year-old, remembering his adolescence, recalled: "I was obsessed with the thought that everyone was always watching me. I was always conscious about what I was doing, just in case someone was watching and would sometimes do things just because someone was watching (or so I thought)."

> "I always felt I was being compared to other girls, that they watched how I walked, ran, sat down, how my clothes fitted, and the type of clothes I wore. At the same time, I was very athletic, but was conscious of what I looked like on the court in comparison to other girls. I even thought that if people were talking or laughing when I walked in a room they had to be talking about me."
> 20-year-old describing her adolescent self-consciousness.

The imaginary audience, as one might suspect from what we have thus far discussed, excites a nervous self-consciousness, a sense of being outside and inside the self at exactly the same instant. Each are seen in the following comment made by a young woman in the superb work of Garrod et al. (1992) on adolescent identity:

> I was always conscious of how other people saw my reactions. It was as though there were two of me. One part was living my life – feeling happy and sad, excited and disappointed. The other part was outside of me watching and noting my effect on others. The outside part enjoyed getting sympathy, attention, and praise. It could romanticize even the worst situations. It put me in the place of the injured heroine from the movies. It was the part of me that imagined what people would say about me if I were to die, and wished to be involved in tragedies for the effect of it. The inside of me did the feelings (p. 176).

The imagination of children, vivid and exciting as it may be, cannot construct the imaginary audiences of adolescence. The child's imagination is bound to first-order scaffolding; the adolescent's imagination is of a more complex, more formal order.

> The main point about the imaginary audience is the fact that it is imaginary, not real. *What young adolescents can do, and what children cannot do, is create such audiences in their head.* Where the young adolescent has difficulty is in recognizing the subjectivity of his or her own mental constructions. The young teenager has trouble in differentiating

between the concerns of others he or she has created and concerns which are properly his or her own. So, the fact that children can infer the thoughts or feelings of others given the situational context, does not really speak to the issue of the imaginary audience, which is mental construction and not social reality.   (Elkind, 1985)

To further reinforce how the imaginings of children differ from the imaginary audiences of teens:

a child reconstructs the thought of an existing person or persons. But an adolescent reconstructs the thought of a person or persons *whom they themselves have created or constructed.* The imaginary audience is a second-order, not a first-order symbolic construction (Elkind, 1985 p. 222-223).

Despite the fact that the imaginary audience depends upon second-order symbolic construction, it is made of much more than mere mental constructs. These audiences evoke fantasies and fears which are fueled by conscious needs and unconscious cravings. They also have a strong affective component which may elicit intense pleasure or deep remorse, or simply quiet satisfaction. All of which indicates that imaginary audiences, though requiring formal thought for their actualization, are also grounded in emotional states. In the words of a 14-year-old boy we hear classic imaginary audience material, blended with fantasy and personal fable imagery:

I dreamt that one afternoon I walked out on our porch headed for the swimming pool when I observed . . . bleachers with some 2000 spectators sitting and waiting for me to swim. I was so taken aback by this event that I decided to favor them by walking on the water. My repeated success in performing such a feat brought the audience to its feet, then its knees in admiration and homage (Thornburg, 1982, p. 106).

The imaginary audience provides the pleasure and pain of a real audience. The task facing the adolescent is to distinguish the real from the imagined; a task which most youngsters do master, at least according to Elkind. "The imaginary audience . . . is progressively modified in the direction of the reactions of the real audience" (1967, p. 1032). What Elkind does not mention is that during the three-to-five-year period when audiences are "progressively modified" to match the real world, the adolescent clings to a belief-system grounded in both reality and in fantasy, and pieces together an understanding of the social world based upon both real and imagined audiences. In by-gone years this blurred perception did not carry the weight it does for teens in the '90s. Today a youngster who confuses fact with fantasy may pay for this confusion the rest of his (her) life.

The fabulous fabulist

"When I say 'I' I mean a thing absolutely unique, not to be confused
with any other."   Ugo Betti

Every person must come to grips with the fact that there is no one
else in the world exactly the same as "me"; developmentalists call this
accepting one's unique singularity. However it is called, it is a tough
assignment during the teen years because the self to be known is
defining and re-defining itself with such a flurry that it is hard for it to
get a solid bearing on itself. Even when we take into account a self trying
to define itself with an incompletely formed mental apparatus, and
without a reliable intimacy partner to share in the adventure, other
obstacles are encountered. Here we shall discuss one of them: the
tendency of adolescents to create fables about their uniqueness, the
teen-ager as fabulist.

Adolescence is one of the most important periods in our lives for
learning to distinguish the illusory from the real. To meet this task the
adolescent has at his (her) disposal the resources of formal thought, the
benefits of formal schooling, and the counsel of parents; impeding the
successful completion of this task is the fable, the *par excellence* mixture
of fact and fantasy, reality, and illusion.

Because David Elkind popularized the concept that the adolescent
mind is structurally inclined to manufacture fables, and because he has
defended the idea as eloquently as anyone, we will start with him.
Elkind believed that the adolescent:

comes to regard himself, and particularly his feelings, as something
special and unique . . . this belief in personal uniqueness becomes a
conviction that he will not die, that death will happen to others but not
to him. This complex of beliefs in the uniqueness of his feelings and of
his immortality might be called a personal fable, a story which he tells
himself which is not true (1967, p. 1031).

From "the personal fable" flows the sensation of being a person
whose experiences are more emotionally profound, whose thoughts are
more intellectually advanced, and whose fears are more fearful than
anyone else's. As a result of this special status, no other person can
comprehend the pain of "my suffering," no one can grasp the profundity of "my convictions," or fathom the depths of "my love." All of this,
since Elkind's classic essay (1967), has been known as *the personal fable*.

From this perch of elevated specialness fabled youth see things
others cannot, understand relationships that baffle others, and experience passions of love and hate far beyond the capacities of their friends,
teachers, and most assuredly, of their parents. Like the imaginary
audience, the personal fable tends to weaken with experience; yet, while
running its course, it exerts tremendous impact on attitudes, expecta-

tions, and perceptions. Will this action lead to pregnancy? Will this action lead to accident? Will this action send me to jail? Will this action cancel my ability to get a job? Such questions affect the course of one's life, and they are questions which, when viewed within the frame of private personal fables, are not always answered honorably. "One characteristic that has been attributed to adolescents is . . . a belief that nothing bad or undesirable (including pregnancy or sexually transmitted disease) will happen to them. This perceived invulnerability to nasty events has been well documented in the case of pregnancy . . . and STDs . . . and is associated with an increase in sexual risk-taking" (Moore & Rosenthal, 1993, p. 18). This issue (the beclouded perception of cause-effect relationships), because of its importance to the entirety of adolescent life, will be pursued throughout the remaining chapters.

While the imaginary audience and the personal fable share egocentric commonalities, they differ in important ways. The imaginary audience is based on the presumption that other people are aware of me, that they can actually intuit what I am thinking, and that they can correctly infer my emotional state. The personal fable, on the other hand, is based on opposite presumptions: that I am so perfectly singular no one could possibly grasp the richness of my thought, or even estimate the depth and power of my emotions. The imaginary audience places me on centre stage, in the spotlight, in direct view of knowing eyes, while the personal fable places me in splendid, heroic isolation. These contrasting self-perceptions alternate with surprising swiftness in the phenomenology of youth, heightening their sensations of self-awareness and mushrooming their conviction of unique peculiarity.

The imaginary audience and the personal fable gain momentum through *affective logic*, which persuades by speaking to emotions, to cravings, to desires. Youngsters are captivated by it because objective reason does not stimulate their passion, or touch their soul. They prefer a logic which quickens the pulse more than one which focuses the mind. This preference profoundly shapes their thought chain.

By its nature the adolescent thought chain tips thought toward the subjective, the emotional, the impassioned, and in so doing inclines the thinker to accept arguments which beg the question, which are based on prestige, which anger an opponent, which employ special pleading, and which attribute prejudice to one's opponent. In short, affective logic is tailor-made for the creation and maintenance of fables.

The fable of invulnerability

"The belief in the recklessness of youth is more than folk wisdom: It is the foundation of our social institutions."   William Gardner

All youth watchers know that North American teens are prone to risk taking which may be injurious, even fatal. The issue before us is not to debate whether teens are risk takers because we accept as a starting point that they are. (The mortality rate, for example, increases by 214% from early to late adolescence, the single largest percent increase in any two consecutive age cohorts in the life cycle; injuries account for most of this increase in mortality. Death rates from motor vehicle injuries increase by 386%, homicide and legal intervention by 587%, and other unintentional injuries by 75% between early and late adolescence. See Irwin, 1993 for further data on this topic.)

Our interest is *why* youth take risks which they themselves recognize as dangerous. We will begin with an observation made by William Gardner:

> Every nation exploits the recklessness of the young by placing them in the front ranks of its military. And not every youth who has gone to war was coerced or fooled: lacking the opportunity for warfare, some will find other ways to place their lives at risk...the extreme risk taking of certain youths requires neither coercion nor ignorance of the likely consequences (1993, p. 66).

Before we look into its importance in the adolescent community, we should acknowledge that risk taking and the sense of being invulnerable to danger are not exclusive to adolescents. Adults also participate in a tragic form of overconfidence where they think of themselves as immune to hazards they openly acknowledge *as dangerous to others*. Ola Svenson, a Swedish psychologist, found that most people rate themselves among the most skillful and the safest drivers in the population. Arno Rethans found in his research that subjects rated their own risks from each of 29 hazardous consumer products like knives and hammers as lower than risks those products posed to others. Ninety-seven percent of the participants in this study believed they would be average or above average in their ability to avoid bicycle and power lawn mower accidents. Neil Weinstein found people to be overly optimistic when evaluating the probability that good and bad life events would happen to them, such as living beyond 80 or of having a heart attack.

One recurring finding is that adults increasingly underestimate dangers which are familiar to them:

> the hazards they underrate tend to be familiar ones in which risks are so low that personal experience of them is overwhelmingly benign. Automobile driving is a prime example. Although poor drivers may drive too fast or tailgate, they make trip after trip without mishap, "proving" to themselves their exceptional skill and caution. Moreover, indirect experience, via the media, shows them that when accidents do happen, they happen to others. Misleading experiences encourage

erroneous conclusions; they can help rationalize a refusal to take protective action, such as wearing seat belts (Slovic, 1986, p. 248).

In their ongoing investigations of intravenous drug users in Alberta, Ann Marie Pagliaro and Louis Pagliaro (1993) found that many of their subjects have a relatively high level of knowledge of HIV / AIDS. The authors conclude that among the more than 800 drug users they interviewed knowledge about how the HIV is transmitted is fairly sophisticated. Nevertheless, users perceive that their own risk of contracting HIV is very low despite the fact that they are participating in high risk drug use and sexual behavior. These individuals, again according to Pagliaro and Pagliaro, "harbour illusions of unique invulnerability" (1993, p. 12).

"Most children, even in adolescence, simply are not able to make sound judgments concerning many decisions, including their need for medical care or treatment."   Chief Justice Berger, Parham v. J.R., 1979.

The research findings of the Pagliaros on adult attitudes toward HIV / AIDS support the findings of Moore and Rosenthal on adolescent attitudes on the same topic. "This is a common theme among heterosexual adolescents in their responses to the threat of AIDS – the 'not-me' myth. It is clear that most adolescents have not personalized the risk of HIV / AIDS, *perceiving the illness as a threat to others, not themselves*. This is consistent with the belief that adolescents' thinking is characterized, in part, by the 'personal fable' " (1993, p. 128). Then, in further support of the basic themes I am here calling "psychic theatre," Moore and Rosenthal observe:

> Adolescents' belief that it 'can't happen to me' has been shown to influence risk-taking in a variety of health-related situations including smoking and contraceptive use. In a recent study of British adolescents, Abrams *et al.* (1990) found high levels of concern about the presence of the HIV virus in the community *but little evidence of concern about their own levels of risk* (1993, p. 129).

Quadrel et al. (1993) concluded that *adults* consistently show patterns of invulnerability, including the tendency to see themselves as less likely than others to experience negative outcomes, more likely to experience positive outcomes, better able to escape detection in ethical transgressions, more likely to win lotteries, avoid natural disasters, pregnancy, and crime. So, quite obviously, we are not looking at an exclusively adolescent phenomenon. However, some unique features to adolescence speak to their tendency to misperceive, to miscalculate the probable.[2]

In some quarters it is believed that once adolescents understand the relevant facts pertaining to any particular risk they will avoid exposing themselves to that risk. Those who accept this point of view believe that when teens take risks they do not truly comprehend the danger, either because they do not have the mental power, or because the appropriate information has not been given to them, or it has been delivered in an ineffective manner. Another interpretation is that adolescents understand the risks but choose to ignore them. They may consider the risk acceptable, given the benefits, or they may enjoy the thrill or social status that come with it.

> "Because they give you demerits and you have to take these [driver awareness] classes."
> 18-year-old, one week after being arrested for impaired driving, responding to "Why shouldn't a person drive after drinking?"

The reader should be aware that research investigating adolescent risk-taking and attitudes of invulnerability have not returned a consistent pattern. Some findings do not seem to support Elkind's concepts of the imaginary audience, the personal fable, or his hypotheses about young people's so-called "feelings of invulnerability." A number of researchers, including Quadrel et al. (1993) have questioned whether the personal fable is the most plausible explanation for the adolescent's tendency to risk-taking.

> Elkind argued that adolescents' personal fable involved a notion of uniqueness so strong that it "becomes a conviction that he will not die, that death will happen to others but not to him" (p. 1031). Elkind noted that his theory was largely speculative, being based entirely on anecdotal evidence from his clinical patients. *Although this article has been cited widely, there is little systematic evidence supporting the theory* (p.103).

They further speculate:

> The most straightforward account of these results is that adults and teens rely on similar, moderately biased psychological processes in estimating these risks . . . both cognitive and motivational processes could contribute to exaggerating one's safety. On the cognitive side, for example, the precautions that one takes (or at least plans to take) should be more visible than those taken by others, especially for active events (where control is more possible). . . . On the motivational side, wishful thinking might deflate perception of personal risk. . . . (Quadrel, 1993, p. 112).

What does all this mean?

Here we are trying to understand the adolescent tendency to strike a posture of indestructibility. This is no easy task. In fact, experts do not even agree as to whether most adolescents possess such feelings. My personal observation: when youngsters think they are immune to consequences, it applies only to selected actions. Virtually no teens (except the most severely disturbed) believe in their complete indestructibility or total immunity. They readily acknowledge, for example, that their house could burn down, that their fathers might contract cancer, or that they could be expelled from school after one further code violation. However, when unknown risks (the probability of having a car accident while driving impaired) *bears upon an immediate desire*, a sense of invulnerability sprouts up. Hence, the adolescent who has been drinking and now wants to drive to the dance is more likely to conclude that an accident will not occur, than an adolescent who also has been drinking but who does not want to go to the dance. The fable of invulnerability distorts those ideas which press upon personal desires, inner needs, or unspoken fears.

Fables of immunity common to North American teens include the following:

- Pregnancy will never happen to me.[3]
- Car accidents will never happen to me.
- Drug addiction will never happen to me.
- Alcohol addiction will never happen to me.
- The police will never arrest me.
- Marriage problems will never happen to me.
- The usual consequences of behavior do not apply to me.

Adolescents do not subscribe to all of these fables: if they did their thought would be so completely irrational, their reality checks so diluted, that hope for them would be pointless. But, then again, it is not necessary for young people to cling to clusters of fables when *any one of them* may produce life-long consequences. In behavioral fact, faulty decision-making is usually caused by only one fable of immunity.[4]

One 16-year-old I interviewed over a four-month period was convinced that she would never become pregnant, despite having unprotected sex with her boyfriend "more than several times" per month, because, in her own words, "pregnancy does not run in my family." However, while espousing invulnerability to the natural consequences of sexual intercourse, she refused to drink alcohol because of the increased risks it posed while driving, she refused to smoke cigarettes because they increase the risk of disease, and she refused to experiment with drugs because she did not want to risk being arrested. All of these struck me as reasoned, calculated viewpoints, which co-habited with pregnancy beliefs which were ill-reasoned and laced with denial. This uneven, selective reasoning is, during adolescence, everyday fare. The lesson to be learned in all this is that egocentric contamination, like temper tantrums, binge eating, and moodiness, appear in episodic bursts. They are not permanent qualities of the adolescent personality – more like uninvited visitors.

Most young people have a friend, or parent, suffering the calamities from which they defiantly claim special exemption. These human tragedies are not denied in their totality, and to perceive adolescent denial in this way is to miss the overall picture. Rather, the adolescent acknowledges these tragedies as facts of human life, but, as facts which affect me differently than everyone else. Why? Because I am so unique that I *am* different. So unique that I live by different rules, am affected by different probabilities. (Such fabled thinking, as we shall see in chapter seven, is the precursor to "the narcissistic attitude.")

Although the personal fable usually claims that the probable will not occur, it sometimes claims the reverse: that the improbable *will* occur. Therefore, some youngsters dwell on the possibility that they will die before age 30, or that they will have a heart attack if they exercise too vigorously. The conclusion that presents itself in this matter is not hard to recognize: adolescents have considerable difficulty with probable outcome. Though this might seem harmless it is not; failure to infer probable outcome accurately can be disastrous. It contributes substantively to adolescent pathology, to adolescent mortality, to adolescent pregnancy, to adolescent unemployment, to adolescent drug abuse, to adolescent gang membership, and to adolescent runaways. Nothing is more devastating to teens than their failure to anticipate accurately the outcome of their actions. Anything which contributes to this failure (including the dynamics of the thought process itself) should concern psychologists, parents, indeed everyone who shares in the stewardship of the young.

Consider that almost all pregnant teens report being "surprised" or "shocked" at finding themselves pregnant. (A. Phoenix, in her 1991 investigation of young mothers, reports that 82 per cent of pregnant adolescent girls had not planned to get pregnant.) When adolescent girls are asked how they "planned" to avoid pregnancy a stunning range of fables emerge.[5] For example:

- the belief that they did not have sex often enough to become pregnant;
- the belief that they did not experience an orgasm, and therefore, could not conceive;
- the belief they were "too young" to become pregnant;
- the belief that they would not be "caught" during high risk days (even when they understood the ovulation cycle);
- the belief that it couldn't happen to "me."

In a superbly documented investigation of adolescent sexual behavior, which Eleanor E. Maccoby of Stanford University described as "by far the best thing that's been written on the subject," Susan Moore and Doreen Rosenthal (1993) make pertinent observations on the adolescent thought process and its understanding of the relationship between pregnancy and contraception. They report:

> In some ways, these young women are reminiscent of the 'invulnerable' adolescents. . . . These are young people who believe that they are unlikely to suffer the negative consequences of their actions, and hence take risks that others would not (p. 149).

The authors then go on to report that Littlejohn, in her Australian research, "found that 20 per cent of pregnant teenagers did not think they needed to use contraception *because they couldn't get pregnant*" (1993, p. 149). Upon close inspection one usually discovers that these beliefs are not acquired from friends, from parents, or from TV; rather, for the most part, they are personal inventions, private creations, neither copied nor stolen, which derive from a *protective intellectualism* as natural to the adolescent mind as propositional thought.

Quite obviously, all thinking about sexual matters, even the serious business of pregnancy, is not fabled thinking. Some thinking blends fable with avoidance. This girl's experiences with unprotected sex indicate such a blend:

> I didn't ask him about it and he didn't ask me about it. It was really strange because I was terrified that I was going to get pregnant. I always thought about it, worried about it, *but I couldn't do any thing about it.*

> Although we didn't use contraception, and we didn't talk about it, I thought about it constantly, and I was scared. I even wrote a paper about teenage pregnancy for a psychology class. I remember working on it thinking, "This could be you, you have to do something about this." I remember having this feeling that I HAD to talk to him about it, but I couldn't. It seemed easier not to say anything and put it out of my mind, to try to forget about it (Garrod, p. 252).

Perhaps things are not really this complicated. Perhaps girls become pregnant simply because they cannot restrain themselves when sexually aroused. Their thinking is not fabled but merely over-powered by lust, by eroticism. Among early- and middle-adolescent girls this explanation is lacking because, according to youngsters themselves, the sexual act is not emotionally over-powering. For them, intercourse almost always has to do with something much more than the sexual. What the "much more" is remains the object of investigation.

> Pleasure does not appear to be a driving force in a teen girl's decision to become sexually involved with a boy; rather girls seem to enter into the relationship as a rite of passage that they must undergo. When a girl says that she feels it's time that she had sex with a boy her decision does not stem from unrestrainable passion (Ayers, 1994, p. 163).

If not from passion, from what? That is the basic question to which we have not as yet discovered a basic answer.

There is, I believe, a compromise fable which Elkind, and other investigators of this topic, have glossed over a bit too quickly. This fable is characterized by the admission that, for example, drug addiction might occur, or a car accident might happen, yet, at the same time, the fabulist concludes *that the usual consequences to these disasters will be avoided.* Thus even if they become addicted to drugs they will overcome their addiction when they choose to do so, and then lead a normal, even enriched life because of the "unique" experiences they will encounter in their downfall; or, even if pregnancy does occur, it will result in a happy child, a happy marriage, or a happy life as a single parent. In essence, the adolescent is fully aware that bad things routinely happen to others, but simultaneously accepts that, at least in certain selected domains, they will not happen to "me." Such is the nature of egocentric triumph within the thought process.[6]

Adolescent idealism: changing a mixed-up world

"The difference between a good man and a bad one is the choice of the cause."   William James

The idealism of youth is, most assuredly, not a "pure" idealism, if indeed there is such a thing. Like their elders, adolescents dream of greater things and hope for better days; but these dreams and hopes are enmeshed with egocentric starting points and self-enhancing premises:

> The reasoning of adolescents who have developed formal operations invariably seems to be idealistic. The idealism can be viewed as "false," or incomplete, idealism. *What looks like idealism frequently, in reality, is reasoning based on egocentric use of formal thought* (Wadsworth, 1989, p. 138).

This "egocentric use of formal thought," as Wadworth phrases it, is of great concern to us in our effort to understand the mechanics of adolescent idealism. Perhaps nowhere is the mix of egocentricity and intellect more potent than in the ideas for social reform held by those youth which Inhelder and Piaget (1958) first called *idealistic reformers.*

Idealistic reformers want to transform society in order to better satisfy their own needs. This egocentricity, in the words of Jean Piaget, is "one of the most enduring expressions of adolescence."

> the adolescent not only tries to adapt his ego to the social environment but, just as emphatically, *tries to adjust the environment to his ego.* In other words, when he begins to think about the society in which he is looking for a place, he has to think about his own future activity and about how he himself might transform this society. The result is a failure to distinguish between his point of view as an individual called upon to organize a life program and the point of view of the group which he hopes to reform.

The defining feature of idealistic reformers is *their failure to differentiate between their needs and the needs of others*: "the adolescent goes through a phase in which he attributes an unlimited power to his own thoughts so that he dreams of a glorious future of transforming the world through ideas. . . . (Inhelder and Piaget, 1958, pp. 343-346). Adolescents consumed with passion for social reform share with narcissists a sense of mission and a desire to be praised and celebrated for the greatness of their reforms and for the improvements in those who benefit from them.

The dreams of idealistic reformers are given fire by what ethicists call "right action," action for which no possible alternative, under the circumstances, is better. The reforms they demand simply are the most fitting for the situation, and as such, every clear-thinking, right-minded person *should* (frequently the ethical "should" evolves into a political "must") support them. The *fervor* which drives idealistic reform should not be downplayed. Strong feelings about ideals are virtually non-existent in children; it is in adolescence that ideas become fused with passion, a fusion which sparks glorious ambitions and heroic projects.

Idealistic reform, for some, is little more than an excuse to reject some disliked feature of one's society, one's school, or one's family. It is alleged that Lenin, upon reviewing the incredible diversity of citizens attracted to his social reforms, claimed: "Revolution attracts the best and the worst from society." In our society, where virtually all young people spend five days a week in school, where no important or meaningful jobs are available, and where parents are landlords, we find a fierce desire among many youth for reform – any reform. Among these youngsters the real agenda is venting anger, obtaining recognition, seeking revenge.

Idealistic reformers are obsessed with talking about their reforms, how they will initiate them, how dissenters will be punished, how these changes are destined by history, by race, by gender. One investigator described a similar tendency among troubled adults which may be worth a moment of our time:

> A sure symptom of this neurosis is the effort such individuals make to be certain that other people know about their unorthodox views as soon as possible on making their acquaintance. They are prone to whipping out their opinions, apropos of nothing at all, merely to flaunt them publicly. Because they value the unpopularity of their ideas, they are unlikely to do much to further general acceptance of these views, regardless of their protestations. They are more interested in shocking than communicating (Putney & Putney, 1964, p. 61).

Ideology and idealistic reform go hand in hand. Ideology is the system of ideas, beliefs, and attitudes which make up a world view; it is the doctrine which guides political and cultural plans, and provides the strategy for putting them into operation. An ideologue adheres to, believes in, and advocates the truth of a particular system of thought. Idealistic reformers, as one might predict considering their egocentric motives, are attracted to ideologies which support, defend, or in any way justify their reforms. In general, something of a dependency circuit exists between these two since effective reform cannot take place without a guiding ideology, and ideology has no power without reformers to put it into action; youth are attracted to the coherence of ideology and ideologs are attracted to the energy of youth. Hence, idealistic reformers and ideologs benefit symbiotically, each fueling the fire of the other.

"Without a revolutionary theory there can be no revolutionary movement." Vladimir Lenin

From what we have thus far discussed, idealistic reformers are a bewildering mixture of devotion to self and devotion to humanity. And how is such a potion brewed? How can the idealistic reformer hold lofty ideas and compassion for humankind and, at the same time, experience so much despair over human actions? Elkind's observation strikes me as especially fruitful:

> For one thing, the young person can conceive of ideal families, religions, and societies and when he compares these with his own family, religion, and society he often finds the latter wanting. Much of adolescent rebellion against adult society derives, in part at least, from this new capacity to construct ideal situations. The ideals, however, are almost entirely intellectual and the young person has little conception of how they might be made into realities and even less interest in working toward their fulfillment (1974, p. 103).

All of which brings to mind H. L. Mencken, the American literary critic and authority on prejudice, who once said: "The objection to puritans is not that they try to make us think as they do, but that they try to make us do as they think." What Mencken said applies, in no small measure, to the idealistic reformer.[7]

The language of psychic theatre

"How can I know what I think till I see what I say?" G. Wallas

One way to introduce the egocentric speech of adolescents is to take a quick look at the same phenomenon in children. The speech of 3, 4, and 5-year-olds almost always reflects their own immediate perspective, their own immediate desires. Their use of language is so privately grounded that they often use words and symbols completely meaningless to everyone else. Since their communications are self-based, preschoolers may speak right past each other without paying any attention to what kids next to them are saying. Elementary teachers know it is impossible to communicate effectively with first or second grade children without first sharing their frame, seeing with their eyes, for these children cannot, with much proficiency, climb out of their own frame, or see through the eyes of the teacher.

Here is how Patricia Miller expressed it:

Children who apparently are talking together while playing in a group may actually be talking, but not necessarily together. Each child's remarks are unrelated to anyone else's. There is a collective monolog, of sorts, rather than a conversation. For example, one child's statement, "I think I saw Superman in a phone booth yesterday," might be followed by "this sweater makes me itch" from another child (1989, p. 58).

The egocentric speech of children reflects their faith that *the listener will decode the intended meaning without the benefit of precise language.* (Under conditions of anxiety or defensiveness adolescents produce the same belief). Thus the child may blurt to mother "She dropped it on him," without explaining who "she" is, what "it" is, or who "him" is. Mothers understand these sentences only when they add to them the necessary information which the child left out; which, of course, they do with remarkable facility.

Thus far we have described egocentric speech as expressed by young children; the egocentric speech of adolescents is different, but particulars are shared.

First, it should be made clear that most adolescents are gifted speakers and effective conversationalists, especially in non-threatening environments. Their command of the rules of conversation (known as pragmatics) is commendable, as is their capacity to convey exact meaning to the people with whom they are communicating. They take their turn in conversation far better than children, and they are usually able to recognize when speech might be lost in the hubbub of confusion or distraction. They know how to use questions to convey commands (Why is everyone talking so loud at the dinner table?); how to deploy articles such as "the" and "a" in ways to enhance understanding (She is *the* person to see if you want a job); and how to tell stories, jokes, and anecdotes to entertain guests of varying ages. Despite these allocentric qualities, their speech is encumbered with many egocentric peculiarities.

Egocentric speech is the precursor to the "socialized speech" towards which it is maturing. In socialized speech the speaker takes into account the frame of reference of the listener; information is presented with less censorship, less contamination, less amputation. Margaret Donaldson hit the mark perfectly when she observed: "For a conversation to go smoothly, each participant needs to try to understand what the other knows already, does not know, needs to know for his purposes, wants to know for his pleasure" (1978, p. 18). This is the basis to functional, considerate speech.

H.P. Grice (1975) claimed that effective communication is governed by a master rule which he calls "the cooperative principle." Four maxims permit the cooperative principle to operate effectively.

- The maxim of quantity: Speak neither more nor less than required.

- The maxim of quality: Speak the truth and avoid falsehood.

- The maxim of relevance: Speak in a relevant and informative way.

- The maxim of clarity: Speak so as to avoid obscurity and ambiguity.

These maxims, of course, represent standards no one can meet all the time. They are standards, however, which we try to meet under specific conditions, especially when information needs to be conveyed accurately and with civility. Attempting to master the cooperative principle, and the four maxims which facilitate it, is an essential task of the adolescent years.

Parallel to the maxims of social language which Grice describes is a quite different form of speech which dwells on a plane of its own. As is true for children, the egocentric speech of teens includes espousing ideas without much concern for the exact meaning of what is spoken, and venting emotion more than expressing ideas. In egocentric speech "I" has the say, and "I" is more important than the say. Self-assertion and self-affirmation are the dominant motives in egocentric speech therefore, it often resembles proclaiming more than speaking. Egocentric speech is a form of self-assertion expressed through the melody of language; it attempts to lay claim to an unsatisfied desire, or an unmanageable impulse, through the articulation of words related to it. As if by ringing a word in circles one actually contains the desire, manages the impulse.

A variant of egocentric speech somewhat removed from what we have thus far discussed, is "pronoun contamination": dwelling so excessively on the pronoun in the sentence as to miss its meaning. Since they persistently attend to references pertaining to the self ("I," "me," "mine," "my") pronoun fixation typifies the speech of adolescents. It is not coincidental that Raskin and Shaw (1988) discovered that students scoring high on narcissism use significantly more first-person singular pronouns (I, me, my) in their spontaneous speech than other students. Plausibly, the egocentrism inherent to the thought process is an ally to the narcissism inherent to the personality.

A few examples may help. "My what good looking sandals you are wearing." "Yes, I am." "What beautiful leather." "I wear them when I'm in a good mood." Such a response to a friendly overture (so typical of early adolescent conversation) deflects the focus away from shoes (the original starting point) and re-directs to "me," the wearer of the shoes, and secondarily to "my" mood. Not infrequently, the adult who initiated the conversation may continue with "Where did you *buy* those sandals?" only to receive, "I call them my mood shoes. I wear them when I'm in a good mood." The conversation partner will encounter greater success when he or she accepts the reflex which governs the youngster's speech and strikes a conversation about the person's mood. Since this is a topic of egocentric concern, the sandal wearer may visit at length on this topic, but tire quickly when it shifts, for example, to a conversation about the partner's mood. Or, consider: "Your father is displeased with you because you skipped school yesterday." "Yes, I know. *He's* always angry about something." Here, the focus transforms from skipping school to father and his anger.

Egocentric thinkers want every interpretation to favor them, every ambiguity translated to their advantage. To this end lazy language is better suited than precise language. "Late" is superior to "1:30 a.m.," since any time can be late but only one time can be 1:30 a.m. "Out," superior to "At John's house" because out can be many places but John's house only one place. Collectively, "Out late" is much preferred to "At John's house until 1:30 a.m." Imprecise language expands freedom, precise language restricts it; loose language encourages self-priority.

"Teaching conversation that sets others at ease gives a teenage girl a useful tool in relationships. When she speaks of her *interests* rather than herself and *helps others to share their thoughts,* she is better able to relate in a way that builds her relationships and her self-esteem."

Lauren Ayers

We might ask ourselves what is being accomplished when someone imposes himself on the topic and thereby alters the flow of the conversation. To this question I would suggest the following: Egocentric speech re-prioritizes whatever the priority of the moment happens to be, replacing the original focus of discussion with a new and improved one, "me." Egocentric speech, in the final analysis, is simply the young person's attempt to make everything which pertains to "me" more important than everything which does not.[8]

Egocentric speech is one part of a strategy to preserve a piece of the world where "me" is greater than "we." It is a defense against the forces of neutrality, bureaucracy, and conformity. It is every young person's rebellion against everything which tries to subordinate "me."

Further observations on egocentrism, the thought process, and theatre of the mind

In this chapter I have dwelled, perhaps excessively, on the adolescent's susceptibility to a variety of irrational thought patterns and belief systems. I have tried to indicate how egocentrism contributes to the self-defeating irrationalities which punctuate adolescent life. Despite my chosen focus on adolescent egocentrism, I do not claim that adults are exempt from elaborate fables, imagined heroics, indeed entire warehouses of preposterous irrationalities. I have no desire to claim that teens monopolize irrationality; to do so discredits the folly of their parents. I have for some time now agreed with Bertrand Russell's assessment:

> Man is a rational animal – so at least I have been told. Throughout a long life, I have looked diligently for evidence in favor of this statement, but so far I have not had the good fortune to come across it, though I have searched in many countries spread over three continents (Egner & Denonn, 1961, p. 73).

My intent is modest: to indicate how illusions evolve from developmental processes and to indicate how adolescent cognition is embroiled in a valiant struggle to balance egocentricity with objectivity, self-centredness with other-centredness, as-if with as-is.

Egocentrism does not destroy intelligence, but merely channels it into domains where needs and cravings, not reason, are sovereign. (And, at the risk of racing ahead of the scheduled flow of ideas, what is true for egocentrism applies still more to narcissism.)

Our investigation of egocentrism and the adolescent thought process has, thus far, led us to three central conclusions:

- egocentrism encourages adolescents to perceive things not as they are, but as they wish them to be;

- egocentrism encourages adolescents to perceive things not as they are, but as they fear them to be, and;

- egocentrism encourages adolescents to perceive things not as they are, but as they have been trained to believe they will be.

Because of its significance to the issues at hand, I would like to now recall a statement written by Rolf Muuss quoted earlier in this chapter.

> Egocentrism in the cognitive structure of the adolescent makes it difficult for the individual to differentiate between his own highly idealistic thought processes (how things ought to be) and the real world (how things are).

This statement underscores what I want to say in this chapter. Its implications are momentous and affect profoundly our whole view of how teens think. What could possibly be more relevant to self-knowledge, to morality, to ideology, than difficulty differentiating between "how things ought to be" and "how things are"? What is more relevant to planning for the future than the struggle between one's own "highly idealistic thought processes" and "the real world"?

David Hamburg, as President of the Carnegie Foundation, and overseer of one of the most constructive youth assistance programs in North America, has thoughts on youth's need for educational mentors and spiritual stewards. What he has to say speaks directly to psychic theatre. I present his thoughts for your consideration here in the closing moments of this chapter.

> There is a crucial need to help adolescents at this early age to acquire durable self-esteem, flexible and inquiring minds, reliable and relatively close human relationships, a sense of belonging in a valued group, *and a sense of usefulness in some way beyond the self.* They need to find constructive expression for their inherent curiosity and exploratory energy; and they need a basis for making informed, deliberate decisions – especially on matters that have large consequences, such as their educational future and drug use.

> The challenge for schools and related institutions is thus to help provide the building blocks of adolescent development and preparation for adult life. Yet most American junior high and middle schools do not meet the developmental needs of young adolescents. These institutions have the potential to make a powerful impact on the development of their students – for better or for worse. . . . We need to develop interventions that can help adolescents cope with several problems at once. . . .

> Early adolescents need attention from adults who can be positive role models, mentors, and sources of accurate information on important topics. . . .They need to learn interpersonal and communication skills, self-regulation, decision-making, and problem-solving skills. Early adolescence is a prime opportunity to teach such skills (1992, p. 241).

Postscript

The conclusions we come to, even if we arrive at them somewhat tentatively, are these:

- The Mozart we call youth is orchestrated by a medley of intellectual operations all of which are influenced by egocentric irrationalities. I gladly and freely remind the reader that these irrationalities are not the only forces guiding the adolescent's intellect; but they are of sufficient importance to warrant our close attention. I have chosen the term "psychic theatre" to characterize these mental operations which include imagined audiences, heroic fables, idealistic reform, and egocentric speech.

- The personal fable and the imaginary audience are similar in their origins, but different in their focus. In the imaginary audience the individual is fascinated with how the audience responds to the leading actor, "me"; in personal fables the leading actor can never be fully comprehended by the audience: standing apart from the rest of humanity is part of the script. Fables nurture the belief that one is grand and glorious, even immune to calamity. Fables embolden and invigorate the narcissism natural to all youth.

- Idealistic reformers channel their internal desires into social reform which may speak to the real needs of real people, but, most frequently, they speak to one's own desires and fears.

- Egocentric speech spices the monolog, the dialog, and, of course, the soliloquy of psychic theatre.[9] It is one of the defining qualities of youth; as it disappears, so also does youth as we know it.

Endnotes

[1] **Distortion**. In human perception distortion takes many forms, and in this chapter we describe only a few. In general, distortions occur when we see others in light of our own needs, desires, and fears. Most typically, these distortions yield three basic outcomes all of which, to greater or lesser degree, degrade clarity of thought.

- They endow others with characteristics they do not have, or have only to a minor degree.

- They cause the perceiver to be blinded towards positive assets in others, such as friendship or devotion, or, cause the perceiver to be blinded toward liabilities such as lying or exploitation.

- They result in the perceiver's being clear-sighted toward certain behaviors within others, and having a keen alertness to certain positive or negative traits. This "clear-sightedness" is focussed into specific domains for reasons specific to the perceiver, and as a result, they preclude an overall perspective. These distortions are not blatant misrepresentations, but rather, subtle re-arrangements and realignments.

[2] J. Arnett (1992) describes adolescent thinking in terms of "a probability bias" in which youth accurately assess other people's susceptibility to a set of conditions, but do not associate themselves with the same susceptibility.

[3] Lauren Ayers expressed it as straightforwardly as anyone. "A young teenage girl has neither the wisdom nor the experience to handle the risks of sexual activity, and the statistics bear out the damage done to young females. The foresight, responsibility, and integrity required for responsible sex come only with maturity and cannot be made to develop earlier" (1994, p. 64).

[4]   This is especially true in teen pregnancy. To reinforce the prevalence of this way of thinking, McGuire's (1983) investigation of teen pregnancy is entitled *It Won't Happen To Me: Teenagers Talk About Pregnancy*.

[5]   We know more about the thinking of girls because of their accessibility to research in programs for pregnant teens.

[6]   Fabulists sometimes think of themselves as "romantics," and this is not without some foundation, as fables tend to share particulars with romanticism and the romantic perspective. Fables, like romanticism, highlight the rebellion of feeling against reason, of passion against intellect, of sentiment against judgment, of solitude against society, of imagination against reality, of passionate love against quiet friendship, of emotional expression against reasoned response, of individual freedom against social order, of young against old, of we against them.

[7]   The cumulative effect of personal fables and social reform are discernible in what Howard Gardner called "interpersonal intelligence." In Gardner's theory interpersonal intelligence refers to *the ability to read accurately the moods and motives of the individuals with whom one interacts*, to assess realistically the dispositions and sentiments of other people. In Gardner's words:

> The core capacity here is the ability to notice and make distinctions among other individuals and, in particular, among their moods, temperaments, motivations, and intentions. Examined in its most elementary form, the interpersonal intelligence entails the capacity of the young child to discriminate among the individuals around him and to detect their various moods. In an advanced form, interpersonal knowledge permits a skilled adult to read the intentions and desires – even when these have been hidden – of many other individuals and, potentially, to act upon this knowledge – for example, by influencing a group of disparate individuals to behave along desired lines (1983, p. 239).

Interpersonal intelligence is only one domain of intelligence. But its significance should not be underestimated in the teen world, a world in which the failure to demonstrate the "core capacity" of interpersonal intelligence invites both exploitation and corruption.

[8]   **Egocentrism and conversation.** Egocentric speech tends to lessen when the self is praised, acknowledged or consulted on a regular basis. With continuous acknowledgement the egocentric core does not insist on *excessive* respect. Some youth, however, so hunger for acknowledgement that they will not participate in conversation unless it is preceded by a series of self-affirming gestures. When the message pertains to immediate needs such preliminaries are less necessary; however, when the message holds no immediate relevance it may be impossible to communicate without some ritualized ego-massage to open the mental air waves.

[9]   **Egocentric speech.** Marlene Webber (1991), who spent two years in the streets of urban Canada interviewing runaways, relates a telling tale of harmless, though typical, egocentrism. In preparing to conduct an interview with a young man, one of dozens whom she interviewed for her book, she had gone to great lengths to explain to him that in her book no

names would be revealed, that anonymity would be maintained through-out, and that, in disappointing fact, because of time and space constraints, most of the youngsters she interviewed would never even be included in the book. After these ground rules had been carefully established and agreed to by the young man, an interview followed. Upon its conclusion a friend of the young man arrived; he was introduced to the author with typical egocentric panache: "This is the lady I told ya about that's gonna write a book about me" (p. 9).

Chapter Four

beclouded thinking

"Generally, youth is like the first cogitations, not so wise as the second; for there is a youth in thoughts as well as in ages."   Francis Bacon

What do we mean by beclouded thinking?

While writing this chapter I encountered an interesting phenomenon that is worth a moment. In my consultations with the academics who assisted and advised me I consistently received a puzzled, noncomprehending look when I informed them that my concern was with the foggy, beclouded thinking so frequently displayed by adolescents. They seemed dazed and confused by the idea of "beclouded" thought; they repeatedly asked me what I was getting at. None of them could find "beclouded" in the index of any of their adolescent psychology texts, and this added to their perplexity. As things turned out, their assistance proved meagre indeed. On the other hand, my 150 adolescent subjects (and their parents) showed no such bewilderment. They grasped the topic immediately; not one of them required any clarification as to the meaning of beclouded thinking. The idea that adolescent thought is sometimes "beclouded" was completely believable to them because their own experiences confirmed it.

"Beclouded" thinking, in my scheme of things, refers to the tendency for thought to become hazy, foggy, blurred, inconsistent, self-serving, and, most usually, inaccurate. In this chapter I will try to outline some of its expressions in the teen community.

One may infer that the opposite of beclouded thinking is clear thinking, but this is not so; its opposite is *critical* thinking.[1] A quick look at what we mean by critical thinking will make this more apparent.

Critical thinking requires one to categorize, infer, and deduce. Critical thinkers must know something about the content in question; for example, to evaluate a reformer's ideas about changing the school system, one must be knowledgeable about the existing school system. Critical thinking, then, relies on having substantive knowledge about the topic to which critical thought is being directed.

But this is not all. A critical thinker must also have solid knowledge about how human thinking works: "Effective critical thinking requires a person to monitor when she really understands an idea, know when she needs new information, and predict how easily she can gather and learn that information" (Seifert & Hoffnung, 1994, p. 532). Critical thinkers must possess some criteria of fairness and objectivity, and enough insight into their own mental operations to know when they are straying from fairness and objectivity. Critical thinking involves skillful judgment as to truth and merit.

The young person's balancing act between critical thought and fabled thought, between objective thinking and emotionalized thinking, between fearless investigation and fearful protectionism capture our interest in this chapter. To assist our investigation, four "beclouding tendencies" are described:

- the tendency to regress to concrete thought;
- the tendency to emotionalize thought;
- the tendency to argue from narcissistic premises; and,
- the tendency to self-deception.

The tendency to regress to concrete thought

"The defining character of thought is its product."   Jerome Bruner

Adolescence, everyone agrees, is an age of transition. By no means, however, is it a transition that flows in smooth, completely predictable progressions. On the contrary, it is a transition where progress advances in clutches and spurts, interspersed with plateaus, and occasionally with backsliding regressions. One outcome of this crab-like cadence is that teens (especially 13- and 14-year-olds) are prone, every now and again, to regress to thought modes which worked effectively in child-hood but which cannot handle the richer and more complex demands of adolescence. Cognitive psychologists refer to this intellectual slip-page as "the tendency to regress to concrete thought." As we recall from materials introduced in chapters one and two, at the "concrete" level of intellectual development children not only accept hypotheses as facts, they sometimes reject facts as if they were mere hypotheses. This failure to differentiate "actual facts" from "mere hypotheses" is a thought deficiency which, especially during adolescence, gets in the way of effective thinking.

When the hypotheses of children are challenged by new informa-tion they sometimes "bend" this new information to better fit their pre-existing viewpoints. Rarely does it occur to them to re-evaluate a belief simply because new evidence fails to support it. Children believe (much like narcissistic adolescents) that because the hypothesis is "mine" it holds a special validity, that it is imbued with its own logical consistency; therefore, it does not seem reasonable to them to change a belief simply because some new information contradicts it. The point to be seized is that even though such thinking is completely normal to children, and that the *ability* to move beyond it is attained with formal thought, this primitive thought sequence appears time and again during adolescence. However, and here the thinking profile of teens again parallels that of children, primitive thought sequences are most likely to occur when the adolescent investigates data, people, or experiences unflattering to the self-concept. And, as one might expect, this tendency contributes to the hit-and-miss quality of teen thought, its tendency to be bright and coherent on one topic, yet dull and jumbled on another.

Among mature thinkers, when evidence fails to support a hypothesis, it is nevertheless re-examined on the chance that something was missed. Children almost never follow this procedure. Thus, an eleven-year-old who believes that he is the best baseball player in the 5th grade, and predicts that he will be the first player chosen when teams are selected, may not alter his belief in his own supremacy even when he is chosen last. He may simply interpret the facts in a self-enhancing way, i.e., "The other players are jealous of me," "I really didn't want to play on this team." The point here is that the belief is not rejected simply because it is not supported.

Adolescents, much more than children, face evidence when and where it presents itself and, as a result, they are more inclined to re-work their beliefs in the light of new evidence. "Maybe the coach is right. I'm not as good as I thought." Nothing heroic here, simply the realignment of a belief to better fit the data; a normal indicator of maturing thought.

"As often as a study is cultivated by narrow minds, they will draw from it narrow conclusions."	John Stuart Mills

Children rarely approach complex questions by analyzing all possible solutions; rather, they generate a conclusion after looking at only a portion of the available clues. Such piecemeal investigation is the result of centrational thought – deriving a premature solution from incomplete data. This predisposition to hastily choose one solution, rather than to investigate further possibilities, diminishes comprehensiveness. This limitation, ironically, allows the child to produce "solutions" to highly complex problems which baffle more advanced thinkers who recognize the difference between any solution and a worthy solution.

Concrete thought does not disappear with the advent of formal thought, but co-exists with it. Concrete thought is the means by which we solve simple, basic problems, i.e., the amount of coal 30 trucks can haul in 30 days if each truck hauls 30 tons per day. Or, how much money you need to buy a loaf of bread and a litre of milk if you know the price of each. More complex problems which require inference, verification, operational definitions are the stuff of formal thought. In the simplest possible language, the tendency to regress to concrete thought becomes a problem when concrete strategies are applied to a problem requiring formal strategies.

The tendency to slip back into concrete thought patterns, (or to use concrete strategies inappropriately) is the first of the beclouding tendencies; it is not, however, the only one.

The tendency to emotionalize thought [2]

"The head is always fooled by the heart."
Francois, duc de La Rochefoucauld

No psychologists has ever claimed, to my knowledge, that adolescents always think logically, or that they always maximize their powers of formal thought. From the beginning, Piaget, Inhelder and their followers recognized this fact of adolescent intellectualism. Piaget hypothesized that while formal reasoning is theoretically available to teens they often do not use it because of a lack of familiarity with the tasks they are required to reason about. He was quick to point out that the power to reason does not exist on a one-to-one relationship with its expression. "Individuals who have developed, and who thus have this type of reasoning available in their cognitive repertoire, may, in fact, prefer to reason on a concrete level, *or not to reason at all in many situations*." Furthermore: "it may be the case that although an individual has developed the competence to reason formally, the individual may not have developed the appropriate strategies or procedures to best access and apply this competence" (Overton, 1991).

As a point of information: La Rochefoucauld was not correct in his claim that "The head is always fooled by the heart." But he was, so to speak, right enough. Our concern is with how emotionality sways the thought process but our focus is not on love, hate, or, for that matter, any of the glorious passions. It is not necessary to look at the extremes of emotion to find its influence on the thought process, indeed, the natural egocentric elements inherent to adolescence are sufficient to becloud the thinking apparatus.

Cold logic, warm logic

The "cold" side of logic is *inductive*; reasoning which produces a conclusion containing more information than the observations or experience on which it is based. For example: "Every crow that has ever been seen is black; therefore, all crows are black." The truth to this conclusion is verifiable only in terms of future experience and certainty in the matter is attained only if all possible instances have been examined. No certainty is afforded that a white crow will not be found in the future, but experience makes such an occurrence extremely unlikely. Inductive logic also is the process by which we conclude that what is true of certain individuals is true of a class, that what is true of part is true of the whole, or what is true at certain times will be true in similar circumstances at all times. It is a method of reasoning by which a general law or principle is inferred from observed particular instances.

Deductive logic is a bit different because it is a form of reasoning where the inference process leads from general to particular statements; it is also the only reasoning where the premises provide absolutely conclusive evidence for the truth of the conclusions. Reasoning "If computers are used for business, then the cost of such a computer merits a tax deduction." "This computer is used for business," therefore, "The cost of this computer merits a tax deduction," is deductive reasoning. If the premises are true, they provide absolute certainty that the conclusion is true.

Inductive and deductive thinking operate on calm reasoning and comparative objectivity. *Affective logic, on the other hand, is a sequence of judgments in which the connection between one judgment and another is emotional.* "Susan is nice to me; she is good." Or, "I received a 'D' in Mr. Wilson's class; he hates me." Affective logic binds ideas to an emotional response; it persuades by speaking to cravings, desires, and fears: "There are too many students in the university; therefore we should keep all minorities out." Affective logic blends rational thinking with subjective desires under the guise of objective thought, fostering the illusion that impartial thought is at work. It directs thought toward things emotional and in so doing *inclines the thinker to accept arguments* which are tautological, beg the question, persuade by style rather than by substance, rely on prestige, insult the opponent, employ theatric pleading, and attribute prejudice to the opponent's point of view. In sum, affective logic is a form of intellectualism in which the thought process is molded by passion and reason combined, rather than by reason alone; this mixture gives it a volatile, "hot-blooded" quality that sets it apart from the more disciplined, "cold-blooded" inductive and deductive reasoning. When the topic under investigation is impassioned, or when the topic holds emotional implications to the thinker, affective logic flows freely and easily.

"The function of reason is to allow the expression of certain passions at the expense of others."   Friedrich Nietzsche

---

Learning to differentiate one emotional state from another, learning to decode the meaning of a powerful experience, learning to carry-on in the presence of unwanted emotional states, are each part of the adolescent struggle for self-knowledge. Mastering this assignment takes on even greater significance for individuals whose affective states are powerful, and for whom assistance is not forthcoming from parents or, for that matter, from any adult. David Wexler, who specializes in the treatment of youngsters deemed, by their own admission, to be emotionally out of control, places this predicament in perspective.

> Perhaps the most important goal of treatment is to help adolescents learn to identify and label internal states. We would like for them to be able to use affect as a form of self-signaling rather than a trigger for reacting impulsively. The chaos of adolescent internal functioning is organized by our clearly explained approach of distinguishing thoughts from feelings. This distinction has never occurred to most of these kids; this new skill helps them establish internal structure. Nor are they skilled at differentiating anger from anxiety from excitement from grief from jealousy from guilt. They know that "something is happening," but are hard-pressed to name the emotion (Wexler, 1991, p. 35).

In short, integrating the truth of reason with the truth of emotion is a necessary achievement in the young person's life. Much of the confusion of adolescence involves the struggle to balance the narcissistic richness of "warm" logic with the neutrality of "cold" logic.

Entitlement-thinking

When a person believes that he (she) is entitled to receive special favors without assuming any responsibilities in exchange for receiving these favors, this person is characterized by *entitlement*. Millon described it as "their inalienable right to receive special considerations" (1981, p. 158). Rothstein said: "they feel entitled to have what they want when they want it just because they want it." (1984, p. 67).

One outcome of entitlement thinking is the preposterous expectation that every difference of opinion *should be* settled to their advantage; that in every dispute they are entitled to receive the benefit of the doubt; that others should always accommodate their beliefs. Further, entitlement-thinking (since it is grounded in the egocentric presumption of self-priority) causes the individual to assume that his (her) ideas and beliefs contain *an inherent truthfulness*, while the beliefs of others must be defended by sound reasoning, by overwhelming evidence. In sum, a double-standard of intellectual accountability beclouds their thinking; others must defend their ideas as in a court of law, whereas "I" am entitled to believe whatever suits my needs and desires.

Although the origins of entitlement thinking are not clear, it is worth underscoring that its themes have a good deal in common with the egocentrism of children, with the selfishness of "the narcissistic attitude," and with the self-serving side of affective logic. In terms of its power to corrupt the thought process, entitlement thinking is among the most profound of all the beclouding tendencies.

Emotionalizing arguments

In its civil expression an argument is a discussion in which reasons are put forward in support of, or against, an opinion, procedure, proposal, or the like; which is to say an informal debate. In reasoned argumentation the participants attempt to demonstrate the truth or falsehood of a proposition, or any idea. This may sound more orderly than it is in real life, especially when the debaters are adolescents and when the propositions bear, in any way, on self-esteem, popularity, humiliation, or any number of emotionally charged realities. Arguments can be "won" and they can be "lost," but in real life rarely is an agreed upon judge present to arbitrate; hence, arguers decide winners and losers on their own, often by the use of criteria which have nothing whatsoever to do with the argument itself.

To emotionalize is to place monochrome ideas in inseparable association with the richness and beauty of feeling; and, to invest thought with a richer payoff because of the muscular, respiratory, and visceral sensations which come with it, the jewels of self-immersion. Adolescents resist "cold" reason because it is concerned more with what is being reasoned about than with them. The impersonal, neutral tone required of objective reason is repulsive to their narcissism.

The strategies for keeping one's ideas, attitudes, and convictions beyond the assault of reason are inventive and numerous; a few are included here for your consideration.

(a) Angering an opponent so that he (or she) will argue badly: ("Of course you think I should be home before midnight, you are a woman-hating male." "You wouldn't understand being in love, you never really loved Dad." "What do you know about homework. You're just a construction worker who didn't graduate from high school").

Angering an opponent is made easier by the use of narrow, antagonizing definitions of everyday words with which the opponent is familiar. For example, defining "teacher" as one who lets the student freely choose his (or her) own course of study, or "parent" as one who slavishly looks after the child's every need; or, conversely, defining "teacher" as a lackey of administrative oppression and "parent" as police officer. Using words in such an inflammatory way seals the real object of investigation from open inquiry.

(b) Accepting or rejecting an idea, not on its merits, but on its popularity with the audience. This tendency carries great weight in peer-group discussions and philosophical "bull-sessions."

(c) Using affect to reduce the listener's concentration on the object of disagreement: "Dad, I know you always want me to be happy and to do what is right for me – well, quitting school and getting a job is best for me and will make me happy."

(d) Disarming the opponent with charm. Albert Camus, the great existential thinker, knew well the power of charm. "You know what charm is: a way of getting the answer yes without having asked any clear question." Charm is an attractive strategy to anyone who has trouble getting the answer "yes" through mere reason or muscle.

(e) Attributing prejudices or undesirable motives to one's opponent: ("You hate Jason because he is white." "Why should I work? Your generation screwed up the world"). Deflecting from the issue-at-hand to the unworthy qualities of the opponent.

(f) Using emotion-laden words to deflect the topic from the question at hand. ("It is hard for me to talk about responsibility when it was you who *divorced* my Dad and *ruined our family*" "Historians are all male chauvinist pigs who leave women out of their disgusting 'brave men and their heroic deeds' stories. It makes me sick." Or after parents discover drugs in the bedroom: "I can't believe you *invaded my* privacy. I feel like I have been violated").

Highly charged buzzwords emotionalize conversation; incendiary language is a specialty of thinkers who utilize affective logic.

The fear of reason

Most teens are not firm believers in the reasoning process. Their faith in reasoned verdicts is tentative because they doubt not only the reasoning process as it expresses itself in others, but as it expresses itself in themselves. And even though they have no choice except to acknowledge their own common sense, they do not necessarily believe that it is completely trustworthy or that it will lead them to their desired destination. The generally accepted explanation for this ambivalence toward their own thought process is that adolescents struggle with knowing when a thought is caused by their own limitations and prejudices and when it is caused by "things as they are." Their emotions are sometimes so diffuse that they do not know for certain when (or if) their thoughts merely mirror their emotions. As a result, they have difficulty with the objectivity required of critical analysis, and the discipline required of a fair, open-minded critique. This does not mean they cannot think critically, or that they cannot assemble a fair, open-minded critique. It means they experience considerable difficulty with these mental exercises, and that they are inclined to abandon them if they do not receive special assistance and encouragement along the way. Their willingness to give up on calm, impartial reason attracts them even more to the rhythm of affective logic.

Another feared aspect of reason is its neutrality. Since it is not grounded in favoritism, reason carries a calm matter-of-factness which many youngsters fear. Reason attempts to read things as they are, to create an image which honestly reflects the issue at hand. It cannot favor one fact over another, consequently, it threatens one's narcissism.

The dominant attitude towards reason during adolescence is cautious skepticism. When it begins to dismantle a belief system, or a fable-system, the youngster may simply reject it. "I don't want to hear any more of this." "I don't care if it doesn't make sense." "Let's not talk it to death, OK?" The hostile relationship with reason may last for years, during which affective logic, cynicism, and blank indifference carry the day. Teens fear reason because they are afraid of being convinced of something of which they don't want to be convinced. After all, what is the point to reason if it takes you someplace you don't want to go!

An additional point is worth a moment. Many youngsters wonder if they will ever attain the common sense that everyone else seems to have in such abundance. They worry about their relationship with reason; they worry about whether they will ever completely control their own reasoning apparatus, if they will ever win all of their arguments with themselves. These fears add up to anxiety over rationality.

> In our society it is assumed that the normal person is *rational*, and can give lucid reasons and justifications for his or her motives, moods, and behaviors. Thus, any indication of an inability to provide some logical accounting to himself, or herself, or others threatens the self-image of the adolescent or adult and generates anxiety. For the adolescent who oscillates from euphoria to depression, from lethargy to frantic activity, from purposeful determination to paralyzing doubt, or from careful, sometimes almost compulsive, planning to impulsive action, without any clearly ascertainable basis in his or her own mind for such fluctuations, anxiety over rationality can at times be very real (Conger & Peterson, 1982, p. 56).

In sum, adolescents do not stand with open arms, waiting for the grace of reason to redeem their intellectual spirit. Nothing within the adolescent personality unfailingly moves them either toward or away from reason. Like most unproven commodities, reason is welcomed in proportion to its utility, its ease, and its social value. When reason proves difficult, unproductive, or unpopular, it often is simply abandoned. This periodic abandonment of reason is a significant factor in the beclouded thinking of youth.

The tendency to argue unfairly

The youthful penchant for unfair argumentation derives from a combination of inexperience with things intellectual (including the art of debate), lack of practice in the smooth transmission of *contested* ideas, and the need to protect the self from the injury of criticism.[3] As E. A. Peel observed in *The Nature of Adolescent Judgment*: "The light of mature reason does not suddenly shed its clarity upon the young adolescent as by a magic wand: the growth from childhood to late adolescence is continuous" (1971, p. 135). He could have, but didn't, add: "And slow."

Among the practical considerations we should take into account when surveying the adolescent thinking process is that when they feel that their knowledge is too weak to answer objections put to them they may respond by casting suspicion on the motives behind the objections. Which is to say, when they cannot handle a problem they may disparage the person who posed it. This reflex, so integral to their intellectual style, is one they must abandon if they are to become critical thinkers.

Here I would like to provide, in no specific order of importance, a few of the more commonly observed outcomes of this frustrating combination of inexperience and protectionism which contributes to the propensity to argue poorly, whether one is six, sixteen, or sixty. But, at least from the limited frame of this author, a tendency exercised more vigorously at sixteen than at either six or sixty.

(a) Making statements in which "all" is implied but "some" is true. Arguing by totality and universality when the question at hand is specific and local. "Everyone does it," when only some are doing it; "I'll be the only one who doesn't have one," when many do not. "Mr. Smith always picks on me," when Mr. Smith only once did so. This tendency is especially prevalent during early adolescence when either/or, black/white, right/wrong thinking exerts a forceful presence in the thought process.

(b) Using proof by selected instances. ("Jane's parents let her use their car and she never crashes it"; "Doing drugs doesn't hurt your grades: I have a friend who smokes pot and he's an honor student"). The youngster who thinks to himself, "I didn't make the team, I'm a real loser" is using proof by selected instances. So is one who argues: "Our principal has a tattoo and people respect *him*!"). The practical advantage of this strategy is to create the illusion that one specific example of one real-life event somehow is adequate grounds for justifying a larger issue. ("If people like me don't get part-time jobs, how will the economy ever turn around?"). This strategy is especially prevalent when youngsters are motivated more to "prove" their point than to evenly evaluate the "proof" in question.

(c) Opposing a proposition by misrepresenting it: ("I am opposed to kids having to do household chores and to all forms of child slavery"; "I don't listen to feminists because they are lesbians").

A favorite ploy is to disagree with what doesn't exist, or with what barely exists. "Abortionists hate babies – babies are our future." This tendency misrepresents an idea in order to better attack it; a common strategy when the misrepresented idea is easier to attack than the original idea.

(d) Diverting to a side issue when one is losing a point; ("You always treat me like a kid." "You said I was old enough to make my own decisions"). Attacking the person who holds the disputed opinion rather than the opinion itself. Arguing with her mother over whether she should be dating an older man, the daughter accuses: "At least I have a steady boyfriend. You go out with a different guy every week." All of this is in accord with the tendency to deflect and distort the focus of the argument in the hopes of gaining the upper hand.

(e) Promoting a conclusion simply because it is the mean between two extremes; claiming that compromise is always just and reasonable. Mother tells the child to be home at midnight; the child replies that she wants to return home at 4 a.m. An argument ensues. The child says: "OK, let's compromise, 2 o'clock." Notably missing from the reasoning process is that compromise involves more than merely halving the difference between two contested viewpoints. Interestingly, enhancing one's position through compromise increases as perspective-taking increases, a point not to be lost on those who claim that understanding the point of view of another always encourages acceptance (or tolerance) of it.

(f) Using a syllogism with undistributed middle term. "She's good at math. Nerds are good at math. She must be a nerd." This is merely part of the larger tendency to argue with unsound form, especially arguing in a circle, or presenting arguments in which the premises and conclusions are identical. Associated with this tendency is arguing so that no other conclusion is deemed plausible: "Only an idiot would believe that disputes can be settled in the United Nations." "Every moral person knows that abortion is murder." Begging the question: "Why should I try to get people to like me; you can't be popular unless you're a cheerleader."

(g) Stating one's position over and over but without defending the *merit* of the position. The use of tautology, the repetition of the same idea in different words. Arguing as if by stating the viewpoint over and over somehow makes it correct; entrenchment through repetition. ("Tremaine quit school and he makes $50 000 a year." "Yeh, but he's a drug dealer." "Yeh, but he makes $50 000 a year". "He might get sent to prison, or get killed." "Yeh, but he makes $50 000 a year"). This form of argumentation holds some parallels with egocentric speech in that its value to the arguer seems to be found *in the act of saying* rather than in the substance of what is said.

(i) Arguing by forced analogy. An analogy is drawing a link between things otherwise dissimilar; an inference based on the assumption that if two things are alike in some respects they will be alike in others. With adolescents (and children) reasoning errors about known alikes are commonplace. "Jane's Mom's letting her have a party, so I should be able to have one too." "Teachers are allowed to smoke at school so students should be allowed to smoke at school." Arguing by forced analogy, like so many forms of emotionalized argumentation, is used because "winning" the argument is more important to the arguer than the merit of the argument.

(j) Failure to say exactly what it is that you are proposing: "School is stupid"; "Teachers are unfair." "I'm tired of being exploited." Employing vagueness in the key terms of an exchange. (In response to the parent's demand to know where the teen was until 2 a.m.: "Out." In response to what were you doing: "Nothing." In response to what do you hate about school: "Everything.") The refusal to use precise language protects against precise rebuttal; a fact of debate most kids learn by grade 6.

(k) Claiming that new "prestige" words are more powerful than ordinary words. This policy contributes to a fascination with buzzwords and clichés: "It's not my fault I drink too much. I come from a *dysfunctional family*, my parents *emotionally abuse* me, I suffer from *unrecovered memories*." A parallel tendency is to gain prestige by the use of pseudotechnical jargon. Both of these habits make it difficult for the young person to distinguish erudition from pretentiousness.

(l) Arguing by "straw-man" – a phony argument set up to be easily knocked down to produce an easy victory; often such "straw-man" arguments have emotional, anxiety-provoking aspects which persuade by diffusing logical thought, by preventing focus on the central issues in question. "Scientists make bombs because they don't care about the people they kill." "Straw-man" arguments are common fare for propagandists; their value to youth, however, is in their ability to produce seemingly logical points which are, in fact, artificial.

In assembling this collection of argumentative strategies I do not mean to imply that only teens subscribe to them. Quite obviously, they are deployed by people of all ages. Among teens, (and children as well) these unworthy arguments carry a certain reflexive quality, which is to say that the arguer usually is unaware of the strategies that he (she) is implementing. From the developmentalist's point of view, this is critical in distinguishing adolescent from adult beclouded thinking. It is one of the tasks of household education (and formal schooling) to help the young person learn to recognize when arguments are shaped by these beclouding maneuvers.

Rationalization

"A great many people think they are thinking when they are rearranging their prejudices."   William James

Thus far I have put forth the modest thesis that data-rearrangement is a natural outgrowth of how the adolescent mind is organized, and, that it is natural to bury from awareness painful and unwanted truths. Here I would like to indicate some of the ways this natural process conjoins with *rationalization.*

The term "rationalization" is confusing because its "rational" prefix inclines us to think it is an objective process. It is not. Objective reasoning attempts to *discover real* reasons whereas rationalization merely *invents acceptable* reasons. The teenage boy who justifies his daily run on bikini beach with "the sand is a better running surface than the high school track" (which is five miles closer) gives us reason to suspect rationalization. So also does the teacher who formerly opposed extra-curricular activities because they are "juvenile," but now that they bring extra pay, believes that they enhance maturity. *Rationalizations provide acceptable explanations which pass for truth,* but their real purpose is, in one way or another, to bolster our self-esteem, to make us appear important, to make us look better in our own eyes and in the eyes of others.[4]

Ernest Jones, Sigmund Freud's famed biographer, introduced the term "rationalization"; he used it to mean finding acceptable reasons to justify an action motivated by something less noble. In general usage, rationalization refers to protecting our self-esteem by finding socially accepted reasons for our behavior, and to the tendency to cushion our failures and our disappointments with a platitude.

Ultimately, rationalizations are for self-consumption since our actions, first and foremost, must appear reasonable to ourselves.

> However unreasonable or immoral an action may be, man has an insuperable urge to prove to himself and to others that his action is determined by reason, common sense, or at least conventional morality. He has little difficulty in acting irrationally, but it is almost impossible for him not to give his actions the appearance of reasonable motivation (Fromm, 1955, p. 65).

Rationalizations are doubted and disputed. If I claim that attendance in my university class is high because I am an excellent lecturer, and a student points out that "It's high because you grade on attendance," my claim has lost credibility. Since rationalizations must be defended in a somewhat reasonable manner, conceptually organized, articulate individuals tend to execute them more effectively than disorganized, verbally inept individuals. When a rationalization does not appear reasonable, plausible, or even possible, it does not advance its author. The intellectual dexterity involved in effective rationalizations led Nancy McWilliams to claim: "The more intelligent and creative a person is, the more likely it is that he or she is a good rationalizer" (1994,

p. 125). A rejected rationalization is nothing more than a bungled attempt to aggrandize oneself.

The most common rationalizations are "sweet lemons" and "sour grapes." Sweet lemon is indicated when one claims that "What I've got is what I want." (I have a lemon, but it is a sweet one, or at least, sweet enough.) Sour grapes enter when one concludes: "What I missed wasn't worth getting." (I don't have any grapes but it doesn't matter because they were sour). The adolescent community, with its unfulfilled hopes and unrealized ambitions, welcomes rationalizations which encourage them to accept what they have and to devalue what they don't.

We cannot help but notice the links between rationalization and moralization since it is one of the more striking instances of how the adolescent mind tries to make whatever one does seem morally superior.

> Moralization is a close relative of rationalization. When one is rationalizing, one unconsciously seeks cognitively acceptable grounds for one's direction; when one is moralizing, one seeks ways to feel it is one's *duty* to pursue that course. Rationalization converts what the person already wants into reasonable language; moralization puts it into the realm of the justified or morally obligatory. Where the rationalizer talks about the "learning experience" that some disappointment provided, the moralizer will insist that it "builds character" (McWilliams, 1994, p. 125).

That every human behavior has several motivations, not merely one, allows creative thinkers to manufacture "good" as well as "bad" motives. Rationalization highlights the good reasons and pushes into the background the bad reasons – making us all slightly grander than we really are.

Lying

Rationalization is not the same as lying, but it shares enough similarities to merit a look. Rationalization is self-deception, lying is other-deception; both distort the truth but they differ in the degree of self-awareness. Rationalization doesn't involve calculated pre-meditation; it is reflexive, involuntary. Lying, on the other hand, is a deliberate choice to mislead another person. Lying "is such a central characteristic of life that its understanding is relevant to almost all human affairs" (Ekman, 1988, p. 229). Lauren Ayers, in her investigation of teenage girls, claimed: "Fibbing . . . is a standard part of adolescent female language."

Following Ayer's line of thinking, Ekman continues: "Some lies are harmless, even humane. Some social relationships are enjoyed because of the myths they preserve. . . . Thus, in some situations self-deception by either the conveyor of misinformation and/or the recipient may be beneficial to one or both" (p. 230). The burden of always "putting one's best foot forward," "interpreting events in the most flattering light," and "attributing one's own personal fears to others," makes it easy to cross the line between rationalization and lying. Lying is a natural, though certainly not an inevitable, by-product of the tendency to interpret the world in ways enhancing to the self.

We cannot understand lying among teens without taking into account the developmental progressions which make it possible.[5]

> After age 10 or 11, children typically begin to recognize in their reasoning the role of intentions in lying and what constitutes a lie. At this level of reasoning, a lie is defined as something that is intentionally false. A full appreciation of intentions in moral judgments begins to develop around the transition from concrete to formal operations . . . *the young child typically views a nonpunished act as necessarily not a lie.* After age 9 or so, there is a separation of the concept of lie from punishment. The concrete operational child typically believes that a lie is wrong even if it goes unpunished (Wadsworth, 1989, p. 131).

I have not spent much time discussing the practical benefits of lying (obtaining something pleasant or avoiding something unpleasant), nor on the vindictive elements of lying (causing someone else to suffer as a result of one's lies) because my intent is merely to point out the connections between the adolescent thought process and the actual event of lying.[6] The conclusion one cannot escape is that rationalization inclines youth to distort information to their own ends; lying is one extension of this natural inclination.

Self-deception as a form of beclouded thinking

> Truth, like light, blinds. Falsehood, on the contrary, is a beautiful twilight that enhances every object."   Albert Camus

Feldman and Custrini's (1988) research into how children learn to lie and deceive is an interesting starting point for this investigation. These authors contend that self-deception increases as mental and social abilities advance, and that it is a normal, inevitable part of the growing-up process. With increasing age children grow in cognitive ability, gain in awareness of their social environment, and develop the ability to put themselves in the position of observer. The net effect of these accumulated advances is that:

> children come to understand that they can fool both themselves and other people. This is due to their growing realization that discrepancies can exist between their inner experience and their outer appearances. They come to see that they have greater access to their inner psychological experience and thoughts than do other people, and conse-

quently are in a position to manipulate the appearance they present to others (p. 41).

From these primitive beginnings self-deception penetrates daily routine; Feldman and Custrini concluded that self-deception is not only a necessary part of mental growth, it *inevitably increases with age*:

> In sum, there is a cogent argument to be made for the position that self-deception will become more pronounced with increasing age. The research on other-deception shows quite clearly that children become increasingly successful in being deceptive nonverbally toward others and in identifying . . . when others are being deceptive. As children's understanding of other-deception grows, however, they are more likely to understand their own instances of self-deception. If this is the case, they are forced to use increasingly sophisticated defense mechanisms to protect themselves. Ability in self-deception, then is likely to increase with age. *It is ironic indeed that the increased skills in understanding others may act to decrease one's awareness of oneself* (p. 51).

In sum, it appears that we adults, and our adolescent children, manufacture self-deceptions to achieve three simple goals: to manage our fears, to reduce our anxiety, and to advance our self-esteem.

Self-deception and facing the future

In every person's development a moment arises when time to come determines more than time gone. One such moment is late-adolescence, where the future attains such prominence that futurelessness, a sense of no hope for the future, becomes, for the first time in the life cycle, a pathological condition.

The conflict between teleology and determinism has not attracted our attention thus far, and here I shall digress only briefly to emphasize its relevance to the adolescent experience. Teleology speaks of being directed toward a definite end, of having an ultimate purpose, especially when these ends and purposes derive from a natural process. Teleology is a belief that natural phenomena are determined not only by mechanical causes but also by an overall design or purpose. Determinism, on the other hand, adheres to the doctrine that everything is entirely determined by a sequence of causes; and, as far as human beings are concerned, that one's choices and actions are not free, but are determined by causes independent of one's will. Cosmic purposes, however, need not be invoked to account for the adolescent's preoccupation with the future; it derives, in great measure, from the increased mental abilities inherent to formal thought, and from cultural demands to prepare for occupation, marriage, and family.

With these points in mind, I put forward two propositions:

- The more optimistically adolescents envision the future the greater their ability to cope with adversity in the present.

- When the future is filled with promise the tension of daily living loses much of its destructive power.

Do not misread the message. Youth are not overpowered by the future; they do not spend every waking moment in its anticipation. The message is more moderate but, nevertheless, crucial. Future time is an essential parcel in the adolescent package; optimal growth does not take place when the future is feared or when it is thought to be unworthy; when the future is perceived as holding chains but never keys, growth falters. Nothing is more relevant to the adolescent's search for a mature, solid identity than belief in the future.

For many young people, however, preparing for the future is beclouded by three critical misunderstandings:

- misunderstanding how property and wealth are acquired and accumulated;

- misunderstanding the amount of money retained by the worker from low-wage employment; and,

- misunderstanding the economics of marriage and child-rearing.[6]

These misunderstandings are brought somewhat into line by first-hand encounters with employment, credit cards, managing a budget, etc.; the practical problem is that, for many adolescents, the decisions made during the period of misunderstanding are either irreversible (e.g., having a child) or they are difficult to reverse (e.g., dropping out of school.)

An informative, and sobering, research project conducted by the Canadian Advisory Council on the Status of Women yielded some remarkable conclusions concerning adolescent perceptions. The study investigated adolescent women's aspirations for the future, and their general understanding of that future. Some of the findings were surprising to the authors of this study (by their own admission), but they were not to those who understand the adolescent propensity for unrealistic appraisal of topics *which touch upon their desires, their aspirations, their self-esteem* (Baker, 1985).

Although about one quarter of the girls in this study said they would probably be housewives at age 30, they saw this as a temporary occupation. The girls did not believe that being a housewife was either physically or emotionally demanding, and their thinking focussed on the most rewarding or pleasant aspects of this role. Such an idealized assessment of the future is a typical early- and middle-adolescent phenomenon. Few girls in this survey possessed a realistic perspective on the low-paying jobs that await them in the work force; that is to say, they simply did not understand how much money was earned in these jobs, nor did they understand whether this income could pay for basic necessities. Few girls thought about the possibility of a long period of unemployment, of getting divorced, or having to raise a family without a husband even though these are widespread problems in our culture and ones which most of these girls had already observed first hand. The author of this study concludes: "In most of their discussions of the future, there was no unemployment, no divorce, no economic need for the females to work when their children were young." Furthermore:

> After interviewing 150 adolescents, we found that many held notions of the future that did not tally with the likely outcomes of their adult lives. Only interesting jobs, adequate incomes, loving husbands, trouble-free children, home ownership, and international travel were on their horizons. Although adolescents are aware on an intellectual level that world peace is in jeopardy, families are breaking up, and many people are living in poverty, *they tend to feel that they are immune to these external forces.* (Baker, 1985)

The authors admit: "Young women need a much greater awareness of present realities of the workplace, of the difficulty raising children as single parents, and on the increasing necessity of two incomes if the materials they cherish are to be obtained." (A widespread fiction held by many teens is that they will be able, somehow, or by some means, to purchase new cars or new furniture, for which they simply do not have sufficient funds, nor do they have any strategy for obtaining these funds). A point not to be lost is that these researchers (like so many scholars who investigate adolescent behavior) seem to believe that these fictions, these misunderstandings, to which adolescents cling with such tenacity, *come into existence merely from lack of education.* This is not the way it is. They come into existence because the adolescent mind *reflexively produces narcissistically comforting conclusions.* Good education can help liberate youngsters from these conclusions, but lack of education does not account for them.

An argument could be made that at least these youngsters have a dream, a vision, a hope for a brighter future. And who will deny that these are vital images to all youth. Dreams are indispensable to charting one's life; an adolescent without dreams is soul without purpose. Sadly, some visions celebrated as real are little more than shimmerings of a contrived world where affective thinking governs one's "philosophy of life." As B. J. Wadsworth phrased it: "What looks like idealism is reasoning based on egocentric use of formal thought."

Cerebral fog

It is not from lack of experience with the hard problems of youth, nor from a lack of respect for young people, that I use "fog" to describe adolescents. I do it because they are foggy. But, like San Francisco, not all the time. What makes fog dangerous (and exciting) is its unpredictable quality; it can roll in unexpectedly, loom ominously on a not-so-distant horizon, then simply vanish, leaving the bright light of the morning sun to radiate what moments before was murky and ill-defined.[7]

A 15-year-old from rural British Columbia whom I interviewed as part of my ongoing research into adolescent life in North America, in response to a rather harmless question about father-daughter relationships, offered: "My Dad thinks I live in the clouds. He's always saying, 'Hey, get down here with the rest of us'." In response to the same question, a 14-year-old from Oregon said. "My dad says I'm in a fog. He thinks I can't see something when its right in front of me." Another teen, again in response to the same question, offered: "My dad calls me Pea Soup." I asked why. "On the coast when the fog is so thick you can't see anything they call it pea soup. My dad calls me Pea Soup because I'm always in a fog."

I was struck by the language these young women (girls) used to describe how their fathers perceived them; and having myself raised two teens, I was curious whether the fathers' descriptions had any merit. Eventually, I began to monitor adolescent self-descriptions which conveyed the idea of being "dazed," "stunned," "blotto," "zonked," "spaced out," "blitzed," "jet streamed," "ozoned," "dhuuhh." This is fog talk. And the surprising aspect of it, at least to me, is the consistency with which teens use this language to describe their own thinking, their own actions, their own selves. ("Stupid" is the word teens most frequently use to describe their own ineffective behavior).

To claim that adolescents always are foggy, of course, overstates the case. Yet, youngsters experience so many disconnected moments in which they are unaware of events in their immediate environment that it is easy to conclude that their vision, and their purpose, are beclouded. Military leaders speak of the "fog of war" and their meaning has some application here. In combat everything happens so rapidly that it is impossible to ever know completely what is going on. Decisions are made instantaneously and impulsively, reason and panic exist side by side in the same person, at the same moment; critical decisions, many of which cannot be undone, are acted out each instant, sometimes with no clear idea or purpose. Heroism and cowardice, brilliant calculations and careless misreadings blur together in the frenetic struggle of combat. Such is the "fog of war" of which military leaders speak. Interestingly, when asked to analyze the actions which take place under such conditions, many teens are not the least bit dismayed by the chaos inherent to combat. They claim that the fog of war describes their own day-to-day existence. This may, in part, be due to the linguistic overkill for which teens are rightfully famous; yet, it contains more than a kernel of truth.

Fog is not an ideal metaphor. "Radiance" might seem a more enlightened premise from which to investigate the adolescent thought process. Those who see it this way do not, in any way, subtract from the views forwarded in this chapter. "Fog," even if not ideal metaphor, is an apt one. As all navigators know, fog is respected because it rolls in at the most precarious moment, because, in an instant, it transforms the harmless into the dangerous. The fog of adolescence descends at the worst possible time: when decisions which yield life-long consequences are in process. But the most important reason behind our investigation of the "fog of adolescence" is a simple fact of adolescent life in the modern era: during adolescence faulty decisions produce far more profound consequences than solid decisions. The most practical challenge of the adolescent years is merely to avoid destructive choices and diminishing decisions. Everything else is secondary.

Helping teens to become better thinkers

One might ask what positive steps can be taken to counter these tendencies. To this question I recall an observation of Raymond Nickerson: "It is not reasonable to expect that we shall discover any time soon how to turn our students into perfectly logical, consistent, thorough, sensitive thinkers. . . . What is reasonable to expect is a gradually better understanding of what it means to think well and how to promote good thinking. . . ." (1991, p. 7).

What, then, can be done to improve the thinking of teens? I would suggest the following as worthy starting points.

Helping them to foster the habit of listening carefully to what other people have to say.

- Helping them to increase their willingness to consider points of view which differ from their own.

- Helping them to restrain their tendency to act impulsively.

- Helping them to use analogies effectively and appropriately.

- Helping them to improve the skills by which they evaluate the merits of an argument.

- Helping them to increase their objectivity when they are analyzing and investigating evidence.

- Helping them to recognize when peers are acting as flattering mirrors

- Helping them to recognize rationalizations in others and in themselves.

- Helping them to recognize when they are defending an idea and when they are defending themselves.

- Helping them to recognize the differences between "cold-blooded" and "warm-blooded" logic.

- Helping them to learn how to double-check the main points in their logic sequence.

Postscript

"Not being clued-in to reality."
The response of a 21-year-old university student to the question: "What was the greatest single problem you faced as an adolescent?"

The themes put forth in this chapter do not represent a completely new set of ideas; rather, they are a speculative response to the adolescent inclination to faulty decision-making and self-diminishing choices. The task we have set out for ourselves is an inherently frustrating one because the more we reflect on the subject the greater appears the distance between the abilities of young people and the dangers they are routinely required to negotiate. We wishfully think of adolescents as junior rationalists but very few of them are; we seem reluctant to admit that each day they make life and death decisions through an incomplete, and, by every standard, immature, intelligence.

The majesty of formal thought is vital to, but not the entirety of, adolescent intellectualism. In addition to the impressive advances which elevate and dignify adolescent thought, we also observe tendencies which distort and darken it. The intent of this chapter has been to indicate how adolescents, because of tendencies built into their thinking patterns, are inclined to think in a beclouded way.

The beclouding tendencies which have been of greatest concern to us in this chapter include the following.

- **The tendency to regress to concrete thought.** We mean that teens are prone to modes of thinking which worked effectively in childhood but which are not suited to the increased complexities of adolescence. Concrete thinkers sometimes accept hypotheses as facts, and sometimes reject facts as if they were mere hypotheses.

This failure to differentiate facts from hypotheses sabotages critical thinking. Children also believe that because the hypothesis is "mine" it holds a special validity; that it is true simply because it is mine. Concrete thinkers manufacture mental conclusions after looking at only a small portion of the available clues. This predisposition to hastily choose one solution, rather than to investigate all possibilities narrows their intellect and diminishes their comprehensiveness.

- **The tendency to emotionalize thought**. Inductive and deductive thinking operate on calm reasoning and comparative objectivity, affective logic, on the other hand, is a mode of thinking where the connections between judgment are emotional. Affective logic blends rational thought with subjective desires. Since it speaks to needs rather than to the question at hand it predisposes the thinker to accept arguments which beg the question, persuade by style rather than by substance, rely on prestige, insult the opponent, and employ theatric pleading.

- **The tendency toward entitlement thinking**. Entitlement thinking represents a narcissistic intervention in the thought process where needs, desires, and self-interest carry more weight than the actual question at hand.This mode of thinking promotes the belief that every difference of opinion *should be* settled to "my" advantage and that, in matters intellectual, "I" am entitled to special benefits and rights.

- **The tendency to emotionalize arguments**. This tendency assumes many expressions. A few that we focussed upon include: angering an opponent so that he (or she) will argue badly; accepting or rejecting an idea because of its popularity with the audience; using emotion to reduce the listener's concentration; disarming the opponent with charm; attributing prejudices or undesirable motives to one's opponent.

- **The tendency to argue unreasonably**. This beclouding tendency speaks to the mechanics of argumentation and debate. In essence, what we observe is the propensity to view intellectual debates with a "win at all costs" mentality, consequently, they bend the rules of fair play. In particular, they are inclined to make statements in which "all" is implied but "some" is true; to use proof by selected instances; to oppose a proposition by misrepresenting it; to attack the person who holds the disputed opinion rather than the opinion itself; to state one's position over and over but without defending the merit of the position; to fail to say exactly what it is that you are proposing; to rely on buzzwords and clichés to make a point; to argue by "straw-man" – a phony argument set up to be easily knocked down to produce an easy victory.

- **The tendency toward rationalization**. Rationalization is a form of intellectual engineering in which we provide explanations which pass for truth, but their real purpose is to bolster our self-esteem, to make us appear important, to make us look better in our own eyes and in the eyes of others. Rationalization is a way of thinking in which we protect our self-esteem by finding socially accepted reasons for our unacceptable behavior. The most common rationalizations are "sweet lemons" and "sour grapes." Sweet lemon is indicated when one claims that "What I've got is what I want." Sour grapes enter when one concludes: "What I missed wasn't worth getting." Rationalization beclouds thought because its function is protective, that is, to protect the thinker. It is the intellectual reflex behind most forms of self-deception.

- **The tendency toward self deception**. An unfolding, growing, developing self cannot know itself with much certainty; the mental operations of understanding fluctuate between assimilating and accommodating, accepting and rejecting, progressing and regressing.

At the risk, then, of over-simplifying an inherently complex and incompletely understood issue, much beclouded thinking during adolescence boils down to a fundamental confusion between that which actually is (what Voltaire called "the world as it is") and the world as one wishes it to be. As Barry J. Wadsworth, the noted Piagetian scholar put it: "The egocentrism of adolescence is the inability to differentiate between the adolescent's world and the 'real' world." Quite a statement! If true, even only in part, it merits the closest possible inspection by anyone who desires to understand adolescence, adolescents, or the adolescent experience.

We remain close to the heartbeat when we remember that the signature of adolescent intellectualism is neither clear rationalism nor murky emotionalism, rather, it is the ebb and flow between concrete thinking and formal reasoning, the intermittent shifts between cold-blooded and warm-blooded reason, and the unpredictable fluctuations between healthy skepticism and crippling cynicism[8]. If it is true, as Herbert J. Muller once claimed: "Only with drastic qualifications can man be defined as a rational animal"; then it most assuredly follows that to define our adolescent children as rational also requires some drastic qualifications.

Endnotes

[1]   Like children, adolescents sometimes see cloudy issues clearly. Hence, the reminders: "It's not that simple." "It more complicated than you think." What teens need even more than clarity of thought is critical

thought, for it is *critical* thought which validates the *accuracy* of one's clear thoughts.

[2]   As is readily apparent from the general tone of this book, I do not defend the idea that either teens or their parents are completely rational creatures; both are speckled with irrationality and anti-rationality. As Robert Ornstein so ably phrased it: "The idea that we have one rational mind seriously undersells our diverse abilities."

[3]   **The penchant for argumentation**. In the following passage Albert Schweitzer describes how his adolescent passion for discussion led him into all kinds of difficulties. In *Memories of Childhood and Youth*, Schweitzer described his penchant for incessant argumentation.

> Between my fourteenth and sixteenth years I passed through an unpleasant phase of development, becoming an intolerable nuisance to everybody, especially to my father, through a passion for discussion. On everybody who met me in the street I wanted to inflict thoroughgoing and closely reasoned considerations on all the questions that were then being generally discussed, in order to expose the errors of the conventional views and get the correct view recognized and appreciated. . . . Thus I emerged from the shell of reserve in which I had hitherto concealed myself, and became the disturber of every conversation that was meant to be merely conversation. . . . If we went to pay a visit anywhere, I had to promise my father not to spoil the day for him by stupid behaviour during conversations (Kiell, 1964, p. 482).

[4]   Perhaps such mental gymnastics is what Benjamin Franklin was thinking of when he penned: "So convenient a thing it is to be a *reasonable Creature* since it enables one to find or make a Reason for everything one has in mind to do."

[5]   Lying. Piaget observed children's understanding of lying generally matures between age 10 and 12. "In the first place a lie is wrong because it is an object of punishment; if the punishment were removed, it would be allowed. Then a lie becomes something that is wrong in itself and would remain so even if the punishment were removed. Finally, a lie is wrong because it is in conflict with mutual trust and affection. Thus the consciousness of lying gradually becomes interiorized and the hypothesis may be hazarded that it does so under the influence of cooperation" (Piaget, 1965, p. 171).

[6]   **Concealment and falsification**. In the act of concealment the individual withholds some information without actually saying anything untrue. In the act of falsification an additional step is taken since the liar not only withholds true information but presents false information as if it were true. "Often it is necessary to combine concealing and falsifying to pull off the deceit, but sometimes a liar can get away with just concealment. If there is a choice about how to lie, liars usually prefer to conceal rather than to falsify." Concealment has its advantages: it is easier than outright falsification and nothing has to be made up: "Concealment lies are also much easier to cover if discovered afterwards. There are many available excuses, such as memory failure or ignorance. Concealment may also be

preferred because it seems less reprehensible than falsifying. It is passive, not active . . . liars feel less guilt when they conceal than when they falsify" (Ekman, 1988, p. 231).

Even though concealing and falsifying are widely used by both children and teens, they are not the only ways to becloud the truth. One can lie *by misdirecting,* that is by acknowledging an emotion but misidentifying what caused it; *by telling the truth falsely,* that is, by admitting the truth but with such a preposterous demeanor that the listener is misled; *by half-concealing,* that is by admitting only part of what is true to re-direct the listener's attention away from what remains concealed; finally, by *incorrect inference,* that is, by telling the truth in a way that implies the opposite of what is said. All of these strategies are usually betrayed by some aspect of the deceiver's behavior.

[7]   I want to make certain that readers familiar with the work of David Elkind do not confuse his idea of "pseudo-stupidity" with what I am calling "fog." Elkind observed that adolescents sometimes seem to behave stupidly when, in fact, they are not stupid at all. Why is it, he asks, that when faced with a simple, straightforward question, adolescents sometimes look at it from a dozen angles, mull it over and grind it up so thoroughly that they are unable to arrive at any reasonable solution? Why, Elkind asks, do adolescents often attribute devious, hidden motives to other people when none exist? Such mental convolutions are not the result of *real* stupidity rather, of "pseudostupidity." Elkind claimed that this kind of thinking is the consequence of accelerated cognitive growth combined with a lack of experience. When adolescents acquire the more sophisticated reasoning skills which come with formal thought, they literally "think too much" about simple problems, about human motives, about almost anything and everything. As they gain greater experience and their thinking becomes more efficient, "pseudostupidity" disappears. Elkind's idea helps to bring into sharper focus some of the befuddlement of teen thought, but the thrust of his idea is not the same as what I am trying to describe. The concept of pseudostupidity is a more specific concept than the pervasive impediment to critical thought I am discussing.

[8]   Differences between skepticism and cynicism. Skepticism is the attitude of questioning and doubting which is based upon uncertainty and the finiteness of human knowledge. As a philosophical doctrine skepticism claims that truth must always be questioned; intellectual inquiry, to the skeptic, is a process of ongoing doubt and examination. (Among the ancient Greeks skeptics believed that humans are incapable of attaining ultimate knowledge.) Skepticism treats doubt and uncertainty as legitimate facts, and, as far as adolescents are concerned, this means that one need not fear the unknown, nor be contemptuous of, or hostile toward, things and people which are not understood.

Cynicism is bankrupt skepticism. Cynics disbelieve the sincerity of human actions and doubt that motivations can be altruistic or idealistic; they even question the value of living. A cynic believes people are motivated only by selfishness, and that the values we aspire to are no better than the ones we discard. Cynicism is the dominant attitude among nihilistic youth, yet it is far more than merely a "negative" outlook; it is a form of emotional protectionism which manipulates reality in order to soothe a frightened identity.

> The cynic plays it safe by not believing in anything with an ethical or moral structure. If he follows a pattern of total disbelief, he is then disappointed in nothing. *Because he believes in nothing, he avoids the heartaches that come from having believed in something that ends in failure.* The device he uses is to deprecate any value which seems to hold forth hope (Bischop, 1970, p. 225).

The ability to formulate a philosophy of life, to construct life aims, to establish a solid sense of oneself – basic demands of the adolescent identity quest – are impeded by cynicism. Perhaps the steepest price youngsters pay for their cynicism is that it cuts away the trust necessary to believe in themselves. As Norman Cousins put it: "the ultimate penalty of cynicism is not that the individual will come to distrust others but that he will come to distrust himself (1981, p. 48). As Furnham and Stacey (1991) claimed in *Young People's Understanding of Society*: "Many studies have shown the lamentable state of young people's knowledge on clearly important issues like economics, law and politics. Some appear to be, and often remain, in ignorance of some of the fundamental processes governing western, capitalist societies" (p. 186).

Section II

some prefatory comments

In chapters two and three I described some of the ways egocentrism influences the thought process. In the next few chapters I want to enlarge the scope of this investigation in order to embrace a wider data base and to permit a broader range of speculation on the nature of youth.

Narcissus was the first reported adolescent narcissist, but assuredly not the last. Ovid's description of Narcissus' self-absorbed character was so powerful, and so convincing, that upon it Freud based his model of narcissism. Narcissus gathers our attention in the next few chapters because he, more than any mythological character, epitomizes the extremes of youthful selfishness.

Chapter five introduces the concept of narcissism, both in its general usage and as it was explained by two of its most important contributors, Sigmund Freud and Karen Horney. Chapter six deals with how the underlying themes of narcissism help us to better understand the adolescent experience. Chapter seven discusses the critical differences between the developmental self-ish-ness which typifies all adolescents and the narcissistic selfishness which sometimes evolves form it.

Some youth watchers, myself included, are increasingly impressed with the evidence supporting the hypothesis that the most serious problems in the youth community stem not from emotional disturbances but from character disturbances; especially from a reduced sense of obligation and an exaggerated sense of entitlement. The investigation of these phenomena have for decades been the dominion of narcissistic theory; increasingly, however, students of the youth culture are taking note of their relevance to the adolescent experience in North America.

A shameful fact of our moratorium culture is that almost everything in it designed for teen-agers (with the exception of the school system) caters to the lesser side of their nature, to the stimulation of their consumer desires and to the deadening of their social perspective. One effect of living in such a diminished environment is an attraction to narcissistic attitudes and beliefs, which, over time, translate into a retreat from "social interest."

The next few chapters speak to a fundamental question: "Does the self-concern natural to adolescence easily erode into a more severe selfishness?"

Chapter Five

narcissism

In Greek mythology Narcissus, the son of the river-god Cephissus, was a beautiful and physically perfect young man who was the object of desire among the nymphs, but in whom he showed no emotional interest. When he reached *the age of sixteen* his path was strewn with heartlessly rejected lovers, for he had a stubborn pride in his own beauty and a ceaseless fascination with himself. One nymph, Echo, who could no longer use her voice except in foolish repetition of another's voice, loved Narcissus deeply and one day she approached him only to be rudely rejected. In her shame and grief she perished, fading away, leaving behind only her responsive voice. The gods, in deciding to grant the nymph's wish for vengeance, decided that Narcissus must also experience the pain of an unreciprocated love. One day, while looking into a clear mountain pool, Narcissus viewed his own image and immediately fell in love, thinking that he was looking at a beautiful water spirit. Unable to tear himself away from his own image, and unable to evoke any response from the reflection, which disappeared when he attempted to embrace it, he grieved until death. When the nymphs came to bury him, he too had disappeared, leaving in place a flower.

Many centuries passed before Ovid's myth attained a niche in psychological theory. Havelock Ellis introduced the term "narcissism" to modern psychology (in 1898) when he referred to it as a normal state which is prone toward morbid exaggerations. In his paper "Auto-Erotism: A Psychological Study," he described a "Narcissus-like tendency" for the sexual emotions to be absorbed into self-admiration. Ellis viewed this phenomenon as an extreme form of auto-eroticism, in essence, a sexual perversion where the individual treated his (or her) own body as a sexual object. Later Paul Nacke, a German psychiatrist, after reading Ellis' paper coined the term *Narcismus* for the "Narcissus-like tendency." And while Ellis was the first to ascribe a specific psychiatric significance to the term we today call "narcissism," it was Sigmund Freud who gave it wings, and it was he who formulated the nuclear premises from which virtually all subsequent writing on the topic has evolved.

Whether Freud explicitly chose the hero of this myth to articulate the ingredients of what we now call narcissism, we do not know. It seems clear, however, that Narcissus was the epitome of everything that we now consider "narcissistic": self-centred, arrogant, obsessed with the visual, fascinated with surface appearances, completely lacking in empathy, and consumed by an attitude of entitlement.

All enduring myths display a wealth of meaning that can never be completely conveyed; they embody symbolic significance for times other than their own, and for minds separated by centuries. The Narcissus myth presents exciting themes to anyone investigating the adolescent experience since the adolescent possesses qualities of the narcissist, and the narcissist possesses qualities of the adolescent. Let us begin this investigation, then, with a brief look at the meaning of narcissism and some of the possibilities it opens for us.

The general meaning of narcissism

In ordinary language narcissism refers to a mixture of self-love and self-fascination; it is widely associated with vanity, illusory love, and hyper self-awareness. Fred Alford (1988) described it as "an infatuation with self so extreme that the interests of others are ignored, others serving merely as mirrors of one's own grandiosity" (1988, p. 2). Some scholars view narcissism in a favorable light: "Narcissism is a positive experience of the self; it is the state of loving, or admiring oneself" (Lewis, 1987, p. 96). Concordantly, Alford offers: "Narcissism is a universal and healthy attribute of personality, when it is understood as a longing for perfection, wholeness...." He then adds: "What is sick or healthy, regressive or progressive, is how individuals come to terms with their narcissism" (p. 3). The various ways individuals "come to terms with their narcissism," as Alford puts it, is one of the critical issues of adolescent life.

The idea that narcissism *can* be positive is widespread in psychological literature: "Favorable narcissism mobilizes behavior to beneficial purposes and is represented by normal self-concern and an adequate level of self-esteem: productive pride, we might call it" (Barrett, 1991, p. 34). Furthermore: "The mighty engine that drives the self in all interaction is abetted by the individual's inimitable stock of narcissistic energy..." (p. 64). Good narcissism fuels positive self-esteem.[1]

Of its healthy manifestations Carl Goldberg writes:

I have come to view narcissism, not as a pejorative concept, but rather as the mainspring of the struggle for human creativity and meaningful human exploration . . . I view *healthy* narcissism as enhancing to the fulfillment of human existence. . . . Narcissistic strivings coexist with mature object love, both confounding and enriching its development. . . . Narcissism, in its positive sense, is . . . a commitment to passion as an enrichment of human experience (1980, p. 13).

In *Narcissism, the Self, and Society*, Rueben Fine claimed: "All people are narcissistic; the difference is only one of degree" (1986, p. 67). This claim is a significant one, and in the following chapters it will remain close to our thoughts. After all, a healthy self-concept without some narcissism is really quite unthinkable. What self could honorably exist without self-love, self-esteem, and self-admiration? We all are characterized by a selfish core which is a vital, worthy part of our being. Erich Fromm, one of the first Neo-Freudians to envision the tremendous implications of Freud's theory of narcissism, claimed: "Even in the average individual . . . there remains a narcissistic core which appears to be almost indestructible." And further, "in the case of normal development, man remains to some extent narcissistic throughout his life." Finally, and perhaps most significantly: "We can say that nature had to endow man with a great amount of narcissism to enable him to do what is necessary for survival" (all quotes taken from Fromm's landmark essay, "Individual and Social Narcissism," 1964).

"Narcissism is a difficult idea that looks easy – a good recipe for confusion." Christopher Lasch

What differentiates the overly narcissistic from the rest of us is not narcissism, *per se*, but rather, the tremendous quantity and the irrational quality of it. And while it is possible to be chronically self-absorbed and genuinely concerned with the rights and feelings of others, it rarely works that way. Narcissism is a "me-first" phenomenon. Unfortunately, narcissists (and here they share so much with adolescents) have great difficulty granting to others the rights they desire for themselves. And, as well, they never seem to learn the secret of giving without losing, of obtaining without depriving.

Narcissists crave praise and they have a great deal of difficulty resisting anyone who provides it. Conversely, they *are repulsed by people, activities, and symbols which, in any way, try to steal them away from their own self-centredness.* Impersonality is anathema to the narcissist within each of us, since by definition, when something is "impersonal" it fails to highlight, praise, or honor "me." Not by chance, narcissists share with adolescents an antagonism toward anyone who tries to blanket "the majestic me" in anonymity.

The starting point for all theories of narcissism is that human selfishness can never be completely eradicated. To deny this fundamental quality of human motivation is folly: "to complain about man's selfishness would be like complaining about his not having been born with wings" (Bloom, 1993, p. 51). Narcissism accompanies all strata of human experience: "The goal of maturity is not the abandonment of narcissism . . . but the integration of narcissism with the various stages of . . . development" (Alford, p. 55). As we shall see, this "integration of narcissism with the various stages of development" is a taxing and strenuous proposition during adolescence.

The psychoanalytic understanding of narcissism

"One of the most far-reaching of Freud's discoveries is his concept of narcissism."   Erich Fromm

Virtually all 20th century formulations of narcissism have as their starting point Freud's landmark essay "On Narcissism," first published in 1914. Scholars do not agree with all of Freud's formulations, but they do agree that he was the modern pioneer of this rich concept. Alford, in his historical overview of narcissism, matter-of-factly observed: "Not surprisingly, Freud's 'On Narcissism' is the basis of almost all subsequent discussion of the topic." The heuristic richness of this original essay is even more impressive when we consider that it was not written for the purpose of formulating either a narcissistic personality type or a narcissistic character structure, but rather to explore variations in the development of libidinal cathexis – that is, where the energy of the primitive self is invested. Most scholars agree that Freud's essay "On Narcissism" remains, after three-quarters of a century, indispensable reading for anyone interested in the subject.

Freud saw narcissism as the turning of love away from the world and inward upon the self; making the self the object of its own investment. In his own words, "The libido withdrawn from the outer world has been directed on to the ego, giving rise to a state which we may call *narcissism*" (1914). Freud claimed that each of us begins life in a blissful state of "primary narcissism" where no distinction exists between self and world; hence no painful tensions from unfulfilled desires, no experience of frustration; a stage of development where the infant has not as yet established any ego boundaries, and thus experiences itself and its environment as one. *Primary narcissism is the most primitive of all emotional states*: the infant is bestowed with a grandiose inflation, with feelings of perfection and power. From Freud's original ideas emerged the belief, still held in some quarters today, that the infant is fused with the mother and the world in a condition of wholeness and harmony. This fusion is a blissful, short-lived state, yet one which registers so forcefully on the evolving psyche that all of us, in certain measure, spend our adolescent (and adult) years trying to recapture, by whatever means, its splendor and glory.

Primary narcissism[2] is neither a perversion nor a defect; it is the stage of psychosexual development where the child's pleasures are concentrated within the self and the body. It is a developmental stage between autoeroticism and object love when distinct autoerotic sensations become fused into one's body, which then, together, become a single, unified love object. This "narcissistic condition" is the libidinal storehouse from which the love of self, and love in general, emerges. Eventually, much of the child's primary narcissism is abandoned in favor of ego development, and in time, the child replaces self-love with love for others. But the love received from others cannot yield the primal satisfaction of one's original self-love. (The significance of this point cannot be over-stated: it implies that shared love is a reduced, less fulfilling than self-love; this primacy of self-love, at the expense of other-love, is the defining feature of narcissism.)

Central to Freud's theorizing about narcissism is the assumption that, in the earliest stages, the infant is at one with the mother and not yet able to distinguish objects or relate to the world.[3] Freud recognized that the developing infant eventually separates self from surroundings and from this separation a primitive sense of tension differentiates *into the experience of need for others.* As the infant grows, its separation from itself allows the merger with other selves; a necessary starting point in the journey toward loving others, toward community, toward all sharing behavior.

> . . . needs put pressure on the developing ego to acquire the skills necessary to fulfill the need, and so the ego adapts to object-reality. *All the energy that in infancy was bound exclusively to the subject in this way slowly extends out and becomes bound up in the subject's pursuit of objects.* The process is essential to normal development (Satinover, 1987, p. 87).

The inherent contradiction of narcissism is the craving to return to an emotional state of self-primacy which can never be regained. *The inherent contradiction of adolescence* is the craving to attain an egocentric self-centredness which cannot be. Hence, during adolescence this injury of childhood, where the self is quite literally torn from its archaic absorption in itself, is re-experienced. The childhood struggle to reconcile imagined greatness with actual smallness is lived again and again during adolescence.

The Freudian position, despite its web of unverifiable starting points, is actually rather straightforward in its understanding of the events which mold the narcissistic character. During childhood, emotional development is dependent upon "giving up" one's basic narcissism; the selfish love we each have for ourselves eventually is directed to, or shared with, others. This extending of self-love creates only partial satisfaction within the evolving personality; cravings persist for complete self-immersion, for the total self-absorption of primary narcissism.

> Freud never altered the basic idea that the original state of man, in early infancy, is that of . . . primary narcissism in which there are not yet any relations to the outside world, that then in the course of normal development the child begins to increase in scope and intensity his (libidinal) relationships to the outside world, but that in many instances . . . he

withdraws his libidinal attachment from objects and directs it back to his ego ("secondary narcissism"). But even in the case of normal development, man remains to some extent narcissistic throughout his life (Fromm, 1964, p. 63).

Furthermore:

Indeed, the development of the individual can be defined in Freud's term as *the evolution from absolute narcissism to a capacity for objective reasoning and object love.* ... The "normal," "mature" person is one whose narcissism has been reduced to the socially accepted minimum without ever disappearing completely. Freud's observation is confirmed by everyday experience. It seems that *in most people one can find a narcissistic core which is not accessible and which defies any attempt at complete dissolution* (my italics, Fromm, 1964, p. 64).

Narcissism represents the struggle to re-experience the primitive self, "a deep longing for a lost state of oneness – that oceanic feeling" (Frosh, 1991, p. 78). As Freud wrote in his famous essay: "The development of the ego consists in a departure from primary narcissism and *gives rise to a vigorous attempt to recover that state*" (1914, p. 95, my italics). These cravings can never be satisfied. Archaic emotional states simply cannot be re-lived; like infancy, they are forever gone. The most we can ever regain of our previous narcissistic glory are fleeting episodes of euphoric self-immersion, periodic flashes of primal grandiosity. Yet, so relentless is the craving for these emotions that any experience which even briefly recalls them is pursued. The narcissist craves immersion in the euphoric primitive self. Flattery, intoxication, love, even the self-absorbing despair of depression, are a few of the pleasures which, because they are imbued in the primal past, are simultaneously craved and feared.

Although perhaps an untimely note here at the end of this brief overview, no known way exists to prove or disprove the vital assumptions which serve as the building blocks for Freud's theory of narcissism. Freud, in his favor, was completely aware of this, as he candidly reports in his 1926 treatise on inhibitions, symptoms, and anxiety: "Unfortunately, far too little is known about the mental constitution of the new-born child to make a direct answer possible. I cannot even vouch for the validity of the description I have just given." On the child's alleged inherent primary narcissism Freud recognized the futility of direct confirmation: "The primary narcissism of the child assumed by us . . . is less easy to grasp by direct observation than to confirm by deduction from another consideration" (1914). The problem, in a nutshell, is that no way exists to verify that the infant, in its earliest psychic state, exists in blissful, perfect harmony with "mother and the world." To reject this assumption, which Christopher Lasch mistakenly called a discovery, is to reject the psychoanalytic foundation of narcissistic theory. Even so, some experts have done precisely that. Rueben Fine states: "the whole Freudian notion of primary narcissism has come under severe attack from the infant researchers, and properly so. The image of the infant as 'narcissistic' or living in a state of 'narcissistic bliss' has to be abandoned" (1986, p. 57). Fine also reports the conclusions of C. Chiland, who claims: "The concept of a purely dyadic relationship between infant and mother is now as unacceptable as the concept of a stage of normal autism." All of these criticisms make clear that the theoretical foundations upon which the theory of narcissism rests, are open to question, perhaps even rejection. However, the focus of this book is upon adolescent behavior not the weaknesses in psychoanalytic theory; therefore, these criticisms of Freud's thinking will infuse caution into, but will not halt, our investigation of narcissism and its relationship to the adolescent community.

Self-love vs. self-hate

Some scholars claim that narcissism is not a manifestation of self-love, but a reaction against self-hate. In the self-hate view, narcissists are thought to be incapable of relating to the outside world because they fear that their hate will elicit a proportional punishment. According to Margaret Mahler,[4] the child "attempts to save the originally all-embracing narcissism by concentrating perfection and power upon the self . . . and by turning away disdainfully from an outside world to which all imperfections have been assigned" (Kohut, 1971, p. 106). Such hatred is sustained by internalizing everything "good" to me and externalizing everything "bad" to others.

> *Self-hatred is more dominant in the narcissist than is self-love.* Narcissists have very low opinions of themselves and this is why they constantly seek approbation. *They consider themselves unworthy and unlovable,* and seek constantly to hide this fact from themselves by trying to get the outside world to proclaim them unique, extraordinary, great. But beyond that they suffer from intense, unconscious envy that makes them want to spoil, deprecate and degrade what others have and they lack, particularly others' capacity to give and receive love (Kernberg, 1978).

For all of these reasons, and a few not mentioned in this condensed foray into the dynamics of narcissism, Louis DeRosis claimed: "Essentially, narcissism is a condition of self-hatred, palming itself off as self-love" (1981, p. 343).

What we see through all this is that what the narcissist really loves is not the self, but a glorified, fabled self; in essence, an invented self. (A point not be lost on students of adolescent psychology who recognize the important role played by the personal fable in the identity project).

The tug-of-war between self-love and self-hate is not portrayed as a dominant struggle in this investigation because it is a struggle where

117

starting points and end points are impossible to ascertain, and because during adolescence normal gestures of self-doubt and self-apprehension carry a ferocity which inclines the observer to believe that self-hate is at work when usually it is not. These tormented gestures often disappear when the youngster receives even small doses of love and affection, leading one to conclude that self-hate, with all its profound implications, is not a *primary* motivation in the lives of most youngsters.

Part of her importance to the history of personality theory is that Karen Horney addressed narcissism from a different angle than Freud did, and as a result, she charted for it a different course.

Karen Horney

Karen Horney originally trained as a psychoanalyst in Berlin, then moved to America to become a member of the New York Psychoanalytic Institute. In 1941 she was dismissed from the Institute because of ideological differences with Freudian orthodoxy; she subsequently founded the American Institute for Psychoanalysis. Horney emphasized social factors in the human personality far more than Freud, and she held a considerably more open and optimistic view of human nature. Her theories relied heavily on several psychoanalytic concepts, such as repression, but her differences with Freud were genuine and significant, especially in her belief that neurosis originated in basic anxiety and disturbed human relationships. And even though most of her writings were devoted to psychotherapy, neurosis, and female sexuality, her insights concerning narcissism were considerable.

Even though she was an effective theoretician she was not a system-builder in the same way as Freud. She explained her theory of narcissism without concepts such as libido or internalized self objects and representations, all of which she believed were clinically unverifiable. Horney's clinical observations did not support Freud's libido theory, which claimed that self-esteem is a desexualized form of self-love, and that persons tending toward overvaluation must be expressing self-love. In a technical sense, Horney believed that narcissism is the identification with the idealized image of the self, a loving of the unrealistically glorified attributes of the self. In a practical sense, she believed that narcissism is *an unjustified egocentric self-inflation, an overdone self-absorption.* This belief, as it turns out, is one of her most important contributions to this topic because it is predicated on the idea that the self-esteem of the healthy person and the self-inflation of the narcissist are mutually exclusive. She viewed healthy self-esteem as based on authentic attributes of an individual, on genuinely positive and pleasurable feelings of pride and worth. Narcissistic self-inflation, on the other hand, is an attempt to disguise one's lack of qualities by pretending to possess capabilities that do not really exist.

In *New Ways in Psychoanalysis* she advanced ideas which speak both to narcissism and to adolescence. To her, in narcissism "the person loves and admires himself for values for which there is no adequate foundation. Similarly, it means that he expects love and admiration from others for qualities that he does not possess, or does not possess to as large an extent as he supposes." She placed great emphasis on the accurate and honest portrayal of oneself and one's abilities, and, by implication, upon the distortions and fables which subvert an honest understanding of self and others.

In her line of speculation, the narcissist is someone whose emotional links to others are brittle, and who, in the effort to protect against further pain, suffers a loss of the capacity to love. Self-inflation is the child's attempt to cope with the loss of the real me. Hence, the overvaluation of self is merely a substitute for undermined self-esteem. *In the course of time, the overvalued self becomes the "real me."* The false, inflated self, simply takes over and deposes the real self.[5]

The overvalued self sees the world in its own unique ways (just as we might suspect) since it values itself more highly than it values the outside world. All narcissists have a critical bias at the core of their perception of the social universe since they see all things through the lens of private interest. Because of this fundamental selfishness within their thought process, and because of the failure of objectivity which flows from it, narcissists are, in a very profound way, learning disabled.

Narcissists, regardless of their age, share common traits and mannerisms. Three of the more relevant to this discussion include the following.

First, decreasing productivity because work is not satisfying for its own sake. Work is never an end, it is always a means to obtain something else, hence "conscientious workmanship" falters.

Second, excessive expectations as to what the world owes the individual without effort or contribution on the part of the individual. That is, "society owes me", or "school owes me", or "parents owe me".

Third, increasing impairment of human relations due to constant grievances, confrontational styles, and overriding feelings of entitlement (Cooper, 1986, p. 121).

(It is interesting to note that even though these observations ring true to modern ears, and sound somewhat like a list of grievances brought forth by a school principal in the '90s, they were first outlined by Karen Horney in 1939).

In the attempt to make clear her divergence from Freud, she wrote: "the correlation between love of self and love of others is not valid in the sense that Freud intends it. Nevertheless, the dualism which Freud assumes . . . contains an odd and significant truth. This is, briefly, that *any kind of egocentricity detracts from a real interest in others, that it impairs the capacity to love others*" (1939, p. 100). As we shall see, the egocentricity which typifies the adolescent experience impairs their capacity for shared intimacy and mature love, just as the pioneers of personality theory (especially Karen Horney and Alfred Adler) predicted.

Some problems with the concept of narcissism

". . . as the word *narcissism* becomes part of our everyday vocabulary, its clinical meaning becomes lost."   Jeffrey Berman

Pulver (1986) spoke to the bewilderment which surrounds the word "narcissism" when he confessed: "there are probably only two facts on which everyone agrees; first that the concept of narcissism is one of the most important contributions of psychoanalysis; second that it is one of the most confusing."

To the reader it should by now be clear that narcissism is not a singular concept held in tow by universally accepted postulates and axioms. Rather, it is so rich in diversity that attempts to condense into a single, tight catechism simply do not work.

> Since Freud first peered over the wall, many psychoanalytic research-
> ers have extended his vision of narcissism. Predictably, there are almost
> as many different interpretations of narcissism as there are interpreters.
> Psychoanalysis is hardly the monolithic point of view its detractors
> have claimed – or that some of its supporters have also claimed, thus
> dismissing any "deviation" from orthodoxy. Narcissism has proven to
> be particularly troublesome to define, explain, and treat. . . . Is narcis-
> sism a normal or abnormal developmental process? Is the patient best
> served by the analyst's cool understanding or warm empathy? Debates
> over narcissism have produced the most fruitful – and rancorous –
> discussions in psychoanalytic circles (Berman, 1990, p. 19).

Some psychologists don't like the term because it is too vague, others because it is too imprecise, and still others, as Pulver (1986) pointed out in "Narcissism: The term and the concept," because it is too confusing. One scholar, who admits to being stretched by its breadth, claims: "That concept has become so broad that it covers almost every-thing and thus has lost most of its usefulness" (Wurmser, 1987, p. 74). Arnold Cooper reported: "Few concepts in psychiatry have undergone as many changes in meaning as has narcissism. . . . It has become increasingly apparent that the term is so burdened with the baggage of the past that it has perhaps outlived its usefulness" (1986, p. 117-118).

For some critics it describes too many different levels of abstraction about the self, and provides too many behavioral outcomes. Pulver's survey disclosed that narcissism, since Freud's classic essay in 1914, has been used to describe (1) a sexual perversion; (2) a mode of relating to objects; (3) a developmental stage; and (4) self-esteem. And this does not even take into account its widespread use as a synonym for relentless self-inflation.

Perhaps the most practical problem with psychoanalytic accounts of narcissism is that its fundamental origins simply are not knowable. Some theorists argue that narcissism is caused by parental rejection which results in the child's defensive withdrawal. Others argue that it is caused by the child's failure to idealize parents because of their indifference. The fact remains, however, that these hypotheses, challenging and insightful as they are, can never be confirmed. No matter how persuasively crafted any particular theory of narcissism may be, we simply cannot know what transpires in the infant's unconscious mind. Nor do we know, with any certainty, how the flow of emotions we associate with narcissism originates. Therefore, all theories of narcissism run smack into the most practical issue in psychological theory: verification. And while some theorists are quite willing to construct their castles on unverifiable foundations, others find the idea entirely preposterous.

Other problems present themselves. Current research on infant behavior simply does not lend persuasive support to Freud's ideas on the fundamental relationship between infant and mother. His theory of primary narcissism (which interestingly, Freud formulated without the benefit of any systematic first-hand observations) is, in general, held in disrepute by developmental psychologists. Daniel Stern (1985) concluded that infants "never experience a period of total self/other undifferentiation. There is no confusion between self and other in the beginning or at any point during infancy" (Berman, 1990, p. 14). Stern also claimed that infants are programmed with a readiness for relating; hence, not only are they more responsive to their environment than Freud's generation of psychoanalysts recognized, they possess a rudimentary sense of self earlier than was previously thought.

We cannot escape, no matter how hard we try, the value judgments assigned to the word itself. "Narcissism" is a word for which the primary connotations are negative. Otto Kernberg associates it with cancer; Erich Fromm speaks of "malignant narcissism."[6]

This judgmental tone of "narcissism" was effectively conveyed by patient Peter Tarnopol in Philip Roth's *My Life as a Man* when he exclaimed to his therapist, Dr. Spielvogel:

"Spare me that word 'narcissism,' will you? You use it on me like a club."

"The word is purely descriptive and carries no valuation," said the doctor.

"Oh, is that so? Well, you be on the receiving end and see how little 'valuation' it carries!"

Peter Tarnopol, of course, was correct. No one wants to be described, or diagnosed, as "narcissistic." Yet, despite the philosophical objections to its broadness, and the personal objections to its essentially selfish tone, virtually all theorists accept Pulver's observation that "the concept of narcissism is one of the most important contributions of psychoanalysis" (p. 91). Why? Because the behavior narcissism spotlights and the emotions it probes are the most powerful in the human drama. The importance of narcissistic theory to an investigation of the adolescent experience is that it helps us to better understand the chronic self-centredness, and the relentless self-preoccupation which both invigorate and degrade the adolescent experience.

Postscript

"He that falls in love with himself will have no rivals."
                                                  Poor Richard's Almanac

I have assembled these ideas in the hope that they would help us to draw fresh conclusions and to enrich our understanding of the adolescent experience. In the present discussion I am putting forth nothing new; the ideas brought to your attention have been as much for review as for any other purpose. However, even in this form, they enable us to conceive ideas important to adolescent psychology.

The theory of narcissism first proposed by Sigmund Freud, drawing upon the classic myth of Narcissus, is the starting point for this investigation. At first, it might seem strange to approach adolescent psychology from such a starting point, but when we look closer it is easy to see how one complements the other. Freud, the father of psychoanalysis and the intellectual energy behind most contemporary theories of narcissism, is a starting point, though not a final destination, in this enterprise. Freud believed that narcissism represents a turning of love away from the world and inward upon the self. During the formative months of psychic stratification the infant is fused with the mother in wholeness, harmony, and bliss – a fusion so perfect that each of us, as we age, strives to regain its euphoric, "oceanic" splendor. Primary narcissism, therefore, is the first stage of psychosexual development, a time when the child's pleasures are concentrated within the body. This narcissism weakens as the child replaces self-love with love for others;

but always, to greater or lesser degree, every person craves the return to grandiose self-love. This passion to return to the immersion of primal self-love is one of Freud's great contributions to our understanding of human nature, and as well, to understanding adolescent self-ish-ness.

Karen Horney's description of narcissism is less eloquent than Sigmund Freud's, but, in many regards, perhaps because of its simplicity and common sense, more closely approximates how most people think of it. Horney believed that narcissism is unrealistic, unjustified self-inflation. The person admires and loves the self for reasons "for which there is no adequate foundation." Such exaggerated self-absorption substitutes for genuine self-esteem; a response to disturbed relationships in early childhood. The narcissistic self, according to Horney, is over-valued, inflated, but most importantly, false. It (mis-)perceives and (mis-)understands the world from an elevated perch of egocentric inflation. (And, as I emphasize throughout this book, the misperceptions and misunderstandings of narcissism overlap in fascinating ways with the misperceptions and misunderstandings typical of adolescence).

Because of her practical bent, Horney stressed the behavioral outcomes of narcissism while Freud was more concerned with infantile origins and psychic infra-structure. As a result she was more attuned to the behavior which flows from the narcissistic stream, especially exaggerated entitlement demands.

The American Psychiatric Association's *Diagnostic and Statistical Manual of Mental Disorders*, fourth edition (generally referred to by practitioners as the DSM-IV), in profiling the narcissistic personality disorder, gives special notice to its clinical contradictions. Notably, how a sense of self-importance alternates with feelings of unworthiness, how the need for admiration fixates more on appearance than reality, and how a fragile self-esteem manufactures outrageous entitlement demands. Such a focus on opposites and contradictions detracts from the straight line coherence we all like to see in our favorite theory of human behavior. Unfortunately for the linearly obsessed, we humans are not a study in uniform progressions; rather, of frustrating contradictions. Theories of narcissism focus on these frustrating contradictions and in doing so provide productive insights into the adolescent character.

Endnotes

[1]   **Benign (beneficial) narcissism**. Once again, we are indebted to Erich Fromm for his insightful elucidation:

> In the benign form, the object of narcissism is the result of a person's effort. Thus, for instance, a person may have a narcissistic pride in his

work as a carpenter, as a scientist, or as a farmer. Inasmuch as the object of his narcissism is something he has to work for, his exclusive interest in what is his work and his achievement is constantly balanced by his interest in the process of work itself, and the material he is working with. The dynamics of this benign narcissism thus are self-checking. The energy which propels the work is, to a large extent, of a narcissistic nature, but the very fact that the work itself makes it necessary to be related to reality, constantly curbs the narcissism and keeps it within bounds. This mechanism may explain why we find so many narcissistic people who are at the same time highly creative (p. 77, *Heart of Man*).

[2] **Primary and secondary narcissism.** Some scholars interpret primary narcissism as the infant's all-consuming wish for attention at a time when object-cathexes have not yet been formed, and the entire quota of libido relates to the newly developing ego. *Secondary narcissism, however, refers to the exaggerated feelings of self-importance and self-love that occur later in life.* Most of the focus in this book is more closely related to the concept of secondary narcissism than to Freud's original concept of primary narcissism. (See Fenichel, 1945, for further elaboration of the important differences between these two core concepts in narcissistic theory).

[3] Freud viewed the personality as composed of stratified layers with consciousness at the top; directly beneath is the preconscious stratum, and beneath that the unconscious layer which is the seat of our instinctual impulses, and the depository of our repressed memories and buried anxieties. Not all theorists agree with Freud's specific formulations, but all psychodynamic theories adhere to psychic "layers" or "strata." Implicit to understanding all human behavior is the image of a fluid personality in which energy flows back and forth, and with this flow each stratum weakens or strengthens depending upon whether energy is entering or leaving.

[4] Margaret Mahler described a narcissism where the infant has no recognition whatsoever that mother is the external agent of their own satisfactions; after a few weeks the infant attains a dim recognition that its needs are somehow being satisfied by someone outside the self, but even in this secondary narcissism where the very young child recognizes that needs are being satisfied from outside "they nevertheless are convinced that *their own desires alone are sufficient to assure their presence*" (Monte, p. 229). In this so-called "autistic state" the child acts out a primitive precursor to adolescent entitlement. Such attitudes, and the behavioral styles they call into existence, when manifested, not in the infant but in the adolescent, undermine every form of community where cooperation, goal sharing, and equitable division of labor are required. Exaggerated entitlements contradict shared community.

[5] The apparent contradictions of narcissism are less puzzling when we recognize the importance of three basic principles.
First, the narcissist's self-esteem is grounded in a perfectionalized image; which is to say that their self-image lacks range and flexibility. The narcissist is *distrustful of anything, or anyone which fails to nourish or praise.* The "false self" is alienated from the "true self," and, as Karen Horney

recognized, this quality of alienation renders the narcissist incapable of genuine love:

> A person with narcissistic trends is alienated from the self as well as from others, and hence to the extent that he is narcissistic he is incapable of loving either himself or anyone else (1939, p. 100).

Second, narcissists "flow" to gratifiers because their needs for approval and admiration are never satisfied. Hence, the self is held captive within the circumference of those who flatter it. Narcissists are never completely in control of their own lives because the self "has" them more than they "have" the self. This lack of control is expressed in their recurring pleas: "I couldn't control myself." "It just came over me." "I just had to do it." Ultimately, this *lack of freedom in regard to themselves* diminishes them.

Third, narcissists perceive criticism as a personal attack. Like agoraphobes who remain hidden within their homes to avoid threats from the outside world, the fear of criticism shrinks narcissists into a protective shell. This defensive style narrows the range of human relationships they are able to experience, and, as we saw in the previous chapter, underlies the attraction to narrowness so typical of the narcissistic attitude.

[6]   In the case of **malignant Narcissism**, the object of narcissism is not anything the person does or produces, but something he has; for instance, his body, his looks, his health, his wealth, etc. The malignant nature of this type of narcissism lies in the fact that it lacks the corrective element which we find in the benign form. If I am "great" because of some quality I have, and not because of something I achieve, I do not need to be related to anybody or anything; I need not make any effort. In maintaining the picture of my greatness I remove myself more and more from reality and I have to increase the narcissistic charge in order to be better protected from the danger that my narcissistically inflated ego might be revealed as the product of my empty imagination (E. Fromm, *Heart of Man*, p. 77).

Chapter Six

narcissism and the adolescent experience

"Narcissistic traits may be particularly common in adolescents and do not necessarily indicate that the individual will go on to have Narcissistic Personality Disorder."   DSM IV

Of the vexing mysteries which captivate adolescent watchers, perhaps the most bewildering is why teens sometimes attach to worthy people and to honorable values and, at other times, to unworthy people and to dishonorable values. This mystery is more than merely rhetorical. Indeed, one might rightfully ask "What is more important in a young person's life than attachment to worthy mentors and peers?" Or, "What is more important than dedication to honorable values?"

In these immediate chapters (5, 6 & 7) much of our focus is on the relationship between the natural self-absorption inherent to adolescence and the unacceptable extremes which flow from it. At the present moment we are at something of a disadvantage in our attempt to decode this relationship because, after six decades of measurement and observation, our theories of adolescent behavior remain tragically minimal. If teens were unable to report their inner feelings and their private motivations, we would know virtually nothing about *why* they behave as they do. In adolescent psychology the unknowns continue to loom infinitely larger than the knowns, a state of affairs I report with frustration and sadness.

Our most serious problem in the investigation of the adolescent experience is that teens, like the rest of us, are far more complex than the crude instruments and unproven theories we must use to investigate them. It is not as though we are using magnifying glasses when electron microscopes are available, or typewriters when computers are in the next room. The tragedy is that we really don't have effective tools in the entire project; a tragedy greatly compounded by the importance adolescence assumes in the global scope of our society.

Because of our limited success in understanding *the profound issues* of adolescence, I began to investigate the classic theories of narcissism. Thus far, the findings have been encouraging. And while it is true that there is rarely anything completely new under the sun, as Noam Chomsky once wrote, there are moments "when traditional ideas are reshaped, and a new consciousness crystallizes, and the opportunities that lie ahead appear in a new light" (1989, p. 45). Hopefully, in this vein, we shall generate some new ideas and fresh insights which permit us to see adolescence, if not in new light, perhaps in a brighter one.[1]

*   *   *   *

Our concern from the beginning has been with the forces which contribute to adolescent corruptibility, the conditions which increase their propensity for self-diminishing choices, and, taken together, why teens to get into trouble when trouble is completely avoidable. These concerns we share with parents, educators, the clergy, coaches, counsellors, indeed everyone dedicated to the welfare and the well-being of youth.

In this middle section of the book we are investigating the idea that inherent to the adolescent personality are a cluster of predispositions which increase the young person's vulnerability to harmful agents. A vital point for the reader to keep in mind is that we are not speaking of pure determinism, or of instinctual, unswerving patterns. Rather, of predispositions and inclinations, of tendencies and propensities. Their significance to the adolescent drama is grounded precisely in the fact that they are not etched in stone, that they are indeed malleable.

How the study of narcissism enriches our knowledge of the adolescent experience

In the previous chapter I presented a brief overview of the basic themes of narcissism; these ideas now serve as our stepping stone into the adolescent self. Let us look a bit further, then, to see what common concerns are shared by narcissistic theory and adolescent theory; and, to see if knowledge of one enhances our knowledge of the other.[2]

- *Theories of narcissism highlight the data of self-experience.* Theories of narcissism recognize that human existence is characterized by heroic contradictions; that the self can feel glorified and inflated while at the same time vulnerable and deflated. Recognizing these contradictions as inherent properties of the self helps us to understand the polarities of mood which typify so many young people. It seems to me that all attempts to understand adolescence, as it is lived in North America, miss the point when they avoid the profound emotionality of adolescent existence. The adolescent struggle with self-discovery and self-definition produces a storm of self-absorption which reactivates the egocentrism and the narcissism of childhood. What David Wexler has to say about this is worth a read:

  adolescence is a period of intensely heightened narcissism and self-preoccupation. The teenager . . . becomes invested in maintaining a sense of self and usually develops an extremely narrowed awareness of others. The self-esteem swings typical of narcissistic syndromes . . . are plainly visible (1991, p. 29).

Another parallel is the rapid shift from one emotion to another, what psychoanalysts call "emotional lability." These shifts may occur in naturally linked domains such as affection and sexuality or unlinked domains such as compassion and hatred. A practical consequence is the overflow of emotional arousal from one domain to another, i.e., passion diffusion. Again, Wexler's observations are illuminating:

> Adolescence is a stage of life that brings out the most intense and labile range of emotional states. Treating teenagers is both exhilarating and miserable, which parallels the internal experiences of these kids. They can be impossible. They are cynical, defended, cocksure of themselves, unpredictable, easily bored, emotionally labile, and lacking in concentration. *These descriptions apply to normal adolescents* (1991, p. 29).

• *The study of narcissism helps us to better appreciate how the young mis-perceive self-other relationships.* Narcissistic theory accepts that every self struggles with its own fears and insecurities, and suffers the anguish of its own anxieties and inferiorities. This, unto itself, is of heuristic value in the study of adolescent psychology. Stephen Frosh put it this way:

> If you are narcissistic, it is claimed, you are struggling to preserve a shaky selfhood . . . you also protect that self by avoiding dependency and real interpersonal relationships. Narcissism . . . is more likely to be a desperate set of strategies for survival in a setting in which the self seems to be in danger of breaking down (Frosh, 1991, p. 3).

In this passage Frosh speaks to the heart of adolescent psychology: struggling to preserve a shaky selfhood, manipulating others in order to stabilize that shaky selfhood, and protecting oneself through the avoidance of intimacy.

The literature of narcissism has uncovered a cluster of attitudes, inclinations and predispositions which hold exciting implications for the study of adolescent behavior. Here are a few.

> Concerning criticism: Teens share with narcissists a confusion between criticism and aggression. Jeffrey Berman observed: "A healthy person is able to integrate love and hate; a narcissist, by contrast, perceives others as shadowy persecutors endowed with sinister powers" (1993, p. 23). Social workers and high school teachers know exactly what Berman refers to because what he describes is daily fare in the teen world. The bottom line is that narcissists and adolescents share an almost paranoic fear of criticism, and from this fear sprouts an anxious aversion to anyone who criticizes.

> Concerning rights and responsibilities: Teens and narcissists share a predisposition to presume that they are *entitled* to receive extra privileges and special rights. This thinking is exacerbated by their unwillingness to accept that with rights come responsibilities and with

entitlements duties. This egocentric isolation is most easily observed among early-adolescents, especially those who have not been socialized to reciprocity and mutuality.

Concerning the receipt of favors: Teens and narcissists share the tendency to presume that they receive favors because of something special within them, not because of anything special within the person who provides the favor. This tendency, so natural to the child, contributes to a coarse indifference to providers, which, in turn, creates hostility within those shunned and overlooked (parents, peers, teachers, grand-parents) who contribute to the welfare of the adolescent.

Concerning self-infatuation and self-centredness: All narcissism involves emotional prioritizing, and the adolescent version is no exception. What has priority is me. Perhaps this is what Kaplan was getting at when she claimed: "The adolescent can epitomize all that is offensively narcissistic. . . . Although contemporary parents have been prepared for the self-centredness, rebellion and other unpleasantness of the adolescent years, the reality always comes as something of a shock" (1984, p. 187). The unique adolescent mixture of self-consciousness, self-indulgence, and self-apprehension produces a self-imbued phenomenology not readily seen elsewhere in other developmental stages.

Concerning envy and jealousy: Teens and narcissists harbor feelings of envy and jealousy which produce resentment and hostility. The net effect is a phenomenology of edginess, of apprehension, of protective vigilance; a need for protective compartments to escape a world charged with negative emotions.

Concerning humiliation and shame: Teens and narcissists share a predisposition to fear humiliation in any way, shape, or form. This fear, in turn, leads to their refusal to participate in activities where humiliation *might possibly occur*. Both groups are overly infatuated with perfection and both share the belief that any less-than-perfect performance will shower shame or ridicule upon them. As well, both groups are inclined to hold self-images they cannot reasonably defend. "Obsession with an image of yourself can make you so sensitive to criticism that ordinary give and take is humiliating and you avoid people. . . . Teenagers trapped with this defense certainly cannot be loose and spontaneous." With regard to shame the same author notes: "An overconcern with your image exacerbates feelings of shame. Some cannot even ask a question, for not to know is to admit being less than perfect. Others cannot acquire skills. To practice a sport means living through a period of looking bad" (Polansky, 1991, p. 74).

Self-consciousness is magnified a hundred-fold by even the remotest prospect of humiliation. Louise Kaplan, fully aware of this phenomenon, claimed: "Another reason for the increased self-centredness of an adolescent is her susceptibility to humiliation. This brazen, defiant creature is also something tender, raw, thin-skinned, poignantly vulnerable. Her entire sense of personal worth can be shattered by a frown.

An innocuous clarification of facts can be heard as a monumental criticism" (1984, p. 189).

The significance of humiliation is found not only in its piercing pain, but in the desperate actions which flow from it. The humiliated one hates himself and wants to punish the object of his hate. A humiliated teen flirts with danger because punishment of the unworthy, pitiful self is what he secretly craves. A humiliated self is predisposed to deterioration and erosion, for in the resulting downward spiral one's own unworthiness is confirmed.

And, of course, one cannot overlook how the presence of humiliation requires adaptive responses from the adults with whom they interact. The humiliated self must be coddled and reassured before it can rebuild. Hence, effective interaction with teens requires that the adult demonstrate a capacity for matter-of-fact reassurance, for calm soothing, for firmness, direction, and clarity.

Concerning "good" people and "bad" people: Teens and narcissists share a predisposition to construct a social world divided into good and bad groups. The basis for the division is fairly simple: the good people are those who support, or nourish, "me" and the bad people are those who don't. From this partitioning of the social order springs a remarkable willingness to love, honor, and obey the "good," and to slander the "bad." Closely related to this predisposition is the tendency to evaluate the "appropriateness" of social behavior in completely moral terms. As a rule, the behavior of good people is evaluated as morally right and the behavior of bad people as morally wrong. Hence, the attraction to good people and the hatred of bad people is reinforced and strengthened through the power of morality. The consistent outcome to this fairly straightforward operation is the polarization of social units into in-groups and out-groups based not on mere personal likes and dislikes, but on moral rightness and wrongness. Moral beliefs are used by adolescents and narcissists alike to render their emotional foes unworthy.

- *The study of narcissism helps us to better understand the adolescent tendency to excessively narrow their range of experiences, to shrink rather than expand their opportunities.* Narcissists and adolescents both hide from the world through self-manufactured narrowness. Why would this be?

The first point to gather our attention is that narrowness forges a lifestyle where physical, mental, and spiritual energies are focussed inward. Narrowness glorifies the self because the narrower one's life the greater is the self within that narrowness. From this basic principle several considerations follow:

(1) Narrowness is simultaneously diminishing and liberating; diminishing in the range of life investments it permits, liberating in its power to justify an unending absorption with oneself.

(2) Narrowness immerses the self in itself, and in this regard it is an updated version of the self-immersion which blesses childhood. A narrow identity prevents one from being transported too far from one's own centredness. During adolescence a lifestyle of narrowness, even when it is racked with pain or failure, even when it incurs the wrath of one's parents and triggers a loss of esteem in the eyes of others, may be more desired than a lifestyle which does not ceaselessly and brightly spotlight "me." Narrowness bonds the self to itself. This, as much as anything, allows us to see it for what it is.

(3) Narrowness insulates youngsters from their deep-seated fear that they cannot attain worth in the no-man's-land of the moratorium.

(4) Narrowness manipulates. With the demand that anyone who desires "my" intimacy must achieve it on "my" terms. And even though this may appear to outsiders as self-defeating, in the adolescent world such demands may produce desired results because the craving for affiliation is so powerful in teen society that everyone who truly seeks a partner will find someone. Not necessarily a mature someone, but always someone. Few teens go without comradeship, even if they must settle for companions living within narrow compartments who, as a condition of friendship, require you to live by their terms. Adults who work with teens know from first-hand experience how frequently adolescent "friendship" begins from such narrow, narcissistic premises.

- *Narcissism helps us to better understand the alternating qualities of self-love and self-hate so frequently observed during adolescence.* For some time now, educators, parents, and psychologists have been pleasantly obsessed with the idea of self-esteem. To them almost everything positive comes from it and everything negative from a lack of it. And I don't want to say too much about this except to suggest that, as a concept, self-esteem lacks the range to do justice to the adolescent experience. Much of what we see in the adolescent arena is not adequately explained by "low self-esteem," or "positive self-esteem" because it is grounded in a deeper, more profound emotionality – in love and hate. About this profundity narcissism offers several insights, the first of which is that during adolescence love and hate intermingle in precarious cohesion. And frequently, one converts to the other.

Self-love is a difficult topic during adolescence, a time of life when the self is changing with such a flurry that simply to "know thyself" is an heroic achievement, and a time when dignified love is so rare that it stirs disbelief in almost everyone, including the love partners themselves. Self-love, in its simplest form, is affection directed upon oneself; in its grander form it is the dignified acceptance and wholesome embrace of oneself. In its lesser form it is little more than self-serving egotism. In adolescence it, most typically, is a bit of each.

While interviewing a 15-year-old, as part of my research into how young people integrate their personal fables into their day-to-day lives, she unexpectedly offered: "You know, I really am my own best friend." She said it with such convincing sincerity that I immediately believed her. However, after consulting my notes, I calmly reminded her that in our interview the previous day she had said, after a lengthy discussion, "I guess you could say that I am my own worst enemy." I brought these conflicting statements to her attention and then asked her if they involved a contradiction. She replied: "No way! Everyone is their own best friend *and* their own worst enemy." Putting aside the implicit sophistication from an otherwise startlingly immature 15-year-old, her comment contains interesting points worth looking into. Of course, being one's own best friend is not the same as self-love, and being one's own worst enemy is not the same as self-hate, but some overlap is easily observed, especially when focussing, as we are, on the narcissistic elements within the developing personality.

At one time I attached some importance to the view that love is an experience which shares nothing in common with its opposite – hate. My study of young people has helped me to recognize that these opposites interplay. In one of the most quoted passages of his landmark essay, *The Ego and the Id*, Freud (1923) observed:

> clinical observation shows not only that love is with unexpected regularity accompanied by hate, and not only that in human relationships hate is frequently a forerunner of love, but also that *in many circumstances hate changes into love and love into hate.*

The classic expressions of self-hate, so richly described in the psychological literature, are familiar to the community of teens, especially in their relentless demands on the self, in their merciless self-accusation, in their self-contempt, and, perhaps most significantly, in their self-destructive actions. Of this adolescent self-hate, narcissism has much to teach us.[2a]

- *The investigation of narcissism helps us to better understand the psychological profile of children raised in a narcissistic culture.* In our culture we provide young people with almost no opportunity for constructive and worthy self-expression. Instead we offer carnival showmanship, street corner theatrics and other juvenile expressions which isolate them from the important machinery of society. Our consumer society encourages youth to define themselves by appearance, by status, by gender, but almost never through legitimate, honest, or meaningful productivity.

If the culture of narcissism diminishes adults, it diminishes even more youngsters vulnerable to consumer illusions and flattering fables of all stripes. The conclusion which presents itself with increasing force is that our society simply is lacking in the human endorsements needed to transport teens beyond their natural narcissism; and equally important to the young person's struggle for dignified affiliation, our society is lacking in any coherent ethical system which rewards communalism more than individualism, "we" more than "me." The tragic outcome, as Christopher Lasch pointed out, is that our culture produces in its adults and in its youth "not an imperial self but a beleaguered, empty and minimal self."

Arnold Cooper, following Lasch's lead, described a "generation of narcissism" where the persona of an entire society has been deformed by consumerism and egotism.

> The high divorce rate, the loss of religion, the inability to maintain an extended family, the abandonment of the home by women who join the work force, the lack of traditional pursuits, which are valued for their own sakes rather than for the material rewards they bring – all of this and more have been cited as causes for, and evidence of, the so-called narcissistic generation. From this perspective, individuals are more than ever self-centred, incapable of self-sacrifice for another person, without deeper moral, spiritual, or emotional values, and capable of experiencing only shallow transference relationships – all of which ultimately subjects them to the perils of alienation, boredom, and insecure relationships (1986, p. 125).

This is the cultural parent to our adolescent children. Can it be that their vision, their style, their attitudes somehow lack the qualities of their elders?[3] Likely not. "The link between narcissistic pathology and narcissistic parenting means that a culture which valorizes narcissism, or at least enmeshes its subjects in webs of superficiality and glamorous but empty exteriors, will be registered psychically and reproduced intergenerationally" (Frosh, p. 113). Less eloquently, but to the same end, Cervantes long ago wrote: "It is nature's law that everything shall beget its like." Frosh and Cervantes, in different ways, ask the same question: What is more relevant to the moral fabric of society than ideological selfishness transmitted from parent to child?

Postscript

To encourage new perceptions about the adolescent experience, I am here suggesting that the core concepts of narcissism, seen in the proper light, can enrich and expand our understanding of adolescent psychology.

I have embarked on this venture because it seems to me that we simply have not made much progress in understanding why adolescents so easily choose self-destructive paths.[4] It is not an exaggeration to say that we simply do not understand why they become involved in relationships destructive to their emotional, economic, and human welfare. We have a long journey to travel before we can understand why teens, as Judith Musick phrased it in her excellent work on the psychology of teenage motherhood, "turn their back on opportunities, deliberately sabotaging their prospects for success" (1993, p. 4).

Some of the questions which occupy our interest include the following:

- Why do teens drop out of school *when they know* this freezes their occupational future?

- Why do teens join gangs *when they know* it increases the risk of injury or death?

- Why do teens engage in sex *when they know* that it will result in an unwanted pregnancy?

What we need, and cannot lay our finger on, is a worthy explanation as to why some adolescents move in self-destructive directions when others do not. Hopefully, our investigation of narcissism will shed some light on this mystery.

The following ideas were given a brief introduction in this chapter

- The theory of narcissism helps us to better understand the adolescent's fascination with uniqueness and individuality, with self-expression and self-assertion, indeed, with all forms of self-focus and self-fixation. It seems especially suited to increase our insight into the opposites within their nature; their brazenness and their timidity; their obsessions with the physical and the spiritual; their sexual indulgences and their ascetic denials; their race into, and their fear of, the future.

- The theory of narcissism helps us to recognize why young people need to inflate themselves in order to offset the pressing fear that they really are nothing.

- The theory of narcissism helps us to better understand how our culture encourages selfish habits in its adolescent children, and how these habits contribute to exaggerated expressions of their natural self-ish-ness.

- The theory of narcissism helps us to better understand the irrational qualities which punctuate adolescent behavior. All theories of narcissism assume that concern for others blossoms only after others have shown concern for us. This assumption, I believe, serve us well in adolescent psychology.[5]

- The theory of narcissism helps us to better understand the young person's need for ego-nourishment. Much more is at issue than self-fascination; the insecure narcissist, like the fearful adolescent, inflates to ward off the fear of not being worth anything. The fear of being unworthy is soothed by flattery, by praise, and by admiration. Therefore, no matter how high the cost, flattering mirrors, admiring audiences, and adoring lovers must be obtained. To these ends all teen resources are channelled.

The conclusions we cannot escape in all this are twofold. The first is that only through compassion, empathy, and constructive participation in real events are young people able to grow beyond their primitive narcissism to share themselves in genuine intimacy and true community. The second is that, in the absence of constructive participation and empathetic sharing, narcissistic investments colonialize the adolescent personality and, in a matter of a few short years, become the dominant force within it.

Endnotes

[1]   Although more scholars are beginning to recognize the important role of narcissism in adolescent life, this is a fairly recent turn of events. Textbooks of adolescent psychology, devoid of soul and passion as they are, rarely include more than a paragraph on narcissism. In what is generally thought to be the authoritative overview of adolescent theory (*Theories of Adolescence*, 5th edition), author Rolf Muuss does not include a single reference to narcissism.

[2]   Every new work dealing with narcissism connects, in one way or another, to Christopher Lasch's pioneer treatise *The Culture of Narcissism* (1978) and, in turn, to the psychological profile born of a narcissistic culture which he described in *The Minimal Self* (1984). In acknowledging the significance of his work, Stephen Frosh reports: "Amongst the various writers who have employed the concepts of narcissism . . . it is perhaps Christopher Lasch who has been both most influential and most distinctively thought-provoking" (p. 63). And while his commentary was not directed immediately to youth, his ideas helped us to see more clearly the shallow roles and the empty illusions which shape their lives. Lasch's writings allowed us to better focus on how our culture (a) excites the narcissism inherent to youth, and, (b) how it promotes the ecology in which narcissism thrives.

[2a]   The minor expressions of self-hatred so commonly experienced during adolescence should not be confused with the more profound expressions which Karen Horney called *self-effacement*, in which the person actually identifies with the despised self and unconsciously idealizes dependency, compliancy, and love. Self-effacement more closely approximates the deep-seated, pathological expressions of self-hate which psychoanalysts

prefer all self-contempt to be. However, it isn't. Especially during adolescence when episodes of self-hate come and go.

[3]   J. Satinover, after searching for a term to encapsulate the narcissistic profile so prevalent in Western culture, settled on "Puer Aeternus" – *the eternal adolescent.*

> It is a personality, on the one hand characterized by . . . a failure to set stable goals, and a proclivity for intense but short-lived romantic attachments, yet on the other hand by noble idealism, a fertile romantic imagination, spiritual insight and frequently, too, by remarkable talent (1987, p. 86).

From Satinover's comments it is easy to see how the stuff of narcissism is, to a captivating degree, the stuff of adolescence.

[4]   **Adolescent irrationality**. We really do not possess any comprehensive explanation of adolescent irrationality. Our understanding of why so many teens (especially mid-adolescents) become pregnant even when they have learned the mechanics of contraception is no more advanced today than it was 30 years ago. Neither do we understand why sexually active young women (19 to 23-year-olds, for example) efficiently avoid pregnancy while sexually active 15-17 year-olds do not? Our understanding of why teens are so influenced by fads, trends, fashions and why they are so pathetically molded by pop culture is no more advanced today than it was 30 years ago. Our understanding of why teens shoot and kill one another is no more advanced today than it was 30 years ago. In regard to these deficiencies, narcissistic theory has, I believe, something to offer because its pivotal concepts speak to the irrational, to the selfish, to the outwardly aggressive and the inwardly destructive.

[5]   The North American disciples of existential psychology were attuned to ideas which speak directly to youth, but, to my knowledge, no one has applied them to the adolescent experience. I found the following precepts of existential psychology especially helpful in my attempt to better understand adolescent behavior:

- Every person is centred in himself (herself) and any attack on this centre becomes an attack on the person himself (herself).

- Narrowness and defensiveness are the methods each individual uses to defend his (her) own centre. The more the self is threatened (or *perceived* to be threatened) the more will be the defensive, protective behavior.

- Every person has a character of self-affirmation and a need to preserve centredness through affirmation. Affirming the integrity of others has an enriching effect on one's own integrity.

- The more an individual is free from threat the more the she (he) exhibits self-affirming behavior which is not harmful to others.

- The more an individual is filled with fear and surrounded by threat the more she (he) exhibits self-affirmation through behavior which is harmful to others.

- All individuals have the need to go out from their centredness to participate in the lives of others.

- Moving out from one's centredness always involves risk. If the individual goes too far he (she) loses centredness and identity, too little of these and growth is shortchanged.

- The failure to participate in the lives of others always, in one form or another, produces emotional emptiness and excessive self-investment.

(For further development of these ideas, see Rollo May's classic work *Existential Psychology*, 1961).

Chapter Seven

the narcissistic attitude

We begin with the generally accepted notion that during adolescence narcissism expresses itself through an intense self-preoccupation which energizes an already heightened self-consciousness. Our concern in this chapter, however, is not with narcissism, *per se*, nor with adolescence, *per se*, but with a unique integration of the two. But before we begin we must first point out the differences between "developmental self-ish-ness" and "narcissistic selfishness."

The normal condition of developmental self-ish-ness

"The teenager who has enveloped himself or herself in a cloud of self-involvement is often engaging in an essential and functional life task." David Wexler

That adolescents are self-absorbed with the demands of physical, intellectual, and emotional development is the starting point of all modern theories of adolescent psychology. To my knowledge, the term "developmental self-ish-ness" is new, but the ideas behind it are given voice by virtually all of the important contributors to adolescent theory. Erik Erikson's concept of psychosocial stages; Anna Freud's theory of psychosexual development; Peter Blos' "second individuation process"; Jean Piaget's theory of adolescent egocentrism; David Elkind's personal fable and imaginary audience; Robert Havighurst's developmental tasks; Arnold Gessel's reciprocal interweaving; and Robert Selman's theory of perspective-taking each, in their own distinct way, speak to the proposition that adolescence is a developmental period in which the individual is consumed by a vital and necessary self-investment.

Developmental self-ish-ness[1] is a term I use to refer to the young person's preoccupation with self-development and self-sensation; it is, in my estimation, a requirement of self-discovery and self-cultivation. I view it as a healthy, wholesome fact of adolescent existence. The term carries no negative connotations; self-ish-ness is as necessary to the adolescent as self-interest to the entrepreneur.

In its general contours, developmental self-ish-ness is easily recognized. Its tenor was captured nicely by Lauren Ayers:

teenage girls are like hit-and-run drivers, barely noticing the wreckage they leave behind them in the family, where they rarely take account of other's needs or feelings and react to most issues solely on the basis of how they will be affected. The ability to empathize, or walk in another's shoes, develops slowly during adolescence.... (1994, p. 127).

The belief that adolescence is a time of "Promethean enthusiasm" was introduced into modern psychology in G. Stanley Hall's classic work, *Sturm und Drang* (1904). But Hall described nothing new. Adolescence has been described throughout all written history as a time of urgency, bewilderment, and excitement. The ancient Greeks provided us with many narratives on the emotionality and excitability of youth; Aristotle, the greatest observer of all the ancients, claimed:

> They are passionate, irascible, and apt to be carried away by their impulses. They are the slave, too, of their passion, as their ambition prevents their ever brooking a slight and renders them indignant at the mere idea of enduring an injury. . . . If the young commit a fault, it is always *on the side of excess and exaggeration* for they carry everything too far, whether it be their love or hatred or anything else (Kiell, 1964, p. 18-19).

And while it is likely that Aristotle exaggerated both the virtues and the defects of youth, there is little reason to doubt that some basis in fact existed for his observations. 2300 years after Aristotle, Anna Freud wrote: "Adolescents are excessively egoistic, regarding themselves as the centre of the universe and the sole objects of interest."

I am here trying to convey a simple idea: that adolescents possess a spirit of self-awareness which invigorates their psychology, indeed, the ecology of the entire teen community.

"Just being in a room with myself is almost more stimulation than I can bear." Kate Braverman

---

The unhealthy condition of narcissistic selfishness[2]

Narcissistic selfishness shares commonalities with developmental self-ish-ness, but, in every way, is an unhealthy exaggeration of it. Narcissistically selfish persons are always anxiously concerned with themselves, always restless, always driven by the fear of not getting enough. They are filled with envy of anyone who might have more; and, important to their friendship patterns, they are unable to give with any pleasure but they are always anxious to take. They lack interest in the needs of others, or respect for their integrity; they judge everyone and everything from the standpoint of usefulness (see Fromm, 1939, p. 521).[3]

What we are calling "narcissistic selfishness," can also be seen in what Fred Alford called unhealthy narcissism:

an exaggerated concern with power and control, the result of which is interpersonal exploitiveness. Typical also is an orientation of entitlement, the notion that one is worthy of great admiration, respect and reward regardless of one's achievements. Pathological narcissism is further characterized by relationships that alternate between extremes of idealization and devaluation. Finally, the pathological narcissist's grandiosity is curiously coupled with great fragility of self esteem (p. 3).

Otto Kernberg believed that unhealthy narcissism arises in early childhood, "as a result of chronically cold, unempathic parents who fail to provide the infant with the love and attention necessary for psychological health. Disruptions in the mother-child bond may bring about a refusion of self and object images, resulting in identity diffusion and an inflated or grandiose (narcissistic) self" (Berman, 1990, p. 24). Most theorists believe that in the narcissistic character the real self has never taken hold. The self-concept remains under the influence of childhood emotional states and the conflicts attendant to them. The more powerful these childhood emotional states, and the more primitive the conflicts within them, the stronger the narcissistic component to the personality.

"Although an accentuated self-awareness is a normal part of adolescence, *excessive selfishness* is dysfunctional in several ways. It can interfere with the formation of friendships . . . and it may give rise to passivity . . . depression."   Lauren Ayers

---

Individuals who exhibit narcissistic selfishness differ from the rest of us in many ways, one being that they cannot maintain any sense of themselves without massive infusions of attention and admiration; without such infusions, their grandiose sense of themselves disintegrates to what Christopher Lasch called "the minimal self."

They also differ on the issue of envy. For example, their obsession with grooming, with physical appearance, and with presenting a beautiful body, rather than building confidence within them, triggers a chronic envy of these features in others. They crave and hate the same thing at the same time: they love stylish haircuts when they have one, but hate them when they are "flaunted" by someone else; they love to walk with confidence but hate the cocky swagger of others who walk the walk. Hence, to the emotional burdens they bring to every interpersonal relationship we add yet another: chronic envy. Its significance cannot be overlooked because envy erodes human connection by casting the achievements and possessions of others in terms of one's own yearnings.

McWilliams opens the window to a better understanding of the free-floating contempt so frequently found among teens:

If I have an internal conviction that I am lacking in some way and that my inadequacies are always at risk of exposure, I will be envious toward those who seem content or who have assets that I believe would make up for what I lack. Envy may also be the root of the much-observed judgmental quality of narcissistically organized persons, toward themselves and toward others. *If I feel deficient and I perceive you as having it all, I may try to destroy what you have by deploring, scorning, or criticizing it* (1994, p. 172).

Narcissistically selfish individuals cannot handle relationships in which "give" and "take" exist in fairly equal portions. Hence, needs which demand equality for their gratification (such as genuine intimacy, basic friendship) are never satisfied. Their self-esteem is quagmired in empty, non-productive investments; hence, they displace their own unworthiness onto others, even when these others are their friends, their parents, their lovers.[4]

In his thoughtful discussion on "the narcissistic course," Ben Burstein asked: "Why do these people need to have so high an interest in themselves?" Answering his own query: "they cannot take themselves (their selves) for granted; *they constantly need to confirm their selves* (Nelson, 1977, p. 17).

It is definitely a two person relationship in which, however, only one of the partners matters; his wishes and needs are the only ones that count and must be attended to; the other partner, though felt to be immensely powerful, matters only insofar as he is willing to gratify the first partner's needs and desires or decides to frustrate them; beyond this, his personal interests, needs, desires, wishes, etc., simply do not exist (Nelson, p. 104).

To this apt reflection we may add an important aside: narcissistically selfish individuals seek relationships in which they are affirmed and praised. This use of companions as providers is a significant force in adolescent bondings.

The belief system of the narcissistically selfish

From the premises which govern their behavior evolves a belief system to perpetuate it.

- The belief that others must always accommodate to my needs, my desires. Hence, the theatre can't be full because I desire to be admitted. My specialness is a "fact of relevance" which entitles me to receive special treatment.

- The belief that my ultimate relevance does not need to be earned or proved.

- The belief that my specialness not only makes me unique, it makes me superior.

- The belief that from my specialness flows a river of entitlements, including unending streams of special concessions.

Each of these beliefs, no matter how much they infringe on the rights or the feelings of others, seem completely legitimate to the narcissistically selfish because, as Millon so effectively condensed it, they "move through life with the belief that it is their inalienable right to receive special considerations" (p. 159). Such a belief system, of course, conspires against every form of community spirit.[5]

Social interest

We can better set the stage by taking a brief look at Alfred Adler's theory of social interest for it represents the theoretical opposite of the chronic individualism to which so many youth are attracted. As we have already seen (in chapter five), all theories of narcissism focus on the selfish side of human nature. In opposition, Alfred Adler claimed that all humans possess an inborn predisposition for sharing and cooperation. Adler rejected self-interest theories as fundamentally flawed since they do not effectively explain cooperation, sharing, volunteerism, or the broad spectrum of "giving without taking" we observe in all human communities. Adler eventually came to believe that the excessive striving for selfish goals is a neurotic distortion of our inborn impulses for social interest.

Social interest is a translation from the German word "Gemeinschaftsgefuhl," which means "social feeling" or "community feeling." Adler, however, used it to mean a pervasive feeling of attachment to all humanity and membership in the social community of all people. In Adler's understanding of human nature, social interest *manifests itself as a natural, inborn impulse toward cooperation.* Adler believed that social interest is an inherent part of human nature which exists as potential to be nurtured and cultivated. It does not spring forth fully blossomed; it is encouraged through parental love, guidance, and sharing during the first five years of life. From these early interactions the lifelong desire to contribute to the social welfare germinates.

Adler opposed Freud's belief that all motivations are, in essence, narcissistic. He claimed that an obsession with self-aggrandizement is evidence that the initial mother-child relationship was not strong enough or loving enough for the child to progress naturally from self-interest to social interest. Narcissism, again according to Adler, is not a reflection of our nature; it is the diminishment of our nature. It is not the starting point, as Freud claimed; it is the rupture point.

Because of our hypotheses concerning the egocentric and the narcissistic predispositions of adolescents, it is abundantly clear that

Adler's theory of social interest is not our starting point. However, without going into it at this moment, it should also be clear that Adler's ideas are vital to our deliberations on this topic. Why? From our investigations of adolescence a fundamental principle emerges: *youth lacking in social interest are guided by the narcissistic inclinations inherent to their nature.* As Adler himself expressed it: "Only those persons who are really trained in the direction of social interest . . . will actually have social feeling.

For youth raised in a culture which limits their social investment and encourages their narcissism, nothing could be more relevant. When all is said and done, youth who do not find someone in whom to invest their hopes, who never build anything tangible, who never volunteer their services or share their skills, who never learn how to contribute to the community on which they totally depend, remain forever absorbed in their natural narcissism

The narcissistic continuum

"All people are narcissistic; the difference is only one of degree."
Rueben Fine

Experts agree that the normal narcissism which lives within each of us exists on a continuum with unhealthy narcissism.

Although pathological narcissism sounds so sick . . . healthy narcissism shares many of the same characteristics. . . . This is explained by a presumption . . . shared by almost all theorists of narcissism that there is a continuum between pathological and normal narcissism . . . (Alford, 1988, p. 70).

My contention is that between the extreme egomania of narcissistic selfishness and the natural self-absorption of adolescence exists an attitude characterized by a bit of each. The narcissistic attitude is not pathological in the clinical sense; rather, it is an attitude which debases others through the unwillingness to honor their rights and feelings. As one might suspect, this attitude sets the stage for a downward spiral in human relationships.

Before we begin a closer look at the narcissistic attitude, it might be helpful to present a brief review:

- Developmental self-ish-ness refers to the natural spirit of urgent self-awareness typical of adolescence.

- Narcissistic selfishness refers to a condition of chronic self-centredness similar to (but not as extreme) what some observers call "pathological narcissism," and what others call "the narcissistic personality disorder."

- The narcissistic attitude refers to a cluster of self-serving beliefs and behaviors which shares features with both developmental self-ish-ness and narcissistic selfishness.

The basic ingredients of the narcissistic attitude

The remainder of this chapter looks into the habits, tendencies, and thinking patterns of the narcissistic attitude. Expressly:

- the excessive demands for entitlements;
- deadness to the feelings of others;
- a reduced capacity to love;
- diminished moral concerns; and,
- a lessened capacity for objective thought.

Entitlements

To psychologists the term entitlement means the expectation of special favors without assuming any responsibilities in exchange for receiving these favors. In the language of governmental agencies, entitlement means receiving benefits without making contributions. Individuals who demonstrate an attitude of entitlement expect far more from others than is reasonable, and they demand far more from their school, their government, and their family than can reasonably be delivered. They view their parents, their schools, their governments as providers; and they view themselves as the *rightful* recipients of everything everyone else can provide.[6]

Individuals guided by this attitude matter-of-factly accept that it is their inalienable right to receive special considerations. They completely fail to recognize how objectionable this attitude is to their friends, their parents, their teachers. "Their self-image is that they are . . . extra-special individuals who are entitled to unusual rights and privileges. . . . Moreover, anyone who fails to respect them is viewed with contempt and scorn (Millon, p. 157).

The narcissistically selfish (and in some instances, egocentric teens in the throes of their own developmental self-ish-ness) "feel entitled to have what they want when they want it just because they want it. . . . They feel entitled to pursue it, no matter how they do so or whom they hurt" (Rothstein, p. 67). And while it is not necessary, in a theoretical sense, to claim that the adolescent desire for entitlements originates within the same subconscious core that psychoanalysts believe produces narcissism, ("The gratifying moments when a child is being overvalued provide the experiences which serve as the anlage for the feeling of entitlement" Rothstein, 1984, p. 71) there is no doubt that, as far as attitudes are concerned, as far as demands are concerned, as far as self-centred preoccupations are concerned, the day-to-day behavior of the "overly-entitled" adolescent is extremely similar to the day-to-day behavior of the classic narcissist.

> "they operate on the fantastic assumption that their mere desire is justification for possessing whatever they seek."   Theodore Millon

Entitlement thwarts self-reliance by demanding that others look after "me," locate jobs for me, make school easy, or fail-proof. The majestic "I" is entitled to special treatment, to special subsidy, to special everything. However, when someone receives someone else must provide. Once young people perceive their peers, and the adults they interact with (teachers and parents) only as providers, the attitude of entitlement has taken hold.

What we are here discussing was a source of great conflict between Sigmund Freud and Alfred Adler in their debate on human nature. When Freud originated the concept of narcissism he had in mind "a protective channeling of energy into the self, a healthy self-interest or self-love." Adler postulated (and in this regard his thought is much closer to Karen Horney than to Freud) that narcissism is really little more than a selfish inward fixation, which diminishes social interest and reduces the desire for extension into the larger community. To Adler, the narcissistic attitude is not innate or instinctual, *but learned or acquired by those who doubt their own strength.* Adler's version of narcissism grapples more candidly with entitlement demands since he recognized from the beginning that excessive self-centredness invariably leads away from genuine interest in the community, and away from the natural impulse toward social interest.

The expectations created by an attitude of entitlement lead one to believe that one *should* be admitted to a theatre after it is sold out, *should* be given permission to take an examination late when such permission is granted to no other student. Boys charged with entitlement sometimes believe that they are entitled to the affection, loyalty, or sexual favors of a girl they know, or date, or with whom they simply share a classroom. When these entitlements are not received the boy may pout, hold a grudge, or slander the girl who failed to deliver. However, it is important to keep fresh in mind that entitlements need not be spoken aloud because they are so firmly accepted as true that articulation of them seems unnecessary. Hence, among the entitled a comfortable smoothness connects expectation with action. Why should one feel self-conscious when taking something to which one is rightfully entitled?

146

An important aside is here worth a moment: vital to the phenomenology of the entitled is that they experience intense pain when their expectations are denied; indeed, pain seems to affirm the righteousness of their demands. In another twist, their peers often respond sympathetically to their pain and try to reduce it by giving to them what they desire.

In our society, entitlement among the young is all too often encouraged by the family and the school (the two most important institutions in their lives) both of whom have granted a wide range of benefits but have set few requirements for how the young ought to function in return. Which is to say that benefits are in place, but obligations are not. There is little doubt that in our present society adolescents live under a regime of social values that allows them to make demands on family, school, and society-at-large far more than vice versa. Perhaps from this tradition of being able to make demands without having to accept duties and responsibilities, irrational and exaggerated entitlement springs (Mead, 1986). At least it jibes with Sebald's observation: "In the forefront of the psychology of entitlement . . . stand the young . . ." (Sebald, 1984, p. 107).

In *Issues of Freedom*, Herbert J. Muller described the links which connect rights to responsibilities. "Almost all societies, from the most primitive to the most civilized, have emphasized duties much more than rights or liberties, and almost all of their members have accepted these duties without protest" (1960, p. 26). If we accept this message, even if only for purposes of discussion, we find discouraging implications for the narcissistic attitude, since its mission is the reversal of the priorities Muller claims have served society from time immemorial. The present discussion, quite obviously, is not the proper forum for a thorough analysis of these concepts but it is a good place to reflect on possible connections. Especially if we see the merit in Muller's ultimate point: that human interdependence demands duty and responsibility in the management of every society, including the society of youth. "The survival of a group depends to some extent on the fact that its members consider its importance as great as or greater than that of their own lives . . ." (Fromm, 1964, p. 78). Exaggerated entitlement, for all intents and purposes, reverses this equation by claiming that "I" am greater than "my" group, and that the purpose of the group is to look after "me and my needs."

Egocentric anticipation vs. narcissistic expectation

Taking into account our earlier discussion of egocentrism (chapters two and three) one might be inclined to think that an attitude of entitlement and egocentrism amount to the same thing. This is not so, and I would like to briefly explain why.

The egocentrism natural to children predisposes them to anticipate that they will be, in general life circumstances, favored. To young children it seems both natural *and* reasonable that mother will provide them with special gifts even when doing so requires great sacrifice on her part. Egocentrism predisposes children to anticipate that they will be blessed with good fortune, that they will receive the benefit of doubt, that they will routinely have exceptions made on their behalf. These anticipations flow so easily and permeate their demeanor so completely that when formal thought begins to impress upon them the concept of impartiality it ruptures their anticipation that they will always receive the lion's share in conflicts of interest.[7] This predisposition to anticipate that things *will* fall in one's favor is the psychogenic precursor to the expectation that things *should* fall in one's favor. The difference between anticipation and expectation is the difference between "is" and "should."

In both children and adolescents the anticipation of good news is tempered by reason, common sense, and by the force of evidence. So, to give a simple example, the child's *anticipation* that he will receive most of the candy is easily brought into line with father's ruling that the candy will be divided evenly. The egocentricity which governs the lives of children is usually reduced by arguments and disagreements, indeed, by all forms of social communication in which the desires of one person come into conflict with those of another.

To summarize: the egocentrism and self-centred philosophy which carries so much weight in the world of children is not the same as the narcissistic expectation of entitlement we see during adolescence. However, the transition from the former to the latter is an easy one.

Deadness to the feelings of others

Certain psychologists who have a prejudice against facing up to the selfish side of human nature contend that people act selfishly only when they are required to do so, or when the rewards for selfishness greatly exceed the pain of its punishment, or when only slight chance exists for being caught. And while I respect the scholars who hold these views, I find no evidence in my experience to support them. Indeed, as far as adolescents are concerned, I find their line of thinking not only naive, but preposterous.[8]

Teachers encounter youngsters every day who, when confronted with a wrong doing, claim they didn't do it. Or, yes, they did it, but they couldn't help it; or, yes they did it but they didn't know they were doing it; or yes, they did it, but so what. Sometimes they don't know what they have done, and at other times they simply disown their actions; a denial which produces an unwelcome mixture of self-alienation and defiance. Nelson (1977) expressed it this way: "The student of today is deeply unaware of the need to be cooperative with others, either students or teachers. He doesn't even seem to be in touch with being cooperative with himself; *some students appear to be unconscious of their very actions* (p. 67).

One narcissistic premise goes like this: if intentions are not bad, neither are the actions which flow from them. When confronted they claim their behavior wasn't bad because they didn't *intend* anything bad. They act "as-if" motives are more important than actions. Such behavior-deadening was conveyed by a sixteen-year-old boy I once interviewed in a youth detention centre, incarcerated after he shot, with a hand gun concealed in his jacket, another teen. To him it was unfair that he had to serve time because he didn't intend to shoot the victim. "He just sort of got in the way." The gunman intended to shoot a member of a rival gang, but "this other dude just started shoving and gettin' involved where he didn't have any right. I shot him but it was no big deal. I didn't even mean to shoot him. If I shot 'D,' like I wanted to, then they would have a case. Just 'cuz some guy gets in the way. It's really more like an accident. I don't think I should do time for that."

These youngsters insulate from their own unacceptable behavior with the claim that only their intentions should be judged. Their logic is simple, though bent: "You can't punish me for what I didn't intend to do." Or, "You can't punish me for what I couldn't prevent." (We gain a certain insight into the narcissistic attitude when we recognize that these youngsters *never* accept this claim when it is made to them by others. As far as their judgments of others are concerned only actions count; motives mean little).

Deadness to the feelings (and rights) of others is also seen in the tendency to become irritated with a friend who couldn't help out with homework because he was sick that day, or with a parent who drives a friend to the hospital and therefore cannot loan the car. When their relationships turn sour, when exploited friends complain or simply walk out, when parents tell them they are sick of being their servants, they are usually taken by complete surprise. Unbalanced relationships are so compatible with their nature that it does not occur to them that their partners feel exploited. From these youngsters we repeatedly hear: "I can't believe you're telling me this"; "How come you are suddenly saying this?"; "Why didn't you tell me you feel this way?"; "How come I'm always the last one to know?"

Being dominated by the narcissistic attitude means that one becomes agitated and anxious when too much time elapses without receiving praise or special acknowledgment. Since these youngsters evaluate adults by whether they are flattered by them, they "respect" adults who praise them, and have no respect for those who don't. Frequently they ridicule adults who don't shower them with attention for the simple reason that being inattentive to "me" proves they *deserve* ridicule. Among their peers these adult-rejecting teens may attain a great deal of acclaim because of their ability to make administrators look like buffoons, teachers idiots, police Nazis, or psychologists neurotics.

Reduced capacity to love

"The most grievous cost of a narcissistic orientation is a stunted capacity to love."   Nancy McWilliams

Individuals driven by narcissistic attitudes are bewildering subjects for investigation when the topic is love. The fact of the matter is that the core definitions of the two are, in great measure, mutually exclusive. Love implies a strong, passionate affection for, an attachment and a devotion to, another person. A narcissistic attitude, on the other hand, implies an excessive self-focus in which the interests of others are perceived as subordinate to one's own.

While individuals with narcissistic attitudes have a pressing need to be loved and admired by others they have no pressing need to *give* their love. Even though they crave love, their most powerfully felt emotions tend to be regressive: envy, anger, and resentment register more forcefully upon them than compassion, joy, or sharing. Their main pleasure in life is the tribute they receive from others, so, as one might anticipate, they inevitably feel restless or bored when no new sources feed their egos.

> Despite the importance of other people to the equilibrium of a narcissistic person, his or her consuming need for reassurance about self-worth leaves no energy for others except in their function as . . . narcissistic extensions. Hence narcissistic people send confusing messages to their friends and families: *Their need for others is deep, but their love for them is shallow* (McWilliams, 1994, p. 175).

How then, do they attract others into their sphere? This question is investigated in greater detail in chapter twelve, so, for the moment, a cursory overview will have to do. These individuals idealize, glorify, and glamorize those who provide emotional supplies; they court affection by convincing their suppliers that it is they who are loved when, in reality, it is the "supplies" they provide which are most craved. This special investment in the "supplier" is made even more powerful by the contempt in which they hold all lesser individuals who serve no such majestic service. Because they feel they have the right to control others, because they feel entitled to their allegiance and affection, they are able to possess them without feeling guilty, or even presumptuous.

And while it is true that they are ultimately dependent on others, it is also true that they never completely depend on anyone because they are fundamentally distrustful.

One might say: "You must love yourself before you can love others," but it is readily apparent that their love is for themselves *instead* of others. The underlying motivation for this emptiness is unclear, but most theorists agree it derives from the numbing pain of rejection, or from the smoldering resentment from being insufficiently loved.

Before closing our look into how the narcissistic attitude stifles love, I would like to draw upon Erich Fromm to connect a few final thoughts.

> Freud said that in all love there is a strong narcissistic component; that a man in love with a woman makes her the object of his own narcissism and that therefore she becomes wonderful and desirable because she is part of him. She may do the same with him, and thus we have the case of the "great love," which often is only a folie à deux rather than love. Both people retain their narcissism, they have no real, deep interest in each other (not to speak of anyone else), they remain touchy and suspicious, and most likely each of them will be in need of a new person who can give them fresh narcissistic satisfaction. *For the narcissistic person, the partner is never a person in his own right or in his full reality; he exists only as a shadow of the partner's narcissistically inflated ego* (Fromm, 1964).

Narcissistically selfish individuals, even when they embrace another person, cannot truly let go of themselves; they lack the *giving* required of loving.[9]

Reduced moral circumference

Moral diminishment is a subject which has not been studied with sufficient care in traditional psychology. And it is with some trepidation that I put forth any ideas on the topic; yet it is so relevant to the adolescent experience that I feel compelled to do so.

Morality, by definition, requires the alignment of one's actions and beliefs *with a principle or a standard greater than oneself.* Such alignment is inherently difficult for individuals harboring narcissistic attitudes because for them moral rightness is determined by how it impacts their own needs and circumstances. This is not to say that they do not believe in good or bad (in fact, narcissists can be extremely moralistic); rather, it means that what they think of as "good" and what they think of as "bad" is gauged by how it favors or disfavors them. Narcissistic morality is by no means an "impartial" morality (if there is such a thing);

rather, it is a brew of pragmatism, egotism, and morality more than a genuine moral system.

> *"I knew it was wrong; so what. Who cares? The worse thing is getting caught.*
> *I sure don't want that to happen again."*
> 14-year-old after arrest for assaulting an elderly paper vendor.

The social contracts which bind children to their parent society might seem straightforward but they are not. Our society is presently locked in debate about the relative weight of rights and obligations. Billions of education and welfare dollars are appropriated, in great measure, by our understanding of how much we owe youth, and how much they owe us. The debate is heated because the ground rules are not clear, and because some of us believe that the entitlements and rights of youth far outweigh their duties and responsibilities and others of us believe the opposite. Even more pressing: some youth believe that they are owed entitlements and benefits far beyond what society at large believes.

It is not universally agreed, for example, what actions youth are morally obligated to perform. What duty do they owe to their parents? What labor should youth be required to perform in our society? Are youth obligated to show respect or deference to adults?

To what extent are youth accountable? Accountable to whom or to what? To what degree can we expect young people to know right from wrong, to be punished for wrongdoing, or rewarded for doing right? Do the responsibilities of youth require them to meet their financial obligations? Can we rightfully expect them to be morally responsible for the consequences of their sexual behavior, financially responsible in their economic transactions, parentally responsible for the children they produce, legally responsible for the people they injure on the highways? These matters of responsibility are not at all clear in our society.

On the other side of the coin: What are the just and fair claims of youth? What are they entitled to by law, by nature, by merit of being young? What claims can they make "in their own right"? Much of the debate reduces to one key question: Do *rights* or *duties* hold greater sway in the conduct of youth?[10]

Rights are especially difficult to discuss in our society because in many people's thinking they are prefaced by "inalienable," which translates into guaranteed, and by "my" which translates into mine but not necessarily yours. Perhaps no concept, philosophical or legal, is as subject to egocentric and narcissistic contamination as "rights." Their first-person relevance makes them attractive to children and teens; teaching youngsters their rights is one of the easiest pedagogical tasks in the books; teaching them about the rights of others is more difficult.

The most difficult, however, is getting them to accept the responsibilities and duties which come with the rights they so eagerly embrace.[11]

Youth obsessively preoccupied with their own rights are, all too often, indifferent to the rights of others. In one of the major understatements of modern social criticism, Laurence Mead, in his analysis of social rights and personal responsibilities says: "Many Americans evidently are less able to take care of themselves and respect the rights of others than in earlier decades" (1986, p. 8). Some critics believe this summarizes well the defining features of youth in modern society: they cannot take care of themselves, yet at the same time, they do not hold any deep respect for those who provide for them. "We were distressed that many Americans are all too eager to spell out what they are entitled to but are all too slow to give something back to others and to the community" (Etzioni, 1993, p. 15). All of which adds up to "a form of citizen infantilism."

The failure to recognize that rights imply responsibilities is more than merely a failure in logic, it also is a moral failure.

> Rights give reasons to others not to interfere coercively with me in the performance of the protected acts; however, they do not in themselves give me sufficient reason to perform these acts. There is a gap between rights and rightness that cannot be closed without a richer moral vocabulary, one that invokes principles of decency, duty, responsibility, and the common good, among others (Etzioni, p. 201-202).

Rights carry responsibilities. About this there is not much disagreement. Individuals imbued with narcissistic attitudes resist this for a simple reason: the balance of payments is too even. These individuals want rights without responsibilities; but for others they expect responsibilities without rights. This view of the world fits perfectly their expectations of entitlements; in fact, they nurture and strengthen each other. Therefore, if one were to speak of the "politics" of the narcissistic attitude, one would clearly see that entitlements and rights are major platform issues.

"Strong rights presume strong responsibilities."	Amitai Etzioni

Reduced intellectual circumference

Individuals dominated by the narcissistic attitude tend to perceive events by how they affect them rather than by the events themselves. This leads to double-standards in both perception and in thinking.

> A person, to the extent to which he is narcissistic, has a double standard of perception. Only he himself and what pertains to him has significance, while the rest of the world is more or less weightless or colorless, and because of this double standard *the narcissistic person shows severe*

defects in judgement and lacks the capacity for objectivity (Fromm, 1973, p. 148).

Teens are more sophisticated thinkers than children because, among other things, they better recognize the gap between the outside world and their private experiences. Like younger children, however, adolescents sometimes "bend" perceptions to fit their needs. To further complicate things, they sometimes simply ignore what they don't want to see. In this regard they are living examples of what in legal circles is called *ignoratio elenchi* – the ignoring, rather than the ignorance, of a contention. *Ignoratio elenchi* is the intellectual style behind every narcissistic attitude because it depends upon ignoring all data which contradict their fable of righteous selfishness. The operative mode is *ignoring*, not ignorance; *inattentiveness*, not unawareness. Rehabilitating the narcissistic attitude requires that the individual quit ignoring the obvious. As every high school counsellor will attest, this is no easy job.

Twist and turn as we may, there is no denying that the narcissistic attitude restricts intellectual freedom. Equally difficult to deny is that individuals who exhibit the narcissistic attitude are the last ones to figure out that their belief system makes them less, not more, perceptive; less, not more, intelligent; less, not more, desired.

What does all of this mean?

The question springs immediately to mind. "Are teens *naturally* attracted to the narcissistic attitude?" Or, for those of you who resist the idea of natural attraction, the parallel question reads: "Do teens *easily* adopt a narcissistic attitude?" To both questions the answer is "Yes." Let me try to explain.

The narcissistic attitude is a primitive attempt to elevate one's importance and to bolster one's significance. It feeds off the egotism essential to every human personality, but in the course of doing so, expands into possessive selfishness which interferes with the ability to extend oneself into the sphere of other private selves, and, perhaps of greatest concern to us at this particular historical moment, to build decent human community.

As to the natural progression from childhood egocentrism to narcissistic selfishness, the evidence is ambiguous. But it seems to me that, under the wrong conditions, this progression comes so easily that one is tempted to think of it as "natural." This conclusion comes as no surprise to anyone familiar with normal growth trends. We know that children do not learn all things with equal ease. If you doubt this, try teaching a group of children to be left-handed, or to always choose celery over sweets; then, try to teach a group of children to be right-

154

handed and to choose sweets over celery. As every parent knows, these are not equal tasks! The predispositions children bring to their experience shape their preferences and guide their inclinations, and, as a result, influence what they *easily* learn. To teach selfish attitudes and self-serving habits to children (and adolescents) is one of the easiest teaching assignments one could possibly have. The egocentrism and narcissism natural to their make-up predisposes them as surely as their neurology predisposes most of them to throw objects with their right hand.

There is not much doubt as to the predispositions of youth. Their egocentrism, their narcissism, and their developmental self-ish-ness, in combined strength, *incline* them, at every juncture, toward self-concern and self-priority.[12]

Such predispositions in youth necessitate a sympathetic attitude in the adults who nurture them, who love them, and who are responsible for their welfare. One cannot provide for the best interests of the child until one comes to grips with the predispositions which chart the child's course; it is through them that we understand their strengths and their vulnerabilities, their resilience and their frailty.

Postscript

As might be expected from the course of developments I have outlined, the relationship between the narcissistic attitude and adolescent behavior is not an encouraging one. The entire attitude is dehumanizing in its use of other people as self-esteem maintaining functions rather than as separate individuals.[13]

We need not repeat in detail what has been explained before, but a few summary points may help us collect our thoughts in a more orderly fashion.

The narcissistic attitude, by narrowing the range of shared emotional investments, and by reducing the circumference of intellectual concerns, impoverishes the adolescent experience in predictable ways. Most notably, by encouraging:

- imperviousness to the feelings of others;
- self-serving friendships patterns;
- presumptions of entitlement;
- indifference to the effects of one's own behavior on others; and,
- the pursuit of rights and the avoidance of responsibilities.

I would like to make clear that all of the problems of youth are not brought into existence by the narcissistic attitude, but I also want to make clear that all problems are deepened by it. The narcissistic attitude is the attempt to maintain the self as the fixed centre of the emotional universe. And while it may prove productive in the short term, it is ultimately degrading because it does not praise the dignity and worth of anything except itself.

Endnotes

[1]   Hyphens, as we all know, do not destroy meaning but they do they alter it. With the term "self-ish-ness" I ask the reader for a certain leniency because I simply have not been able to locate a term from self-psychology, from personality theory, from the insufferable expanse of psychologese and creative neologism, which adequately conveys the *vital spirit of vigilant self-protectionism* which ignites the adolescent experience. I have settled on self-ish-ness, despite its bulkiness, because of its ability to convey a series of ideas rather than only one, and to suggest a connective thread weaving through self, selfish, and selfishness.

[2]   What I call "narcissistic selfishness" is known to H. Kohut and O. Kernberg as "pathological narcissism," to Fred Alford as "regressive narcissism," and it parallels what the DSM IV calls "the narcissistic personality."

[3]   To better understand the meaning behind narcissistic selfishness consider this:

> In some of us, concerns with "narcissistic supplies," or supports to self-esteem, eclipse other issues to such an extent that we may be considered excessively self-preoccupied. Terms like "narcissistic personality" and "pathological narcissism" apply to this *disproportionate degree of self-concern*, not to ordinary responsiveness to approval and sensitivity to criticism (McWilliams, p. 170).

[4]   Individuals consumed with narcissistic selfishness may respect the feelings of others when it leads to their own gain or gratification. This is not to be confused with respect for people as people. Their respect is what behaviorists might call "instrumental" respect since it is grounded more in pragmatism than empathy, more in receiving than in giving, more in efficiency than compassion.

[5]   A different view of narcissistic selfishness is presented by Robert Bellah, et al., in their analysis of individualism in modern culture.

> By the end of the eighteenth century, there would be those who would argue that in a society where each vigorously pursued his own interest, the social good would automatically emerge. That would be utilitarian individualism in pure form (p. 32).

In their profile of the selfishness which grips the modern era, *utilitarian individualism* is front and centre. I encourage the reader to investigate the particulars this concept shares with narcissistic selfishness.

[6] Sir Bertrand Russell, a man by no means enthralled with narcissistic selfishness, once wrote: "The man who loves only himself cannot, it is true, be accused of promiscuity in his affections, but he is bound in the end to suffer intolerable boredom from the sameness of the object of his devotions."

[7] To narcissists *impartiality* is feared because of its unacceptable assumption of fairness; impartiality implies that I do not possess any inherent advantage over those who want the same things I want. Impartiality contradicts the entire idea of narcissism, indeed, of every form of human selfishness. If you want to lose a narcissistic friend, simply show impartiality in all matters that pertain to him (her). In the absence of favoritism, narcissism withers.

[8] Arthur Schopenhauer (who grappled with the inherently selfish qualities within our being as tenaciously as any of the pre-Freudian thinkers) once claimed: "Egoism is so deeply rooted a quality of all individuals in general, that in order to rouse the activity of an individual being, egotistical ends are the only ones upon which we count with certainty." The extreme flavor of Schopenhauer's statement has been debated in many quarters, but whether we accept or reject his view of human nature no one doubts that *many* individuals are motivated exactly as he described.

[9] Erich Fromm once claimed: "The ability to love depends on one's capacity to emerge from narcissism." In this section we are looking at some of the reasons which support this statement.

[10] Etzioni's analysis of rights and responsibilities is particularly relevant to this discussion.

> When Communitarians argue that the pendulum has swung too far toward the radical individualistic pole and it is time to hurry its return, we do not seek to push it to the opposite extreme, of encouraging a community that suppresses individuality. We aim for a judicious mix of self-interest, self-expression, and commitment to the commons – of rights and responsibilities, of I and we (1993, p. 26).

[11] See Amitai Etzioni's *The Spirit of Community* (1993), for further elaboration of these ideas.

[12] What concerns us are the different ways that narcissism and egocentrism cast the thought process to their own ends. Several suggestions were made in chapters three and four, including the tendency to argue ineffectively because of narcissistically imbued logic, and the proliferation of rationalization as a form of intellectual warping.

[13] **The soloist and the choir**. Harold D. Grovetant, in an informative essay on the integrative demands of adolescent identity (1993), subtitled his essay "Bringing the soloist to the choir." In this article he puts forth ideas which share commonalities with ideas put forth here, especially, the tenet that every young self is engaged in a struggle to balance the legitimate

needs and demands of the group with the legitimate needs and demands of "me." The key words, however, are not "group" and "me," rather "balance" and "integration." Grovetant writes: "Metaphorically, the interplay required for musicians to produce a coherent, balanced performance is not unlike the interplay required for the orchestration of one's sense of personal identity; both involve blending and integration" (p. 121). Individuals steeped in narcissism enjoy their role as soloists but fail to recognize that without the choir they have no place to sing. For them "balance" and "integration" mean something quite different than to the choir members, who view the soloist as one voice in a chorus of many.

Section III

some prefatory comments

If we can retreat for a moment to certain ideas communicated in the Introductory chapter, we will recall that youth in Canada and the United States share a "moratorium" culture in which they spend virtually all of their out-of-household hours in the presence of one another. But, despite their age-segregated world, adolescence is also the time of life when young people must emerge from their protective cocoon to explore, to investigate, and to master the larger world in which children have no real part.

Learning the ropes of the social world, cultivating friends, nurturing intimacy, falling in love – this is the human business of the adolescent years. To understand it requires more than merely watching it in action. In fact, much of what we see when we are watching it is impossible to make sense of until we recognize the needs, cravings, and desires which drive it.

In the upcoming chapters I provide the reader with ideas not readily found in the mainstream literature of adolescent psychology. And while the general themes are generic (approval, friendship, intimacy), my treatment of them, hopefully, is not.

In Chapter Eight, I discuss the dynamics of teen relationships, especially the need for friends to nourish one another's self-esteem. These needs, especially when skippered by an immature thought process, take many unexpected twists and turns.

In Chapter Nine I discuss the most significant intrusion of the past three decades into the young person's struggle for approval: consumerism. And, how the acceptance of consumerism creates another corrupting influence in the life of teens: work-for-pay.

Chapter Ten investigates the adolescent's search for intimacy. Its significance to the adolescent is that it represents connection with the deepest core of another person; its relevance to society is completely different. In the adolescent arena intimacy goes hand in hand with sexual intercourse; sexual intercourse with pregnancy; pregnancy with motherhood; motherhood with single-parenting; single-parenting with welfare and poverty. In North American society, nothing strains the social contract between youth and society more than teen pregnancy.

In Chapter Eleven the concern is with how certain "hungers" influence teen bonding. We are especially concerned with mirror-hunger, the need to be the object of attention; ideal-hunger, the need to admire someone great and grand; and alter-ego hunger, the need to dominate.

In Chapter Twelve the adolescent attraction to the selfish and the self-centred is our concern.

Chapter Eight

friendship and companionship

"Of all the things which wisdom provides to make life entirely happy, much the greatest is the possession of friendship."   Epicurus

As far as I am able to judge, after attending to the subject over the past four decades, there is no simple or efficient way to address the topic of adolescent friendship. This, in great measure, is due to the fact that there are no comprehensive theories which focus on this worthwhile topic. And what we do find often lacks the economy of explanation and the range of accountability we look for in a good theory. Rolf Muuss, in his authoritative *Theories of Adolescence*, claimed that since no theory of adolescent friendship is available, its elucidation requires "several different theoretical perspectives that are compatible and mutually supportive" (p. 300). I completely agree, and in these chapters I follow Muuss' advice by presenting a range of ideas which, when taken in their entirety, hopefully will provide some insight into the phenomenon of adolescent friendship.

As is true for adults, the richness of teenage personalities and the vitality within their community is simply too great to describe with universal generalizations. Yet the question of teen relationships is a fascinating one which is given even greater significance by compulsory schooling, by pop culture, and by our society's pseudo-glorification of all things youthful. The intent of these chapters, then, is not only to summarize the research and theory relevant to adolescent relationships, but also, to present to the reader some of the frustrations of teen relationships.

"Without friends, no one would choose to live."   Aristotle

Generic observations

W. W. Hartup and Susan Overhauser, in their overview of adolescent friendship in the inaugural edition of the *Encyclopedia of Adolescence*, make several interesting observations which will serve as starting points for my treatment of this topic. They observe: "The essentials of friendship are reciprocity and an enduring commitment between individuals who see themselves more or less as equals." They also report that when asked to describe their friends, younger children "emphasize common interests and a sense of mutual attachment along with an appreciation that equality in their encounters with one another can be taken for granted." But with the onset of adolescence "expectations emerge attesting to the importance of trust, loyalty, self-disclosure, and mutual understanding."

In their investigation of friendships and relationships among Canadian young women, Holmes and Silverman report:

> Friendships and its commitments are deeply meaningful to young women . . . it is clear that they count on their friends for much more than the sense of conformity they are often said to pursue. Adolescent women turn to friends for the same kind of support they say they need from their families. They want to speak out, to be heard, to counter what one 14-year-old described as "the fear that nobody is going to be around when you really need someone to talk to and confide in" (1992, p. 35).

The authors also report that in the Canadian Youth Federation survey, "both sexes listed friendship as the highest of their goals and named friendship as their greatest source of enjoyment" (p. 36).[1]

For most youngsters friendships are vital because they support and nourish.

> Most adolescents perceive their friends as supportive . . . frequently more so even than family members. When dealing with routine concerns, adolescents go more often to friends than family members or other adults for discussion and support. . . . Friendships may also constitute a buffer against daily stresses. Young adolescents with supportive friendships report having fewer bad hassles and more good "uplifts" in the course of a month than do children with less supportive friendships (Hartup & Overhauser, p. 251).

Non-generic observations

An investigation of adolescent friendship cannot be concerned only with how adolescents feel about their friends, or with the positive benefits of the friendship, although these certainly are necessary concerns. It must also take into account the motives which impel companionship, and the consequences of being without friends in the teen community. We need to know not only why friendships are formed, but also why they are dissolved and abandoned.

All human relationships are made of much more than the initial attractions which brought them into being; of adolescent friendships we know a good deal about initial attractions but almost nothing about why relationships fizzle and fall apart. As is true for so much of adolescent psychology, the experts have focussed almost exclusively on surface issues such as popularity and peer pressure, and have chosen to turn away from subtler, more profound topics.

A first consideration in all this is that in the teen community the *absence* of friends may signal impending catastrophe. In a peer-dominated world, to be without friends is to be nobody. Youngsters not accepted by their peers are much more likely to drop out of school, to engage in delinquent behavior and criminal acts, and to develop psychopathology later in life. Low levels of friendship support are related to depression and other symptomatology during adolescence, especially for girls. *Who* one's friends are also is important since friendship with deviant peers is highly correlated with delinquency, fighting, and antisocial attitudes. And, as we discuss later, attraction to narcissistic peers brings additional problems.

This investigation starts with the belief that all youngsters need friendship, companionship and love, but because of their natural narcissistic tendencies, adolescent relationships all too often are concerned too little with the needs of the partner and too much with the needs of me. Although teens very much want to experience meaningful relationships with friends and lovers their expectations about giving and receiving often lead to their partners' dissatisfaction. These expectations about giving and receiving, and the confusions which naturally flow from them, unfortunately, are given virtually no consideration by the researchers currently investigating the adolescent experience. An exception is Louise Kaplan, who writes:

> most adults . . . tend to imagine the adolescent years as brimming with opportunity. They see the adolescent as having infinite possibilities for love relationships, friendships, interest in dance, music, clothes, learning, work. They do not always understand why the new loves and friendships, the passionate new interests, usually prove to be unstable, transient, and heartbreakingly disappointing (1984, p. 151).

Much of the effort in this chapter will be spent trying to explain why teen companionships are so often "unstable, transient and heartbreakingly disappointing."

In the past, several of my graduate students (professionals who work with "normal" and "disturbed" youth) have resisted some of my ideas on the nature of adolescent companionship. Their resistance, I believe, is based on two assumptions. The first is that spite, jealousy, and anger play only a small role in human relationships. The second of their assumptions is that adolescent alliances exemplify the highest ideals of friendship; that, in the words of Graham Allan, their friendships are "based solely on their personal and voluntary commitment to each other"; and, that such bondings are "unfettered by any selfish or instrumental concerns. Each gives what the other needs, without thought to cost or reward, simply because of the fact of their friendship" (1989, p. 13). Such a portrayal of friendship is idealized, and as far as adolescents are concerned, considerably less than accurate.[1a] Adolescent friendships are sometimes molded from necessity, sometimes from desperation, sometimes from emotional hunger, and sometimes from the dignified core of a beautiful, sharing self. But, most typically, from a little of each.

To lend some organization to those readers who may prefer to skip certain sections, or to dwell more fully on others, four general themes are discussed in this chapter in the following order:

- How the adolescent social arena is typified by frustration and hostility, and how these experiences shape friendships and alliances.

- How friendship is influenced by reciprocal rationalization and by flattering mirrors.

- How adolescent relationships are influenced by hypocrisy.

- How gang behavior contributes to corruptibility.

Tension, frustration, hostility

"Friendship is almost always a union of a part of one mind with a part of another; people are friends in spots."   George Santayana

A certain amount of what I am here trying to convey (or, at least, the tone of what I am trying to convey) has been effectively presented in Edgar Friedenberg's classic work *The Vanishing Adolescent*. Friedenberg was fully aware that adolescents are not angelic, that they often behave like self-serving junior executives, and that the cement which holds them together is not necessarily mortared by ideal friendship.

> Groups of juveniles are not friendly; and strong-felt friendships do not commonly form among them, though there is often constant association between members of juvenile cliques. They are not there to be friendly; they are there to work out a crude social system and to learn the ropes from one another. To some extent they behave like the gang in an office, jockeying for position within a superficially amiable social group (1959, p. 44).

More condensed, but to the same point, Weiss claimed that "adolescent conformity to the peer group is of necessity, not enjoyment" (1980, p. 254). The key is *necessity*, and when it is considered, our attitude toward the nature of teen social life shifts somewhat. Friedenberg and Weiss both recognized dynamics which must be taken into account if one is to understand teen friendship at a deeper level than mere platitudes allow. First, there are important differences between "being friendly" and the attainment of genuine friendship; second, among the young sociability may derive as much from the setting as from the relationship itself; third, while sharing time with comrades brings laughter, even deep emotion, it does not follow that these experiences are the same as real friendship.

Sue Lees (1986) investigated teen friendships first-hand, interviewing adolescent girls over a five year period, and in doing so distilled a more personal assessment of adolescent friendship than is usually reported in the psychological literature. (Freidenberg and Weiss, it should be pointed out, did not base their conclusions about adolescent life on data they themselves gathered from teens as much as from their personal insights into the adolescent personality and how it operates within its social world). Lees also investigated the adolescent's social world, but she was primarily concerned with how power relations constrict the adolescent experience, especially for girls; her strategy was "to take the girls' own descriptions and raise questions about the way they describe their lives, their experiences, their relationships . . ." (p. 157).

One of the more intriguing findings in Lees' investigation was the extent to which teen friendships are burdened with grinding antagonisms and uneasy alliances. Although the girls in her study very much desired unconditional acceptance, genuine intimacy, and "true love," they also faced a day-to-day peer world with stinging demands for acceptance, popularity, and reputation. Lees reported that all of the girls she interviewed agreed that friendship is characterized by loyalty and sticking up for your friend. However, it is not that straightforward: "The other side of the coin is bitching and spreading gossip and rumours. Bitching is constantly referred to as something that girls are particularly adept at and as the source of aggravation and even fights among girls" (p. 65). One girl in the study says: "Sue, one moment she can be really nice but the next moment she can be really bitchy. Sue will use what you say against you." Another girl reports: "There are boys that bitch as well – but on the whole I think girls have more character for bitching." Another says: "Girls get pretty ratty and annoyed with each other and say things about each other. Whereas boys . . . don't bitch about each other behind each other's backs so much."

The adolescent community, as described by teens themselves, is one in which the all too human failings of betrayal, gossip, and slander are facts of daily life:

> That's why you have to be careful who you hang around with, who you speak to, because even the slightest thing you tell them, they can change what you said and get you into a lot of trouble. You might say something to them, 'Don't tell anyone what I just told you.' The next morning the whole school knows it (Lees, p. 68).

The vital issues of trust, reputation, and integrity intermingle in precarious cohesion. "One reason why so few girls talk even to their closest friends about sexual desire or actual sexual behavior is through fear that their friend might betray them and gossip – spread the rumour that they were a slag [promiscuous]" (Lees, p. 68). Lees reports that slander among teen-age girls is everyday fare: "A more vicious type of devaluing aspects of other girls is to cast doubt on their sexual reputation, which is why much of the bitching characterized by girls involves sexual abuse [slander]" (p. 66). According to one subject in the study, girls who desire a boy-friend but have difficulty attracting boys are the most bitchy. Lees suggests that "bitchiness seems to be a way of devaluing aspects of other girls that you wish to signal as 'not you'. It is a way of marking differences between other girls and yourself." One girl, describing herself says: "I am bitchy. I say 'oh she's so fat'. You say it in front of friends for instance to see if they say 'You can't talk, you're just as fat' or to see if they agree with you." From what we have learned from Lees we can better understand why John Churton Collins claimed: "We make more enemies by what we say than friends by what we do." An aphorism to be sure, but one which drives home an important message in the community of teens.[2]

The significance of what is at stake should not be taken lightly. In the teen world reputation is currency, and anything which inflates or deflates it is big business. Reputation cannot, in any real way, be separated from integrity. Slander, therefore, is a vital issue, especially for girls, because, as Lees puts it: "an attack on a girl's reputation is an attack on her personal morality and integrity which only she can defend" (p. 72).

I do not want to convey an exaggerated impression of the trials and tribulations of teen social life; neither, however, do I desire that this book join the stream of sterile treatises which *claim* to describe (but do not) the adolescent experience; nor do I desire to add to the vacuous manuals of classroom management which build education around a Pollyanna vision of teen society which promotes the preposterous belief that every youthful disruption must be caused by defects in the social environment, by unloving parents, by incompetent teachers, by stultifying rules and regulations. Youth have their own deficiencies, their own immaturities, and their own vulnerabilities which account for much of their social and behavioral difficulties. None of us benefit from the denial of this fact.

*　*　*　*

An ocean and a continent away from Sue Lees in England, Myrna Kostash in Alberta conducted her own investigations of friendship patterns among adolescent girls. Interestingly, though not surprisingly, Kostash's observations parallel in striking ways those made by Lees:

> This is not, however, the whole story about the relationships girls strike among themselves. Through much of the language they use in talking about each other runs a streak of unmitigated nastiness, a shrill and

cold-hearted aggression designed to wound. At the very least a vague and free-floating anxiety seems to charge the air when more than two or three are gathered together, as though something unpleasant were about to happen, but from which quarter no one is quite sure. One girl described it as not being able to "trust" your friends fully, fearing that, when your back is turned, they will "put you down"; or fearing that something is planned from which you are to be excluded, or that the other two "know" something you do not. More extremely, girls hurl obscene epithets at and about each other – slut, bitch, sleaze – and cruelly disparage each other's bodies – so-and-so's tits hang down to here, and so-and-so's thighs are gross and check that hairdo, a rat's nest, no kidding. They pass along damaging and probably spurious tales about each other's sexual behavior and reputation (who does "it", with whom, and how many times) (Kostash, 1989, p. 37).

The social toughness observed by Lees and Kostash (and by virtually every investigator who actually participates in the lives of youth rather then merely reports the results of paper-pencil tests) harkens to mind Mark Twain's observation: "It takes your enemy and friend, working together, to hurt you to the heart; the one to slander you, and the other to get the news to you."

Flattery friendship

"What I liked most was that he liked me." 16-year-old's response to the question: "What most attracted you to your first boyfriend?"

Adolescents are attracted to companions who overlook their limitations, or even better, perceive them in a favorable light. With the passage of time youngsters whose friendships start from this unspoken agreement develop a profound desire to be with one another because it is only in each other's company that defects become virtues, weaknesses strengths, and personal failings the failings of others.

Reciprocal rationalization

In reciprocal rationalization each partner is attracted to the other by reassurance and flattery. The cement is each partner's willingness to give approval and support to the other. In its psychogenesis, this is an alliance of emotional dependence, and as such there is invariably a great deal of resentment. And while adolescents passionately defend these friendships as true and pure, as they attain greater insight into their motives they eventually come to see them for what they are. I have discovered in interviews with university students over the past three decades, that many young adults (19-22-year-olds) candidly and freely admit that their early- and middle-adolescent friendships were, in many instances, self-serving and egoistic. Rather than being embarrassed by this fact of social engagement, they accept matter-of-factly that such egocentric immaturity is simply part of "growing up."

"He was older and more mature than friends my age – he was like a trophy for me. I found it very flattering for somebody in high school to want to be with somebody in jr. high. He even gave me his football jacket." First year university student's response to the question: "What most attracted you to your first boyfriend?"

Genuine friendship requires a clear knowledge of where one stands in relation to the friend. Individuals with fragile, shaky bondings may call their partner friend, but the word "friend" has lost its meaning since any argument, any rumor may arouse not only doubts but shake the very foundation of the relationship.

Daniel Goleman adds some thought-provoking ideas to the issue of friendship when he claims that some groups (especially families) engage in "synchronized self-deception" for purposes of mutual emotional protection, where they "tacitly agree not to notice, and not to notice that they do not notice" (1986, p. 274). Goleman is convinced that friends, family members, and lovers learn to protect one another by failing to acknowledge buried secrets which, if uncovered, would force everyone to face unflattering and painful facts. Henrik Ibsen, the Norwegian dramatist and poet, called these buried secrets "vital lies" because they dim our awareness of disturbing realities.[3]

One peculiar consequence of mutual denial is the willingness of peers to synchronize their self-deceptions into a web of *acceptable intrusions into each other's emotional lives*. From this web an alliance of social cohesion is attained, but at the expense of honesty. All of which leads Goleman to observe: "When some aspects of shared reality are troubling, a semblance of cozy calm can be maintained by an unspoken agreement to deny pertinent facts, to ignore key questions" (p. 279).

It is helpful to recognize the advantages of such an arrangement. Any group which honors "unaskable" questions (questions never to be raised in the presence of the protected person), which operates on the principle that personal limitations should, whenever possible, be overlooked, affords young people a certain measure of growing room, and a latitude in which their real strengths can be paraded and exercised while undeveloped qualities remain dormant. The struggle for personal identity (especially for self-knowledge and self-understanding) parallels, in important ways, the struggle for national identity in that it requires a blend of honest disclosure and public acknowledgement with an unacknowledged bureau of hidden secrets and private files. To such devious, yet functional, ends reciprocal rationalization is channeled.[4]

Teens, for the most part, are impressed with loyalty, and recognize it as the cornerstone of good relationships. One girl put it this way: "If you have an argument, your friend sticks up for you even if she doesn't agree with your point because she's your friend." Then further: "You can't argue with a friend" (p. 64).

When young people make up after a quarrel a curious twist often characterizes the reconciliation: namely, that no real reconciliation of *the actual disagreement* has taken place. Surviving a disagreement often means (a) the partners have reassured each other; (b) that they each admit to being sorry that they quarreled. What we usually see in such reconciliations is juggling with words more than the clarifying of disagreements. This accounts, to a certain degree, for the recurrence of the same disagreements among teens; they have only limited skills at slicing to the heart of a disagreement. As a result, when they claim that their disagreements "have been worked out," what they often mean is that they no longer are angry with one another, or that their alliance has been resumed. (The adolescent glorification of loyalty is due, in part, to their pressing fears of abandonment and betrayal. See [5] for further elaboration).

Flattering mirrors

To meet the demands of a world far more intricate and immeasurably more demanding than childhood, adolescents require friends who give reasonable advice, and who honestly describe their actions; in other words, they need accurate mirrors. In all friendships, it is the duty of each friend to help the other be a better person, to hold up a standard and to count on a true friend to do likewise. This moral component of friendship helps one not only to better meet the demands of daily living, but also to become a better person. In the society of teens, morale boosting and partner improvement are integral to friendship. (See [1] for its importance in developmental friendships).

An accurate mirror, important as it may be, is cold and matter-of-fact; it reflects only what is. On the other hand, a *flattering mirror*, is warm and complimentary; reflecting what one desires, it is not constrained by the painful narrowness of the real world. And even though "the opposite of a friend is a flatterer, who tells one what one wants to hear and fails to tell the truth" (Bellah, 1985, p. 115), the role of the flatterer is an important one in teen culture. In the real world of teen friendship the role of certain individuals is nothing more than that of the flattering mirror. And, it is a role for which many kids willingly audition and eventually learn to act out with great proficiency.

"We hung out together, drank, and partied together. He complimented me lots. He made me feel great. He was a bit older. Everyone thought he was so great." 17-year-old's response to the question: "What most attracted you to your first boyfriend?"

In the course of time, flattering mirrors become an indispensable part of the flattered person's social network and integral to their sense of well-being.[6] Such an exchange, praise in return for affiliation, is often perceived by teens as deep friendship, and in a certain limited sense, it is; but in an equally certain sense, it is not. As this emotional collusion continues each youngster gives approval and support, an alliance further bolstered by non-aggression pacts, and solemn agreements to do nothing which will hurt or embarrass the other. The pact serves as "proof" of their dedication to one another. Such pacts, however, usually rule out blunt observations, or unwanted candor, that might lead to hurt feelings, or to a loss of status. This would nullify the protective value of the pact; hence, in such alliances honest criticism is regarded as a hostile attack not only on the person to whom the criticism is directed, but on the alliance as well.

To some observers (especially parents) this dependency relationship is hard to understand because on the surface youngsters who need flattery and flattering mirrors may look confident and self-assured, but internally they have a boundless need for reassurance that they are admirable or valuable. They sometimes admit that they don't really know who they are or what they believe in; what is of most concern to them is simply being reassured, on some kind of ongoing basis, that they really matter.

Peter Blos, more so than other psychoanalysts, emphasized the vital role of the peer relations in the transition from parental dependency to independent selfhood. He recognized that one of the most important tasks to be mastered during adolescence is to recognize in a realistic way the shortcomings and imperfections within one's self, a task which early- and middle-adolescents are diligently working at, but by no means do they have it mastered. Their tendency toward unrealistic images, and their need to glorify friends in order to magnify their own self impedes an honest awareness of their own limitations and perpetuates their blind-eye to the shortcomings of their friends.

Blos also recognized that adolescents use friends in "make-believe" relationships in order to work through developmental changes in their own personalities. Fantasy-friends serve as representations more than as persons; their primary function is to provide reassurance. The point not to be lost is that fantasy friends are grounded in both friendship *and* fantasy, however, the adolescent must convince himself (herself) that it is friendship only, pure and simple. The adolescent-as-

170

thinker, however, usually will not condone mere fantasy-friendship, but, amazingly, by drawing upon deeper, emotionally rich sentiments, will fable-ize the partner so convincingly that he or she becomes worthy of anything and everything.

Hypocrisy and its impact on teen relationships

Adolescents face squarely the realization that how people treat you depends on what they think of you.[7] From this grows the further realization that it is in everyone's best interest to positively influence how others think of them, and that this influence is best effected through behavior. In a nutshell, adolescents know it is to their advantage to present themselves so that other people draw positive conclusions about them. It is, therefore, with impression management that adolescent hypocrisy is usually concerned.

Three categories of behavior can justifiably be described as hypocritical:

- the tendency to pretend to be what one is not;

- the tendency to pretend *not* to be what one is;

- the tendency to talk negatively about peers in their absence but positively in their presence.

The adolescent participates in these hypocrisies for numerous reasons, some of which are developmental and, with counsel, are likely to be outgrown, some of which are grounded in the personality and, as a result, are highly resistant to extinction. Our concern is with the former.

To be hypocritical one must recognize the distinction between public appearance and private experience and understand that it is possible to manipulate the conclusions other people draw. Hypocrisy requires the ability to remember accurately and plan systematically a complex series of actions and thoughts, always distinguishing within one's own mind that parade, charade, and fact must appear to the observer as equally genuine. Hypocritical behavior, in most respects, is beyond the developmental capacities of the child, especially the pre-school child, who does not clearly understand that thought is private and cannot be read infallibly by outsiders. The adolescent, on the other hand, is aware that thought is private, that motives are ambiguous, and that deceit may go undetected. Teenagers are able to transact hypocrisy because they possess the mental tools required for its effective execution. (Youth characterized by a narcissistic attitude are even more inclined to hypocrisy than ordinary kids because all of their predispositions are geared to engineer opinion to their own personal advantage, one further reason peers gravitate to them).

Adolescents can be relied upon to document the daily hypocrisies of elders, but the intelligence which allows insight into the behavior of others does not as adroitly investigate itself. In fairness, we must report that insight into adult hypocrisy is often sophisticated and, on occasion, exceeds that which adults themselves possess. The issue I believe to be of most concern, however, is not how accurately adult hypocrisy is perceived by teens, but how inaccurately they perceive their own.

Adolescents constantly confront situations where they are expected to pretend to be what they are not: to be content with school when they are not; to be honest when chastisement is the response to honesty; to conform to parental expectations they do not believe in. They constantly are expected to be other than what they are; hence the stage is set for one type of hypocrisy: pretending to be what one is not.

The converse, pretending not to be what one is, also is commonly observed in the adolescent arena: expected not to be angry or resentful when they are; expected not to engage in behavior which will hurt their parents; expected not to feel hatred, jealousy, or possessiveness even though these feelings surge through them. In essence, the adolescent is expected by peers, adults, parents, and teachers *not to be, not to feel, not to desire* the very things which constitute a legitimate stake in their emotional life.

Adolescents are, in a very real and practical sense, what Vance Packard long ago described as "status seekers" and "pyramid climbers." Especially during early adolescence they are driven by the need to belong, and to power politics to satisfy this need; they become perfect prospects for the web of survivalism we associate with junior executives. When the need for group acceptance becomes overwhelming, as it indeed does for many adolescents, the ability of the group to manipulate is proportionately increased; on the other hand, when the group strongly desires to admit a particular person, the greater is that person's ability to manipulate the group. Adolescents who find themselves on the weak side of the exchange, constantly seeking admission, incessantly proving themselves, are easily enticed into behaviors to which they otherwise would never consent. Of the extremes to which an adolescent will go in order to win group acceptance, hypocrisy is among the more moderate.

A common ploy is to debase, to ridicule, or in general to dehumanize peers competing for acceptance, thereby elevating one's importance at the expense of a fellow. If the peer group values honesty, it is an easy matter to point out the dishonest nature of a competitor; if the group values toughness, it is elementary to point out the frailties and weaknesses of a competitor seeking acceptance. Adolescents, like their parents, are not above lying, slandering, and defaming others if such actions produce a more secure footing on their slippery social ladder.

> *"Perhaps Liz and I became good friends because we were both incredibly sensitive to the propensity of the "popular group" to just drop people, to turn on them for no apparent reason. We were both afraid and angered by this possibility."*   A. Garrod

The final hypocrisy we shall address is the tendency to do whatever is immediately required: the hypocrisy of expediency. The adolescent who says only what the school principal wants to hear, who behaves as the gang leader expects, who feigns sincerity to win confidence, in other words, who acts out a role for the returns that role brings, is participating in the hypocrisy of expediency. Role playing, in itself, is not hypocritical; however, when one attempts to persuade another person that the role being played *is an accurate portrayal of one's real self when it is not*, then one is hypocritical. On this count, adolescents are guilty time and again.

Samuel Johnson was partly correct when he stated that "no man is a hypocrite in his pleasure." His intention was to point out that people, if nothing else, are forthright in pursuing their pleasure. One is tempted to surmise that Johnson's insight is geared more to adults because adolescents are steadfastly hypocritical about their pleasure, convincing themselves that they like things which they don't, and assuring others that they don't like things which they do.

Adolescents tend to outgrow their unique brands of hypocrisy, replacing them in time with adult variations. Adolescents are comparatively exempt from the universal adult hypocrisy which decrees that others should do as I say, not as I do. Adolescents believe in doing their own thing, and tend not to be overly prescriptive about what others (especially peers) should do. Therefore, this form of adult hypocrisy irritates them no end. Adolescents generally pretend to be what they are not if it will help them to avoid chastisement; adults, on the other hand, often pretend to be what they are not to achieve a sense of superiority. Teen-agers are quick to advise adults of such hypocrisy and to encourage them to be themselves and not to worry about being superior to others. On the whole, good advice.

All in all, the demands of self-presentation and the requirements of management impression are so strong during adolescence that it is generally to their advantage to strategically manipulate the opinions and reactions of others. When these manipulations involve deception and trickery, or downright falsehoods, we have hypocrisy. Adolescence is impossible without a certain amount of it.

Gang membership and peer corruptibility

"If you live with a lame man, you will learn to limp."   Plutarch

Since our concern here is with "normal" youth living in what might be thought of as "normal" environments, I do not want to get involved in the phenomenon of gang membership in those communities where crime is so rampant and criminal behavior so commonplace that gang membership is essentially a survival mechanism. In these communities (and they exist in the hundreds in North America) the facts of violence supersede the facts of youth, the necessities of survival outrank the requirements of growth. In these conditions gang membership has more to do with crime, violence, and survival than with youth itself.

The questions we are investigating are better served by looking at gang membership among those youth where adolescence itself, not the demands of survival, is the object of discourse. An incident which took place during the summer of '95 serves our purposes well.

In a small Oregon community a group of boys, aged 11-16, were charged with raping an 11-year-old girl who had been roller skating in a city park. The boys were members of a neighborhood gang. So, at least in terms of peer affiliation, they were easily tagged. However, as sons, as students, as members of Christian youth groups, and as employees, the day-to-day behavior of these boys was completely different from their day-to-day behavior as gang members. The following newspaper story describes the boys, their gang, and their life inside and outside of the gang; it paints a painfully graphic picture of peer corruptibility. Of special interest to us is the degree to which the behavior of seemingly otherwise good kids erodes in the presence of their gang brothers.

The gang described in this article is, without question, morally less than the sum of its parts; an organic contradiction not at all rare in teen collectives. But only one of many such contradictions which add to the adolescent's vulnerability.

He's 14 and a familiar face at Our Lady of Angels Roman Catholic Church. He regularly attended Mass. He belonged to a Catholic youth group. Whenever his family couldn't find him they telephoned the church.

"His mom called for him several times, and so did his grandmother, looking for him here," recalled the church secretary.

But the youth also belonged to another band of angels, a Hispanic street gang called "Angelitos Sur 13," or "Little Angels of 13th Street." He and at least seven other Angelitos, with their trademark baggy pants, blue bandanas and flannel shirts, are accused of abducting an 11-year-old Portland girl as she rollerskated in Victory Square Park in Hermiston's west end July 5.

174

Police say the youths led the girl to a unit at the nearby Golden Manor Apartments and took turns raping her.

Now, a youth is in the Umatilla County juvenile detention centre in Pendleton, charged with three counts of first-degree rape, first-degree kidnapping and burglary. Five other youths, ages 13, 14, 15, and 16, also are in custody, and more arrests are likely, police say.

The "Angelitos Sur 13" claimed the park as their turf, along with the narrow lawns of an adjoining low-income housing project. During the past two years, the Angelitos smashed windows, vandalized cars and menaced their neighbors, residents say.

But the twist is that when the Angelitos weren't hanging out together, some were getting good grades in school, working at part-time jobs and taking part in church groups, say school officials, police and church members.

It is that Jekyll-Hyde flip-flop that perplexes so many in this northeastern Oregon farming and food-proces[s]ing town of 10,330. Shannon Gordon, principal of the junior high school where many of the Angelitos attend classes, knows the accused youths' problems well.

"Each of these kids is a separate person," said Gordon. "To say they are all bad kids, that they don't do well in school, is not correct."

C.E. Huffman, Hermiston Police Department's gang enforcement officer, said you can't paint a black-and-white picture of the youths accused of the rape.

"We have guys who have [been] courted into gangs that are A and B students in school and are still in school. We have gang members, working in almost every minimum-wage job here, that are good people. You look at them, they are just like any other teen-age boy."

Regular kids they may be, but police, school officials and church members say the youths are transformed when in the presence of other gang members, when subject to the peer group dynamics and pressures. And the transformation isn't subtle.

"I'm scared right now," said a 19-year-old woman sitting near the tennis court in Victory Square Park. She nervously fiddles with the hem of her blouse as she waits for her husband to pick her up.

She and her husband lived in Dean Holmes Plaza until about a month ago. She watched gang members break windows, throw rocks at passing cars and, most terrifying of all, hold a gun to the head of a small child, she said. Frightened, they moved to nearby Umatilla.

The woman will speak only on condition of anonymity.
"You don't know when they are gonna do something to you."

Still, she seldom frets about one-on-one encounters with gang members. "When they are a lot of gangsters is when they do the stuff. Look at what they did to that girl. They think they are not bad? I think they are."

The 14-year-old that church secretary Edwards knows behaved like a gentleman at church.

"He's certainly not a child from hell," she said. "You don't shudder when he walks into a room. But I would be fearful if they were all together."

Maria Sanchez belongs to one of the 400 Hispanic families registered as members of the congregation of Our Lady of Angels. She knows many of the town's gang members and said their parents often work in food-processing plants or in the fields all day. When they come home, they often have little energy left to supervise active teen-agers, she said. Many parents don't know or refuse to believe their children are in gangs" It becomes common knowledge that they are gang members but the parents will still deny."

But the common denominator for every gang member in this arid, sparsely settled corner of Oregon is that they paid their dues with their fists. Street gang members must be "courted in," meaning each must fight six to eight established gang members simultaneously in a bareknuckle free for all.

When they want out of the gang, and many do, an even tougher rite of passage awaits, said Huffman.

They must be "beat out," which can mean fist-fighting an entire gang, perhaps 15 people, he said. It's daunting, dangerous and can be side stepped briefly but never avoided altogether.

"They'll hunt you down," said Huffman. "It's easier to get in than it is to get out."

Huffman believes most gang affiliates lose interest in the gang lifestyle after a time and would like to quit. But the prospect of being "beat out" keeps many from getting out.

Even so, the gangs continue to influence younger, more impressionable children, even as they attend Christian youth groups.

Sanchez thinks the magnet is a chance to belong to something, plus the protection that the gang affords and the potential to be respected as tough and dangerous.

"People are scared of them," she said. "They feel powerful that way."

Joining a gang also is a way for an insecure teen to assume a brand new identity. Getting "beaten in" is like being "reborn," after which gang members are renamed, said Huffman...

How do you sum up the phenomenon of dozens of "regular kids" who can turn predatory and dangerous?

Gorhom speaks of wrong choices.

"This was a group of boys who ma[d]e a very wrong choice, one of the worst they could make," she said. "And now there's a young lady who has to deal with the consequences of that choice, and I feel bad for everyone."[1]

[1]The mother of one of the accused boys claimed that the girl requested the group sex after she heard that was how they initiated gang members. (story by Richard Cockle, Correspondent, *The Oregonian*. July, 25, '95.)

Assuming for the moment that this article describes honestly the situation (which, of course, requires more than a small degree of faith) we are struck by several trends in the behavior of these boys which accord almost perfectly with the propositions brought forward in the Introduction chapter. Notably, that young people all too easily become less than what they could be, and that their potential is *easily* eroded and diminished; that their eagerness to contribute to their family and to their society can be suffocated by the impulse to negate and to destroy; that their capacity for clear thought is easily contaminated by peer pressure; that their ability to accurately envision the long-term consequences of their behavior is underdeveloped and easily manipulated; and, finally, that without constructive adult intervention youth are easily transported into a downward spiral in their behavior and their sociability.

Postscript

I am sure that long before the reader has arrived at this point, a crowd of difficulties will have gathered; therefore, it may be worthwhile to repeat the important themes of this chapter.

Some of the most glorious moments in our entire lives are shared in youthful friendships. Everyone knows immediately the select, chosen few with whom such intimacy exists, and everyone remembers instantly those few with whom such treasured closeness existed in time past. As Myrna Kostash so ably phrased it: "The best friend is she who has the right to your time and attention and the privilege of hearing your confession. Never again in life will there be someone quite so unambiguously interested in you" (p. 31).

Adolescent friendships can be a splendid and beautiful experience, but all friendships are not made of such stardust. This chapter has spoken almost exclusively to the less grand and less glorious dimensions of adolescent relationships. And though this approach does not romanticize youth in the manner to which we have become unfairly accustomed, we do well to remind ourselves that when discussing something as fine as friendship there is no honor in denying its less noble elements.

The behavior of all young people is influenced by their tendency to *perceive* the world in ways which flatter their selves, and by their propensity to *experience* the world in ways which nourish self-absorption. However, what we see is not always what we get in friendships because the subterranean motives which heat and meld them are as vital to their duration as the reasons which justify them. Adolescents sometimes recognize the discrepancy between motives and justifications, but sometimes not. Acknowledging such contradictions is one of the many adventures in self-discovery which vitalizes the adolescent experience; acting upon these contradictions, learning to reconcile them within the expanding circle of one's identity, is the heart of the identity project. Since so much of the adolescent's difficulty with forming genuine friendships is also seen in the narcissist's struggle with self-other relationships, perhaps this is a good time to reflect on an observation forwarded by Nancy McWilliams in her excellent work *Psychoanalytic Diagnosis*:

> A therapist who is able to help a narcissistic person to find self-acceptance without either inflating the self or disparaging others has done a truly good deed, and a difficult one (1994, p. 181).

Everyone who works with teens recognizes that this statement applies not only to therapists and their narcissistic clients: it is, word for word, a truism which advises the upbringing of all youth.

"I was attracted to her because all of my friends thought it was so cool that I dated her." 17-year-old's response to the question: "What most attracted you to your first girlfriend?"

In abbreviated form, I have suggested that the following principles mould, shape and define adolescent relationships.

- Many young people are too insecure and too frightened to unreservedly share their self with another person; hence, their relationships tend to be conditional, tentative, "wait and see." Since adolescents are "in process," many of the qualities they bring to their relationships are susceptible to change, realignment, and improvement.

- Many young people desire a flattering mirror far more than an honest mirror; friends are meant to bolster their self-esteem, and if the "friend" fails in this function, so also does the friendship.

- Adolescent relationships are, in part, designed to help young people to "learn the ropes" of their social system. Hence, friendships are simultaneously instrumental and personal, utilitarian and sharing. Friends are bonded by many forces other than the human qualities of the partner. These forces cannot be overlooked in an investigation of the adolescent experience.

- Adolescent friendships may require one to give approval in exchange for approval being returned. Convincing a friend that his or her defects are really virtues in exchange for his (her) doing the same is what I call "reciprocal rationalization." Reciprocal rationalization is not the pillar which supports all teen friendships, but it certainly is a buttress without which many would collapse.

- Adolescents (especially early- and middle-adolescents) are weak at reading the motives of others, a weakness which dims their insight into the unspoken agenda of their friends, and ultimately increases their vulnerability to manipulation and exploitation.

- Hypocrisy is one expression of the natural desire to position oneself advantageously. When transacted by social neophytes (which adolescents are) struggling with refinements in morality, intellect, and self, the end product may be crude and primitive. Adolescence, at least as we know it in North American culture, is really quite unthinkable without hypocrisy; it is, after all, the portrayal of one's defects as less than they are and of one's virtues as greater than they are. Hypocrisy is the art of self-promotion. Teens, embroiled as they are in the battle between appearance and reality, cannot resist the rewards of such a narcissistic enterprise.

Endnotes

[1]   **Developmental friendships**. A special form of adolescent friendship which we are not going to investigate in this chapter is known as developmental friendship – bondings in which one friend has unusual qualities *which assist in the development of the other*. Such friendships promote togetherness and loyalty in a way ordinary friendships cannot. For many young people developmental friendships usher in a higher level of personal integration.

> Fred had certain qualities particularly lacking in Bob and required by him for his own development. Two of these qualities are prominent: Fred's interest in and evaluation of ideas and all that we mean by the "liberal arts" in education and his freedom to oppose and criticize authority. Bob was badly in need of being opened up to intellectual, cultural and human values and freed from the overly technical and materialistic outlook he had on education when he came to college. Bob needed to break out of the constraints of parental obligation and to oppose such authority. Fred was an expert at rebellion (Madison, 1969, p. 117-118).

[1a]   It is interesting to note that Norman Polansky, the noted psychotherapist, encountered similar tendencies among young professionals. He ob-

served: "Just as social work students, most of whom are straightforward people, commonly underestimate the presence of spite as a motivation in clients, they also overlook narcissism" (p. 72).

[2] **Accurate appraisal of peers.** What we have been addressing from a variety of angles condenses to a few basic questions: "Why are teens, under one set of circumstances, inclined to appraise their peers accurately, and, under another set of circumstances, inclined to appraise them inaccurately?" Parallel to this: "Why are teens, under one set of circumstances, inclined to appraise themselves accurately, and under another set of circumstances, inclined to appraise themselves inaccurately?" To assist in tackling these questions, B.B. Brown, M.S. Mory, and D. Kinney (1994) have assembled thoughtful ideas. As with all investigators they began with a question, namely, how can teenagers maintain an image of peers "that is avowedly inaccurate?"
Drawing upon principles of social identity theory, Brown, et al., claim that teens: (a) accentuate differences between their own group and other groups, (b) overstate the positive characteristics of their own group, and (c) overstate the negative characteristics of others groups.

[3] **Defensiveness and protectionism during adolescence.** The inescapable fact of adolescent life is that defensiveness highlights both behavior and emotion; so much so that it is impossible to understand adolescent behavior without understanding the techniques of self-protection upon which it relies.
Defensiveness refers to an excessive sensitivity to criticism, whether real or imagined; equally important, it is *a style of processing information* which enables one to reject, deflect, or deny criticism. Defensiveness does not result in the young person merely absorbing criticism in hurt silence, rather with defiance or negativism. This style of self-protection is employed when personal security is threatened, when boundaries are infringed upon, or when the self simply feels exhausted or frightened. It is really little more than a counter-measure to affirm the self. It may or may not be successful, and it may or may not alienate those who are affected by it.
Defensiveness during adolescence is often expressed as a somewhat reasoned, yet emotional argumentativeness, and a persistent counterattack against all criticism, even when it is offered in a constructive vein. Interestingly, this same defensiveness surfaces when someone with whom the adolescent identifies is criticized, and this, in great measure, accounts for their tendency to defend their friends against all accusations.

[4] **Defense mechanisms tend to follow three general paths.** First, they may weaken or disappear as the anxiety which calls them into existence lessens its grip. In terms of the psychological well-being of the adolescent, this is the most ideal outcome. Second, the defense mechanism may become even more powerful, heaping upon the adolescent increasing distortions. Third, and perhaps most typical during the adolescent years, the initial defense mechanism may be replaced by a less distortional mechanism. This occurs when some progress is made reducing anxiety, but not enough to completely shed the defense mechanism. For example, youth who during early adolescence shelter themselves from rejection by

denying that they desire acceptance, may discover that as their interpersonal skills increase they are better accepted, held in higher esteem, and in turn have less need for the denial which cushioned them in earlier years.

In sum, defense mechanisms distort and deny to lessen the waves of negative emotion we call anxiety. They are employed by all adolescents, and in and of themselves are neither good nor bad. Defense mechanisms are inherently self deceptive since their basic responsibility is to distort; and while it is true that they may be understood by the conscious mind they are not controlled by it. They cannot be reasoned out of existence.

[5]   **Betrayal** hits young people with such crunching force that it shakes their faith in friends and friendships – especially when it comes from a parent, a hero, or a loved one. Betrayal may come from abandonment, as when a friend deserts you or simply forgets you exist; or in the form of rejection, as when excluded (symbolically or physically) by peers, parents, or teachers.

Betrayal opens the floodgates to the separation anxiety dammed since infancy. John Bowlby claimed that separation anxiety is the deepest and the darkest of our deep, dark fears. To be betrayed resurrects the painful childhood fears of losing mother or father, and casts into doubt one's desirability, for, by definition, one is desired less than that for which one is betrayed.

In her study of runaways who end up as street kids Marlene Webber (1990) reports: "Betrayal is the most common experience among them. . . many street youths feel profoundly betrayed by significant adults, usually one or both parents, or surrogate parents assigned by the state . . ." (1990, p. 28). Paradoxically, the pain of betrayal elevates the significance of allegiance and loyalty in the adolescent's value system.

[6]   Some of what is meant by "flattering mirrors" parallels what Jones and Pittman (1982) called *ingratiation* – making oneself likable in another's eyes. On this phenomenon, John Sabini makes some interesting observations:

> One way is simply to agree with what other people think. Another is to praise your target's accomplishments, personality, and so on. But these strategies require subtlety to succeed; pushed too far, they give way to their purpose. And they have one further problem. The target of ingratiating behavior is often easier to fool than observers are. . . . *Because we believe our opinions are correct, we're not terribly suspicious of the motives of people who agree with us* (1995, p. 203).

[7]   As we have already discussed in Chapter Two, the perspective-taking required to effectively anticipate the reactions of others is, for the most part, beyond concrete thinkers. For example, younger children have only a very limited ability to step outside a two-person exchange and imagine how a third person might perceive the interaction; 10 and 11-year-olds are not gifted at recognizing that beliefs are influenced by unacknowledged assumptions.

Chapter Nine

consumerism and corruptibility

Consumerism and the psycho-economics of teen approval

> "... we have an innate propensity to get ourself noticed, and noticed favorably, by our kind."
> William James

In North American culture the approval-obsessed are, with monotonous regularity, fools for consumerism. Since they cannot autonomously define themselves they desperately rely upon the approving judgments of others. Hence, for them, the "right" commodities, the "right" labels, and the "right" people are everything, not only for the anticipated approval they will bring, but because, by definition, right commodities and right labels require wrong commodities and wrong labels. In its most primitive manifestation, the psycho-economics of teen life reduces to a simple equation: the "right" goods bring approval, "wrong" goods bring rejection.[1]

Consumer goods render criteria visible. And while this has some advantages, it is punishing to the fearful and to those so anxiously dependent that they dare not scorn anything which has the potential to bestow, however briefly, approval. This, I believe, is what Christopher Lasch had in mind when he observed: "The state of mind promoted by consumerism is better described as a state of uneasiness and chronic anxiety. The promotion of commodities depends ... *on discouraging the individual from reliance on his own resources and judgments* ... of what he needs in order to be healthy and happy" (my underlines, 1984, p. 28). Decoding the nebulous, but very real, relationship between approval and ownership is a task made even more difficult by beclouded thinking, by inexperience, by changing fads, and ultimately, by the fact that there is no sure way to achieve it. It is an individual problem presented in a mass setting which requires individual solutions from individuals who have not as yet worked out their own individuality.

Ours is a consumer culture and the impact of consumerism on our psychology is everywhere observed, perhaps nowhere more blatantly than in the fictionalized lives of approval-obsessed teens. The personal fable encourages the illusion that goods will not only attract, but mesmerize; the fable that everyone will notice every new purchase is, of course, the shared theme in all advertising. Youngsters who accept these fallacies, and they exist in staggering numbers, find themselves emotionally locked into dependence on consumer goods not so much for the approval these goods elicit from others, but for approval from themselves because they are so hooked that without material goods even self-approval is impossible. This phenomenon exemplifies what, in social psychology, is known as "the looking-glass self"; seeing ourselves through the eyes of others, and incorporating their views into our self-image, our self-concept, even our sense of purpose, our destiny.

Whatever one's judgment may be about purchased goods, there can no doubt that their primary function is to produce illusions and to sustain images:

> Commodity production and consumerism alter perceptions not just of the self but of the world outside the self. They create a world of mirrors, insubstantial images, illusions increasingly indistinguishable from reality. . . . The consumer lives surrounded not so much by things as by fantasies . . . (Lasch, 1984, p. 30).

The need for illusions to sustain self-image is grounded in the elementary fact that most teens are not satisfied with either their appearance or their "image." The Canadian Advisory Council on the Status of Women (Holmes & Silverman, 1992) reports that only 13% of adolescent girls are satisfied with their appearance. Which probably is not surprising for young women living "in a society which stresses the ideals of feminine beauty and thinness, places a higher value on beauty for females than for males, and minimizes the value of women's other qualities" (p. 18). All in all, the tendency is for image to replace substance. Eventually, "the self one shows to the world becomes more vivid and dependable than one's actual person" (McWilliams, 1994, p. 170).

"I constantly cared about how I looked – especially my clothes. Everything I owned had to be name brand – if it wasn't, I wouldn't wear it. It all had to do with what others thought of me. I always wanted to be the best and others to think of me as that – and I often was."
18-year-old university student describing her preoccupation with appearance during her early adolescent years.

In reality, of course, the picture is more complicated than I have presented it. I am here highlighting only one contradiction: that youngsters who try to bolster their self-concept with purchased goods soon discover that their dependency on image does not strengthen their self-concept, but weakens it through the fear that the goods they now own are no longer image-enhancing and must be replaced with newer, more glittering goods. By putting oneself on display one begs for approval, a gesture of subordination which increases dependency on those who dispense approval.

An all-too-frequent outcome of obsession with trendy consumer goods is not an increase in self-esteem, but an increase in envy for those who possess what "I" do not, or contempt for those whose image is more beautiful when decorated with the same possession. Perhaps, in the vortex of these confused cravings we can sift some understanding from Don Marquis' lament: "Ours is a world where people don't know what they want and are willing to go through hell to get it."

Almost everybody allows himself or herself some entirely unjustifiable generalization on the subject of consumerism. I hope that what I have said thus far does not strike the reader as fitting this trend. Before concluding, however, I would like to introduce one or two further ideas about the connections which bind adolescent approval to the consumer society in which we live.

Young people are constrained by their limited capacity for social initiative and by a lack of skills, or perhaps more accurately, by a lack of confidence. As a result, they experience great difficulty introducing themselves to others, complimenting others, offering congratulations to someone who has achieved an impressive goal, or even striking up a casual conversation to pass the time of day; in essence, teens have trouble negotiating what clinicians call "moving toward others." Because the force of their personality is weighted toward the egocentric, they are disposed both emotionally and socially *to receive* overtures more than to offer them. The magnet which helps to pull them out of this impasse is *the visual symbol*; recognizable enticements which melt the barriers separating them from other kids equally constrained by their lack of overture skills. In this sequence, any enticement which encourages one individual to make an overture to another is valued. It seems to me that the real significance of commodities is in their power to elicit reactions and to create overtures. A new sweater, a stylish haircut, a designer label which fails to produce these desired reactions is essentially worthless. (Which is one reason why kids sometimes suddenly trade, or throw away goods which only a month ago were thought to be a life necessity).

"He was friendly, easy-going and he was good looking and had a nice car. Initially, these are the aspects I liked in him but now I really cannot see what I liked in him because the only things I could come up with are superficial." Response from a 19-year-old girl to: "What most attracted you to your first boyfriend?"

Youth flow to the visual because it is voiceless, personless: deficiencies which provide the very freedom teens need to utilize their own speech, to express their own person, to advance their own agenda. The visual rescues them from the weighty encumberment of their own self-consciousness by creating an opportunity to respond and to be the object of response. The visual allows voiceless Echoes to display without speaking, self-absorbed Narcissuses to respond without leaving themselves. The visual object is valued precisely because it is an object; if it fails the test of desirability it can be discarded. The relationship is one of utility and, as such, it holds appeal when one is attempting to solve a practical problem.

The visual, in addition to being the medium of acceptance, is also the medium of rejection: the wrong image can elicit as much condemnation as the right image acceptance. This part of the equation also plays an important role in the dynamics of teen popularity, but, even more crucial to the point I am trying to establish here, it contributes to the teen's almost paranoic fear of rejection.

The impact of work for pay on teen society

During the '70s and '80s an attitude prevailed among educators, youth watchers and most teens themselves that young people would benefit from greater participation in the world of work-for-pay. (By "work for pay" I mean work for which teens receive an hourly wage; it stands in contrast to volunteer work, community service, or any activities for which labor is provided without cash compensation). This attitude was encouraged by parents who resented the anti-establishment attitudes of youth in the '60s, and who were fearful that a similar lack of motivation might strike their own children. Thus, the call to teen-age employment was encouraged by parents, and welcomed by youth tired of their school-only menu. On the practical side, this movement was encouraged by the avalanche of employment opportunities presented by the fast food industry and a wide range of minimal competence "clerk" jobs provided by the growing service industry. The President's Science Advisory Committee (1973) endorsed youth employment as sound in principle because it encouraged adolescents to venture out of age-segregated schools into the world of adult roles, habits, and expectations.

Thus, a massive number of adolescents entered the part-time labor force while remaining full-time students in the school system. One researcher reported that about 60% of Grade 12 students, and about 40% of Grade 10 students are working at any given time during the school year. This contrasts with 1940 where only about 2% of similar aged youngsters were enrolled simultaneously in the school place and the work force (Greenberger & Steinberg, 1986, p. 14). This historically unique phenomenon, though complex in its social genesis, was given impetus by four critically important sets of forces:

- the profound set of economic and occupational changes that swept Postindustrial societies;
- an ideology about the meaning and value of work in American culture;

- the encouragement of youth gratification;

- the increased emphasis on consumerism and materialism in our society, which is stimulated by television and directed to all youth populations (Greenberger, xv).

Interestingly, few social scientists investigated either the motivation for entering the work force, or the practical consequences of doing so. Greenberger and Steinberg (1986) were among the first researchers to investigate these topics, and their findings jolted an inattentive public. In subsequent years, (1986-1995) no real progress has been made in our understanding of *the underlying motives* which impel youth to join the work place.

The beliefs *held by adults* who support youth-employment are consistent and earnest. They include the belief that work-for-pay is good for youngsters and that it helps them "to get their feet wet in the real world"; the belief that work helps kids assume responsibility; the notion that working youth contribute to the financial welfare of their household; that income permits young people to "pay their own way"; that learning about work smooths the transition to the harsher, less personal world of adult work. Thus, youth employment is validated by those who govern the adolescent moratorium – adults.

The research findings did not support hopeful expectations. Most distressing were the findings that employment consistently undermines the quality of young people's education; that employment leads to increased spending, especially on luxury items; that working tends to promote, rather than deter, certain kinds of delinquent behavior; that youth employment often leads to increased alcohol and marijuana use; and, instead of fostering a respect for work and the work place, it tends to generate cynicism and scorn for all "lower-level" work.

Findings such as these have led most researchers to conclude that the benefits of adolescent work-for-pay are overestimated while its costs are underestimated.

The mathematics of student employment simply do not fit the 168 hour week. Working teens spend about 34 hours a week in school, about 30 hours per week at their job (including travel time), about 49 hours per week in sleep, about 8 hours doing homework, and 10 hours eating (minimum). With this average schedule, they have remaining only 37 hours per week for *everything else in their lives.*

"The demand to 'make something of yourself' through work is one that Americans coming of age hear as often from themselves as from others."   Robert Bellah

For most teenagers it takes only one semester for their schedule to create undesired symptoms; but, most youth are so sturdy that it takes a year or more before they develop chronic tiredness. During that one year period a fateful event occurs which attains a significance greater even than the chronic tiredness which follows: the purchase of a car.

The automobile allows young workers to provide their own transportation to work and to school and thus lessens parent exhaustion. At least that is the hook that parents bite, not recognizing that such logic makes the car the cause, not the effect, of work. The *real* reason for the car is elevation in esteem and an increase in popularity. The real outcome is a bank loan. Most youngsters who own cars work to overcome indebtedness even though the word is not in their vocabulary. Work becomes servitude. It is hard to believe that neither adolescents nor their parents see the inherent contradiction in this sequence of events. They eventually feel it, pay for it, sometimes even fall apart from the pressure of it, but they rarely see it.

It was wishfully believed by parents, educators, and youth themselves that work for pay would enhance self-cultivation, that it would provide an economic head start, that it would resemble an "apprenticeship" in the traditional sense of that word. No such luck.

> Today, fast-food chains and other such places of work (record shops, bowling alleys) keep costs down by having teens supervise teens, often with no adult on the premises. *There is no mature adult figure to identify with, to emulate, or to provide a role model or mature moral guidance.* The work culture varies from one store to another. . . . Rarely is there a "master" to learn from; rarely is there much worth learning. Indeed, far from being places where solid work values are being transmitted, these are places where all too often teen values dominate (Etzioni, 1993, p. 111).

One reason youngsters and adults alike were so wrong is that the work place is different than it used to be, and not only different, but *different in a way that conspires against meaningful work.* Youth work is work in which skills are rarely transferable to worthwhile work. Most work environments where teens work are filled with other youth (just like school); their exposure to adults is limited to those adults who, for whatever reasons, are still working in the dead-end, low-paying jobs monopolized by kids.

"That's easy. To get money to buy stuff." Working 16-year-old's response to: "Why do you work every day after school?"

Work is purposeful activity performed in producing goods or services whether for remuneration or not. It may or may not contribute to personal meaning, and it may or may not enhance self-esteem. No matter how we slice it, youth work rarely stacks up as meaningful, and young workers are fully cognizant of this before they enter the work force. They knowingly sell their labor for cash. There is little self-deception about the nature of work, except perhaps among Grade 10 students who are inclined to be misperceive almost everything for which they have no first-hand experience. Adolescents know the difference between what philosophers call meaningful work and what Marx called exploitive work, and they enter willingly into work devoid of meaning because they recognize it for what it is: short-term effort for short-term gain. They do not think of work as meaningful in its own right, or as an activity which engenders meaning; therefore, selling their labor (in the beginning) is not emotionally deflating. The research consistently finds that adolescent workers view their labor as a commodity to be sold on the open market, that it has no intrinsic value unto itself, that its purpose is to increase consumption. These young workers think they know exactly why they are working, but they don't. They know what they want to buy, and this inclines them to think that they know why they are working. The tragedy, of course, is that they do not understand, in any meaningful way, *why* they desire what they desire. Sadly, many of them never get much of a clue. In the absence of solid adult guidance, it is a very difficult puzzle for young people to solve.

Youth recognize and accept that they are engaged in future-less work for immediate wages. In their mind this is a fair exchange. What they usually do not understand is that the goods they purchase with their earned capital tend to be over-priced, over-hyped paraphernalia which they hope (sometimes correctly) will enhance their desirability and their status. Their failure to understand is not due only to developmental immaturity, although this contributes in serious measure. With remarkable consistency their parents are equally non-comprehending, equally impelled by an ideology of acquisition, and similarly incompetent at distinguishing the real from the contrived. These are, after all, the parents who make up what Neil Postman called "the culture of trivia," and what Carl Bernstein called "the idiot culture," a whirl in which social life is a perpetual round of entertainments and public conversation is little more than baby-talk. In sum, according to Postman and others persuaded by his message, our culture has produced in its youth the same illusions which permeate our entire society.

Judging by spending habits, young workers are motivated far more by the desire to consume than to lend financial assistance to their family. Virtually all research confirms that the majority of earnings are spent on status items and youth-industry products.

> Today's teen pay may be low by adult standards, but it is often substantial. Especially among the middle class, it is largely or wholly spent by the teens. That is, the youngsters live free at home and are allowed to keep considerable amounts of money. Where this money goes is not quite clear. Some use it to support themselves, especially among the poor. Some middle-class youngsters set money aside to help pay for college or save it for a major purchase, like a car. But large amounts seem to pay for an early introduction into trite elements of American

consumerism: trendy clothes, trinkets, and whatever else is the fast-moving teen craze (Etzioni, 1993, p. 111).

One researcher concluded that youth money goes toward maintaining automobiles, for rock concerts and variations on the pop music industry, and fashion clothing (Greenberger & Steinberg, p. 30). A separate study determined that half of Grade 12 students do not save for their future education, and only 1 in 10 youngsters save half of their earnings. Among males, automobiles are the biggest expenditures. Over half report that they make no financial contribution to family expenses of any kind.

> Money can be disposed of on luxury items (designer clothing) rather than necessary items (food, rent) because so many young workers come from families situated in the top 25% of the income distribution. Thus, money earned is not spent on family necessities, but on "self" items (Otto, 1988, p. 389).

And, as one commentator put it, perhaps this is "only fair and square: the youngsters are just being good . . . consumers, working and spending their money on what turns them on." Yet, "an educator might bemoan that these young, as-yet-unformed individuals are driven to buy objects of no intrinsic educational, cultural, or social merit" (Etzioni, 1993, p.111).

The picture painted here is too splashy, but the image is essentially correct, especially for middle and upper-middle class youth who hold the majority of work-for-pay jobs. The net effect is that we need to look soberly at how youth employment relates to societal contribution and to personal dignity, and not merely as an avenue to consumerism. If we have learned anything from our investigation of teen employment it is that young people work not to attain necessities, but to purchase what they hope will, in one form or another, bring approval.

Postscript

> "A real understanding of the behavior of any human being is impossible without a clear comprehension of the secret goal which he is pursuing."   Alfred Adler

The ideas which have been the object of our attention in this chapter do not lend themselves to quick and tidy summary. The larger themes are not new to adolescent psychology (the need for approval has been investigated empirically since the '50s), but the sub-themes, how the need for approval deteriorates into an obsessive fear of rejection, and how the need for approval is corrupted by market forces, are neglected in mainstream analysis. In introducing these ideas I have no intention of taking a step backwards in our understanding of young people and the dilemmas which spice their lives; rather, it is my hope that this crab-like progress, in which an idea advances while seeming to go backward, will ultimately enrich our understanding of the adolescent experience.

The ideas given greatest attention include the following.

- Rejection carries an awesome weight in the teen community. Every form of rejection humiliates the insecure and demoralizes the frightened; which is to say some youth all of the time, and all youth some of the time.

- The link between approval and consumerism is fascinating but unclear. Quite obviously, reasons other than a hunger for approval contribute to the young person's willingness to toil in the work force. However, the pervasive belief held by virtually all teens that they *must* work, must spend, and must consume is in serious need of re-analysis by both teens and adults. At this moment it appears that neither youngsters nor their parents are of a clear mind as to *why* the young should work. Until clarity is reached on this matter, the adolescent mind will interpret the question from its own frame and on its own terms.

It helps to stand back for a moment if from the distance gained by such a retreat we attain improved perspective. Approval for the teen (and for the child as well) is far more than mere approval in the generic sense of the word. The assembly-line inspector approves the quality of work which passes before him; he says this is OK, this is faulty, this requires touching up, this is rejected, and so on. The approval which teens pursue is often of this technical, surface variety, notably in matters of clothing, hair styles, and social deportment. A deeper craving, however, also dwells within; a craving for validation of "me," an affirmation of the self-under-construction, an acknowledgement of the me who cries and sings and feels the sadness of my own loneliness, the experiential me, the grandiose me, the majestic me. This vital "me" is the heart of the adolescent's real self and it clamors relentlessly for praise, for affirmation.

When we take this "deeper me" into account we see that the quest for approval is a struggle in which the stakes are higher than meets eyes trained only on the symbols and gadgets youngsters manipulate in the hope of receiving profound approval. It is understandable why kids disintegrate when approval is not forthcoming when they perceive lack of approval as rejection of their deeper self. The teen's plea for approval is the cry of a self striving for validation. *The absence of validation* creates a vacuum which nature always fills, but, sadly for the young person, nature takes no responsibility whatsoever for who, or what, fills it.

Endnotes

[1]   **Perfectionism**. A decidedly fixed certainty for many young people is that they think they must be literally "perfect" if they are ever to amount to anything worthwhile. Because of this obsession they are fearful of making any mistake, of being criticized for even the slightest offense; to compensate, great lengths are taken to appear impregnable and infallible. The youngster searches for flaws to cover up before anyone else detects them. Early and middle adolescents are especially inclined to believe that the slightest error invites the greatest catastrophe. The anxieties inherent to this misapprehension are magnified further by the belief that one's emotional security and that one's prospects for meaningful relationships are completely dependent upon *being accepted by a limited group of specific people*. As a result of this belief, arguments and disagreements among peers assume enormous significance since to be rejected, in any way, may cause irreversible damage. In their eyes, they are lost forever. This is quite a burden to bear. The painful process of learning that such beliefs are preposterous, and do not reflect the way things really are, represents, not only a breakthrough in self-understanding, but, as well, a breakthrough in understanding the nature of social relationships.

When they fall short of meeting a goal they say to themselves: "*I shouldn't have* taken a rest on Saturday." "I *ought to* know better than to visit too long." "I *must never* phone her again." All failure acquires a moral quality, and perfectionists do not recognize mistakes simply as mistakes, rather, they *condemn themselves for making them*.

Ironically, despite their high standards, and often high levels of performance, perfectionists see themselves as wasteful of their time and talents. They falsely believe that other individuals achieve their goals and meet their deadlines with little or no effort, with minimal soul-searching, and with no errors. Their consistent misuse of "never," "always," "every," "none," "nobody," "everybody," "totally," "completely," and "forever" carry such finality that every situation appears more grave than it is.

Chapter Ten

intimacy

"You can't worship love and individuality in the same breath. Love is a mutual relationship."   D. H. Lawrence

Adolescent intimacy is grander than anything which comes before it. The passion, the eroticism, the fascination with one splendid partner have no childhood equivalents. The metamorphoses from companion to confidant, from playful peer to erotic partner, from friend to lover, are among the most profound in the entire life cycle. As one nineteen-year-old expressed it: "With intimacy, life begins to happen to you in a hurry." To the intimacy experience the adolescent brings eros, fidelity, clarity, and befuddlement: indeed, the entire package of virtues and vulnerabilities we call youth.

To understand adolescent intimacy is no easy assignment because very little research has been directed to it:

> Despite the seeming importance of romantic life in early and middle adolescence, scientific research on the topic is surprisingly limited. . . . Some investigators have studied opposite-sex friendships but they did not distinguish between platonic and romantic ones. . . . Certainly, much important work has been done recently on adolescents' sexual behavior, but this work cannot substitute for research on romantic relationships. . . . Particularly absent is a theoretical framework to guide research on adolescent romantic relationships (Furman and Werner, 1994, p. 169).

Intimate relationships exist on many planes. In terms of *intensity*, some intimate relationships are very intense while others are calm and tranquil. In terms of *commitment*, some relationships are sealed by a strong commitment to longevity while others are brief. In terms of *emotion*, feelings run the gamut from ecstatic joy to agonizing despair. In terms of *sexuality*: "Sex and psychological intimacy are independent factors. Some intimate relationships are sexual, some are not. Some sexual relationships are psychologically intimate; others are not." In terms of *gender*, men and women (boys and girls) often take different approaches to intimacy. And, as well, intimate relationships exist between same-sex partners and between partners of the opposite sex (Brehm, 1992).

At the heart of every intimacy relationship is a deep concern for the partner. In *The Interpersonal Theory of Psychiatry*, Harry Stack Sullivan claimed that intimacy requires: "a clearly formulated adjustment of one's behavior *to the expressed needs of the other person* in the pursuit of increasingly identical – *that is more and more nearly mutual – satisfactions"* (1953, p. 246). I have underlined two phrases in this well known quote to draw attention to concern for the *genuine* needs of the partner, and the pursuit of *mutual* satisfactions. Intimacy requires care, responsibility, respect, and responsiveness to the partner's growth and happiness.

As religious feelings are not the same as religion, intimate *feelings* are not the same as intimacy. Intimacy, at least as it is dealt with in this chapter, implies much more than deep feelings, more than sexual involvement, more than romantic exhilaration, all of which teens tend to confuse with intimacy. Dignified intimacy is a deep and profound mutual relationship based on a genuine concern for the needs of the partner. Sadly, mutuality and concern for the *real needs* of the partner are the Achilles heel of adolescent relationships.[1]

Intimacy and identity

"In order to establish intimate relations with others, one must first know who and what one is."   Jerome Dusek

Since the prolific and persuasive writings of Erik Erikson took hold in North America it has been widely accepted that a fairly solid sense of identity is a requirement for intimacy; after all, it is one's identity which is shared in intimacy. Summarizing Erikson's stance on this issue, Adams and Archer write:

> intimacy involves a capacity to make commitments, even in the face of tempting and desirable alternatives. Without an active form of identity, the individual is thus thought not to possess the necessary components of a healthy personality and is unable to make commitments to others or to abide ethically by commitments made. *Put another way, fulfillment of intimacy requires a sense of shared identities* (1994, p. 194).

Erikson, as one might expect, also said it clearly himself: "It is only when identity formation is well on its way that true intimacy . . . is possible" (1968, p. 135).

In sum, intimacy requires a maturity of identity.

> In order to establish intimate relations with others, one must first know who and what one is. . . . If one is to reveal the inner self to others, one must know what the inner self is and have self-acceptance; for if one cannot accept the self, how can one ask others to accept it? Those who have not resolved the identity crisis . . . have trouble developing intimate relationships for they continually fear that they will reveal they have no firm sense of self (Dusek, 1991, p. 152).

Our understanding is enhanced by what Erikson's calls the "peculiar strain" of the intimacy quest.

As the young individual seeks at least tentative forms of playful intimacy . . . he is apt to experience a peculiar strain, as if such tentative engagement might turn into an interpersonal fusion amounting to a loss of identity and requiring, therefore, a tense inner reservation, a caution in commitment. Where a youth does not resolve such a commitment, he may isolate himself and enter, at best, only stereotyped and formalized interpersonal relations; *or, he may, in repeated hectic attempts and dismal failures, seek intimacy with the most improbable of partners* (Erikson, 1968, p. 167).

Teens do bond, connect, embrace, and love. This is not a matter of dispute. Their relationships are intense, sincere, and erotic; neither is this a matter of dispute. However, they have difficulty with sustained mutuality and durable reciprocity. The point to be grasped is elementary but nevertheless vital: because their identities are in process, because their self-knowledge is in flux, because their need for mirroring is intense, adolescents have difficulty sustaining relationships in which the rightful and necessary needs of the growing self can accommodate to the rightful and necessary needs of the partner. Adolescents who successfully resolve these issues are capable of genuine intimacy, and, of course, many do resolve them. Equally true, many do not. I believe that during the early and middle phases of adolescence it is extremely rare to find reciprocal intimacy of much substance.

"In grade 9 (14 years old) I went out with two people. I liked the first guy's looks and athletic status. The fact that he found me attractive was really nice too. I liked the happy-go-lucky personality and the smile of the second guy. At 15 (grade 10), I liked Trevor's eyes and view of the world the most."
19-year-old describing "first attractions."

Ironically, many young people find themselves desperately craving love and affection, yet unable to satisfy either because they are incapable of giving themselves in a way which will encourage a loving response from others.

Primitive identity, primitive intimacy

"He liked me; he paid attention to me; he was cool; he was a show off; he was cute." 15-year-old girl's response to the question: "What most attracted you to the first guy you had sexual intercourse with?"

As part of my ongoing research with adolescents I interview early-adolescent girls (12-15 years-old) who are pregnant, or who have recently given birth.[2], [3] Many of these girls (young women) tell relationship stories which hold special relevance to the intimacy experience. In this line of research it is not unusual to meet a young mother who refuses to talk to the man (boy) who fathered her child because she feels betrayed. The stories these girls have shared with me hold a surprising consistency. The boy is often two or three years older (during early- or middle-adolescence this amounts to a tremendous psycho-emotional advantage). At the beginning of the relationship the boy praises, pursues, and woos the girl with earnest aggressiveness. The girls perceive these actions as motivated by "love" (sometimes they believe that the actions, unto themselves, are love). The girl accepts the boy's persistence as a singular interest in her, even when she has been forewarned by her girl friends, her mother, and sometimes, even the boy's friends. Their involvement becomes sexual, she becomes pregnant, he becomes gone. She feels betrayed; she trusted him and he turned out to be fraudulent. Her betrayal transforms into shame, then anger, then on-going resentment.

The self-ish-ness, quite obviously, does not exist solely within the boy. The girl does not (or cannot, depending on your assessment of adolescent aptitude) distance herself from the praise, the pursuit, the eroticism. These girls all too often discredit their own reality checks. At a certain level they know that love is not what is happening; but knowing does not prevent hoping. The young mother, while deploring her mate's desertion, also sings his praises, foremost of which was his willingness to praise her. This point must not be lost: in the primal acts of praise and flattery adolescent relationships are forged; with the loss of praise and the cessation of flattery they deteriorate.

A fifteen-year-old mother in rural Washington described her boy-friend this way: "He was a liar most of the time, but he made me feel good. He was always nice to me so I can't be too mad at him." Her best girl friend, age sixteen, also has a baby. Of her boy friend she said: "I'm glad I didn't have to marry him but I wouldn't want to have never met him. He was a nice guy, just not dependable. I kinda thought this [becoming a mother] might happen, but I never thought much about it." A seventeen-year-old from Portland, Oregon offered this: "I liked it when he was nice to me. I don't know if I ever *loved* him, even though I told everyone I did. I just liked his always wanting to do things for me, and his always saying nice things to me."

"I suppose I was attracted to him because I thought he was funny, cute, and popular." 19-year-old's response to the question: "What most attracted you to your first boyfriend?"

When speaking with adolescents about intimacy (interestingly, they rarely use this word in ordinary conversation), one cannot help but be struck by their entrenchment in egocentric speech. This entrenchment is partly due to their lack of skills in explicit communication, but it is also more than that. One gets the sense that, at their stage of identity formation, they have sculpted a tentative patch of turf which they call their own, and have then sent out "feeler invitations" to a prospective partner to come in and share it. With youthful charm, the invitation is rarely explicit and, with youthful protectionism, the acceptance is always guarded and low-key.

> *"The relationship was very superficial; he seemed to like to be dating me just to have a girlfriend not because he particularly liked me. He treated me fine around friends but completely ignored me otherwise."* First year university student's response to the question: "What most attracted you to your first boyfriend?"

Mature intimacy requires a vocabulary which allows the partners to express the richness and the beauty of the experience they share. Teens lack the means to put into words their affection, their respect. In a phrase, they have no language of love:

> Eros requires speech, and beautiful speech, to communicate to its partner what it feels and wants.... It is almost impossible to get students to talk about the meaning of their erotic choices, except for a few artificial cliches that square them with contemporary right thinking. . . . What one cannot talk about, what one does not have words for, hardly exists. Richness of vocabulary is part of richness of experience . . . to make love humanly, the partners have to talk to each other (Bloom 1993, p. 25).

What Bloom describes in the abstract teens themselves report in the concrete:

> When I love someone and want to know him better, I am afraid to tell him of my feelings for fear that his reaction will disappoint me. He may not love me back.... So, I may stifle my feelings of love because I don't want to handle the disappointment of being refused the real love that I would eventually ask (DeVaron, 1972, p. 342).

Keep in mind that many youngsters know so little of real love, have seen so little of it in their household, and have received so little of it in their personal lives that they have great difficulty differentiating the desperate clutching of hunger-bonding from the earnest embrace of genuine love. To compensate, they create their own fables about real love and convince themselves that this is the love they are experiencing.

In sum: primitive identity, primitive intimacy.

> *"He was charming; a sweet talker. I was attracted to him because he thought I was hot. He treated me nice."* 18-year-old to the question: "What attracted you to the first boy you had intercourse with?"

The dynamics of allegiance

> "Teenagers search for relationships . . . where the primary experience sought is not so much the personal bond as it is the sharpness of affect . . ."
> David Wexler

Perhaps the greatest mystery to shroud teen relationships is how young people come to be loyal to one another, to give their allegiance and dedication to one chosen partner. In the next few pages I want to investigate two concepts which speak to the issues of loyalty and allegiance, both of which, at least in my estimation, represent important pieces in the intimacy puzzle; each of them speak to what one scholar called "the choreography of we-ness."

Fidelity

Erik Erikson believed that during the adolescent years loyalties are shaped by a *predisposition* to faithfulness and commitment, and by the *desire* to give oneself and one's allegiance. "When you reach a certain age you can and must learn to be faithful to some ideological view . . . without the development for a capacity for fidelity the individual will have what we call a weak ego, or look for a deviant group to be faithful to" (Evans, 1967, p. 30).

Fidelity, as I am here presenting it, is not the same as the concept is expressed by James Marcia, who described it as a commitment to a vocation, or a set of important values, or to a sexual identity. The broader use which I apply does not refer to the actual decisions which have or have not been made, or even to the commitments which have or have not been finalized; rather *fidelity exists as an impulse to join, to affix, to commit oneself to someone or something*. Fidelity expresses itself through the *desire* to bond, a free-floating urge to attach oneself to someone or something. The "urge" to affix cannot be randomly grati-fied; since one's validity is measured by the greatness of those with whom one associates, attachments must be to someone grand and glorious.

Erich Fromm spoke of the readiness and the willingness to share oneself through love; he called it "the basic sympathy to love." He believed this "sympathy" is a predisposition to search out a person to bond with and to love. "Love . . . is rooted in a basic attitude which is constantly present; a readiness to love, a *basic sympathy* as one might call it. *It is started, but not caused, by a particular object.*" (1939, p. 520). And it is precisely this final point which here concerns us.

Robin Simon and her colleagues (1992) report the juvenile expres-sion of this phenomenon with welcome candor.

> For some girls, the onset of their first romantic attraction was the beginning of a continuous state of being in love, often with frequent changes in the object of their feelings. *In fact, simply having romantic feelings may have been more important than the actual boy to whom these feelings were directed* (p. 42).

198

This final comment, assuming its basic correctness, speaks volumes to the dynamics of teen attraction. Further to it, the authors report the following anecdote about one of the young girls in their study:

> a researcher noticed that a girl had "I love" written on her hand and asked her about it. Although this girl's romantic feelings had no particular target, she explained that she was ready to add the name of a boy as soon as a suitable target was found (1992, p. 42).

Further to this theme: "when girls realized that a boy they had been going with now liked someone else, they often redirected their romantic feelings toward someone new" (p. 42). What is being described here, it seems to me, is the predisposition to attach through romance. It is not a predisposition to love, at least not as love is generally understood, but perhaps the early adolescent version of it.

Fidelity is an inward craving seeking outward expression. The person to whom it is directed is not its cause, only its recipient.

> The important point, however, is that love for a particular *object* is only the actualization and concentration of lingering love with regard to one person; it is not, as the idea of *romantic love* would have it, that there is only *the* one person in the world whom one could love, that it is the great chance of one's life to find that person, and that love for him or her results in a withdrawal from all others (Fromm, 1939, p. 520).

This idea is so rich in its implications that I cannot, as yet, leave it. Since fidelity lives *as a constant readiness* it cannot be understood as being *caused* by a particular person, no matter how splendid the person may be, (and no matter how much the teen wants the loved person to be its cause). In this regard, it parallels any number of other organic predispositions:

> the erotic person, has a basically erotic *attitude* toward the world. This does not mean that he is constantly excited sexually. It means that there is an erotic *atmosphere* which is actualized by a certain object, *but which is there underneath before the stimulus appears*. What is meant here is not the physiologically given ability to be sexually excited, but an *atmosphere of erotic readiness* . . . (Fromm, 1939, p. 520).

From all this it seems to follow that the atmosphere of erotic readiness, the basic sympathy to love, and the predisposition to bond, are the dynamic forces behind adolescent intimacy.

"I am in a relationship right now where we are committed to each other. We have been together since the summer after grade nine, so that is nearly three and a half years. All through high school, and now university, with all the selection of people to choose from, we have remained faithful to each other. We both love and respect each other in a way that I feel is quite mature. I love our relationship and wouldn't just throw it away to experience something new. Our parents try to tell us we should "play the field", but I can't just rip my heart away to try going out with other people – it doesn't work that way. I figure if I have something

Overestimating the greatness of the object of one's allegiance
increases vulnerability to charlatans, impersonators, and self-serving
narcissists: "the adolescent is vulnerable to fake ideas, he can put an
enormous amount of energy and loyalty at the disposal of any convincing system" (Evans, 1967, p. 34). On the positive side, fidelity increases
the young person's capacity to sustain love relationships; it lessens
egocentrism by focusing energy outside oneself; it opens the door to the
companionship and promise of others.

As with many of Erikson's fertile ideas, the concept of fidelity
leaves important questions unanswered. For example: How does fidelity come into existence? Does it have to be nurtured? Does it shine
naturally? Does it express itself in easily recognized ways? Do gender
differences shape fidelity? Do some youth fear fidelity (and intimacy)?[4] What happens when it merges with another force such as
eroticism, nationalism, or religion? Does the concept of fidelity allow us
to better explain behavior which is ineffectively explained in current
theory?

Particularization

William James was very much concerned with our tendency not
to see what we do not want to see. In his classic essay, "On a certain
blindness in human beings," he claimed: "Our judgments concerning
the worth of things . . . depend on the *feelings* the things arouse in us."
James' message is simple yet profound: as positive feelings ascend so
also do our judgments about the particular people associated with those
feelings. This truism is the basis for the concept of particularization.

Particularization equates the means of satisfaction with the need
itself. Or, to put it in a slightly different light, particularization is the
belief that the person with whom an experience is shared is the cause of
that experience, *without this particular person, the experience could never
be.* Rather than attribute the experience to their own inner feelings, their
warmth, or their sexuality, the experience is attributed to the partner.
In this way the partner attains a splendor (and a power) beyond what
is known in ordinary friendships.

Young people are remarkably attracted to the idea that the best within their nature cannot surface on its own; that it must be nurtured into existence by a special, wonderful person. In North American culture youth are especially keen on the idea that only one person can elicit deep love, and this one person is wonderful beyond anything we deserve. Of course, to lose this person would be a disaster which must never, ever occur. The young, as often is true for the elderly, are inclined to believe that only one person can create love in their world and when that person is gone so also is love.

When a youngster profoundly experiences himself or herself with only one particular person that person attains life-and-death urgency. Thus, if the lover or friend is lost, if the relationship is broken, an overpowering loss is felt, for in losing the person one has forever lost the experience. Or so it appears. When such an experience is exaggerated by the fable that "my love" is more profound than all other love, the stage is set for the adolescent's willingness to make any sacrifice for the beloved partner. And from this scenario heroic acts of loyalty and selfless giving are inspired.

"When I entered my first relationship at 15 the relationship did take on a life-death urgency. I thought that the only reason I was happy was because of my boyfriend, Daren. But this may also be due to the difficult year I had at 14. At that age I never before experienced so much loneliness. I was completely miserable, I had no friends, I was at a new school, my family was broken up. Things were shaping up, when I met Daren things were never better. All I wanted was a true friend and when he gave me that, I attributed all my happiness to him. I can even recall calling him my angel. Still, because I thought he caused my happiness I didn't think of him to be perfection. I saw his faults and I knew the qualities that I disliked. Even with this I thought he was the one who made me happy. With time we began to be more and more absorbed in each other. Then I thought it was him who brought out my sexual desire. With experience and time I've come to learn that I could be just as passionate if I were with someone else I loved. It's inside me – he didn't create it, but I know he helped to bring it out."

19-year-old describing "first love."

On close inspection we observe an interesting reflex. Whenever you, or I, or an adolescent, elevate the nobility of another with whom we are intimately connected we simultaneously elevate ourselves. This unintentional, yet real, elevation plays no small role when the self is engaged in an on-going struggle to dignify itself. Perhaps nowhere is this more clearly evidenced than in the way younger adolescent girls perceive their sexual partners. Not unfailingly, but with remarkable consistency, they view their boyfriends as more committed to them than they are, and more in love with them than they are. In most regards these girls hold accurate perceptions, but when it comes to "love" and "relationships," their perceptions are remarkably amiss. Susan Moore and Doreen Rosenthal provide us with some interesting background:

> we found that young women were more likely to define their sexual encounters as occurring with a regular or steady partner than with a casual partner, while young men were more likely to regard *what must be essentially the same encounters* as casual . . . in fact the male interpretation of what is going on may be closer to reality. The girls are interpreting, as an indication of love and commitment, encounters which will often turn out to be short-term (1994, p. 98).

Perhaps this is why Lauren Ayers claimed "teenagers are not able, as a rule, to be mature and responsible about sexual relating" (1993, p. 164).

To be the object of particularization is tailor-made for narcissistic youngsters. What better way to have one's grandiosity nourished than by the spellbound allegiance of another (usually younger) teen. Indeed, one of the traits of narcissistic youth is to encourage peers to perceive them as special beyond special, beautiful beyond beautiful; such adulation reinforces their own sense of greatness, and diminishes their own insecurities.

"All my life I've desired to have a "Bosom" friend One who I could confide in 100%, spend all my time with etc. When this finally happened to me I attributed all my success to her because I felt that she had a tremendous influence in everything I did. I gave her credit for my popularity because "she" helped me be out-going! Then her father got transferred and she moved away. I immediately made up my mind that I would now have no social life and no friends. I totally doubted my abilities to meet new people because I thought that my best friend was the one who gave me this ability."

17-year-old student describing the importance of best friends.

Postscript

In adolescent life intimacy is the pinnacle of shared affirmation. Since it speaks to the core of the growing personality it is awarded the highest possible significance. For these completely human reasons intimacy is romanticized, fabled and feared. And frequently, neither the adolescent, the adolescent's partner, nor the adolescent's parents can distinguish the romance from the fable.

"I was attracted to the first guy because of his status in the school – popular athlete, and his looks and height. The second I wasn't really attracted to at first – I just didn't want to hurt him by saying no. He was attractive however and fun to be with. I don't know what attracted me to Trevor. We just hit it off. We enjoyed each other's company, looks, personalities, and we just meshed really well."

18-year-old describing "first attractions."

In this foray into youthful intimacy I have invited the reader to follow several lines of speculation, which, for convenience, are here briefly summarized.

- Intimacy is a condition of human fusion *optimally* characterized by mutuality, by open and honest communication, and by emotional commitment. In the words of H. S. Sullivan, "a clearly formulated adjustment of one's behavior to the expressed needs of the other person."

- It is unfair to suggest that "genuine" intimacy is *never* experienced during adolescence; but it seems clear that during early- and middle-adolescence it is rare.[5] As Sondheimer put it: "the mid-adolescent . . . generally remains too self-involved to undertake the mature responsibility of deeply caring for another peer" (1982, p. 224). Along similar lines, Gallatin reported:

  > Both in middle and late adolescence, girls defined their friendships in terms of virtues like loyalty, the ability to keep confidences, emotional support, and common interests. The researchers concluded that older subjects were much more capable of establishing a relationship with another person, of truly sharing experiences and being responsive to their friends (1975, p. 127).

- The most influential of all the thinkers specializing in the adolescent experience, Erik Erikson, claimed that adolescents must resolve the psychosocial crisis of identity *before* they become intimate. Other theorists, perhaps the most notable being Carol Gilligan (1982), claim that Erikson's understanding of the identity process fits the experiences of males more than females; the "adolescent" experience, is really, in Gilligan's rebuttal to Erikson, the "male-adolescent" experience. Her reasoning goes like this: the experience of being raised female in our culture prepares girls to define themselves through their relationships with others; hence, for girls *intimacy contributes to their identity*. Erikson, more attuned to masculine roles in culture, failed to recognize the importance of this sequence; his claim that solid identity is a necessary precursor to real intimacy does not sufficiently honor the demands (nor the outcomes) of female socialization.

Attaining competence, one of the key demands in the adolescent identity project, requires different skills for boys and girls. Accordingly, R. L. Josselson (1987) argues along lines similar to those sketched by Gilligan when she describes the "interpersonal track" which shapes the socialization process of young women in our culture. The implications for intimacy are immediate. For boys "individualizing oneself" is part and parcel of identity since separation from mother is essential for the development of masculinity. For girls, however, feminine identity does not depend on the achievement of separation from the mother. Jeffrey

Berman summarized it this way: "Since masculinity is defined through separation while femininity is defined through attachment, male gender identity is threatened by intimacy while female gender identity is threatened by separation. Thus males tend to have difficulty with relationships, while females tend to have problems with individuation" (Berman, p. 260).

Exciting as these theoretical formulations may be, research findings neither conclusively confirm nor irresistibly refute either, keeping the controversy alive and vital. Research throughout the '80s and the '90s has thus far yielded mixed returns; the very extensive and finely detailed research efforts of Dyk and Adams, for example, "found no simple gender difference in the relationship between identity and intimacy" (Cobb, 1992, p. 435).

In this chapter I have placed only slight emphasis on gender differences because I am concerned most with the shared commonalities of intimacy. Gilligan, Josselyn, and others have ably advanced their position concerning male-female differences, and in the process they have given us even greater insight into Narcissus-Echo relationships.

- Fidelity and particularization represent a significant part of the adolescent intimacy experience; any attempt to understand adolescent intimacy which does not take them into account, it seems to me, is incomplete.

"Every powerful emotion has its own myth-making tendency."
Bertrand Russell

Endnotes

[1] It is interesting to report that in *Personal Relationships During Adolescence* (1994), a scholarly work representing Volume Six in Advances in Adolescent Development series, I could not find a single reference to how *normal developmental characteristics* impede adolescent intimacy. This failure, I believe, accords with the unwritten mandate of the nineties forbidding any phenomenon to be explained by a limitation or even an immaturity within the person in whom it is experienced.

[2] **Pregnancy during adolescence**. Even though we know the incidence of sexual behavior at virtually every developmental level, we have no clear understanding *why* teens are so inept at avoiding pregnancy. Nor do we understand why teens invent, then cling to, irrational beliefs about pregnancy – especially the "It can never happen to me" fable.
Mothers under age 15 experience a rate of maternal deaths two and one half times that of mothers aged 20-24. Teen mothers also have a higher rate of nonfatal complications than non-teen mothers; the younger the mother the higher the risk for such complications of pregnancy as toxemia, anemia, prolonged labor, and premature labor; teen mothers are

92% more likely to have anemia, 23% more likely to experience premature birth than mothers in their 20s.

Teenage pregnancies more frequently end in miscarriage and stillbirths than pregnancies of women in their 20s. Babies born to teenagers are more likely to be premature, to have low birth weights, to have low Apgar scores, and to die within the first month and within the first year. Low birth weight contributes to cerebral palsy, mental retardation, epilepsy, and is a major cause of infant mortality. The Carnegie Council on Adolescent Development (1989) reports that medical costs for low-birthweight infants average $400 000. (By the time you read this these figures they will be much higher).

[3] **The adult years following teen pregnancy**. The impact of teen motherhood was effectively summarized by Arthur Campbell:

> The girl who has an illegitimate child at the age of 16 suddenly has 90 percent of her life script written for her. She will probably drop out of school; even if someone else in her family helps to take care of the baby, she will probably not be able to find a steady job that pays enough to provide for herself and her child; she may feel impelled to marry someone she might not otherwise have chosen. Her life choices are few, and most of them are bad. (From Ginzberg et al., 1988)

By age 29 about 50% of women who had their first child as a teen had obtained a high school diploma, while over 95% of those who did not have their first child until after age 20 had obtained a high school diploma. Mothers without a high school diploma are twice as likely to live in households receiving Aid to Families with Dependent Children. Women whose first child was born in their adolescence produce more children in their lifetime than women whose first child was born after adolescence.

> Teenage mothers pose a substantial cost to the state. "A major source of new applications/acceptance on welfare rolls is the young teenage mother who, in the absence of a wage-earning male, frequently has no other source of income to cover living expenses for her child and herself." A significant factor for teen mothers is longevity: "Although many adults who go onto the rolls leave within a relatively brief time (less than two years), many teenage mothers remain for a decade if not longer" (Ginzberg et al., p. 30).

[4] **The fear of intimacy**. All forces within the personality do not push toward intimacy; much within it is resisted, even feared. Certain life experiences inspire what Erikson called *distantiation*: "the readiness to repudiate, isolate, and, if necessary, destroy those forces and people whose essence seems dangerous to one's own." For many youngsters distantiation increases after attempts at intimacy fail, or when the self is too long unacknowledged, too long undesired, too long unloved (Erikson, 1968, p. 136).

Intimacy triggers pre-existing weaknesses within one, or both, of the partners, which may have gone unnoticed during previous conditions of isolation or pseudo-intimacy. These pre-existing weaknesses strain the relationship. Therefore, the new intimacy partner not only encounters the strain of adjusting to another person, but must come to grips with deficiencies within his (her) own personality silently filed away, or defensively avoided. Intimacy brings joyous connections but it also may expose some of the least desired aspects of the youngster's personality.

[5]   Douvan and Adelson's research suggested that *pre*adolescent and *early* adolescent girls are not overly interested in the personal qualities of their friends, but more concerned with sharing activities with them. When asked to describe "what a friend ought to be like," *early* adolescent girls mentioned considerably fewer personal qualities than older girls.

> Both in middle and late adolescence, girls defined their friendships in terms of virtues like loyalty, the ability to keep confidences, emotional support and common interests. The researchers concluded that *these older subjects were much more capable of establishing a relationship with another person, of truly sharing experiences and being responsive to their friends* (Gallatin, 1975, p. 127).

Chapter Eleven

hunger bonding

"We consider it incompatible with our idea of love when we find a person using another . . . because he fulfills certain needs."

Karen Horney

That youth, like adults, bond to one another to better satisfy their own needs is certainly not a new idea, as the quote from Karen Horney at the top of this page suggests. It is, however, one whose implications are largely overlooked by scholars and researchers of the adolescent experience. In this chapter I would like to look a bit closer at some of the underlying reasons *why* teens connect and bond, but with a special focus on the "hungers" which drive them to attach for reasons other than genuine friendship.

The ideas of Heinz Kohut are of interest to many scholars for many reasons, but to those of us who investigate teen relationships, his insights are of special significance.[1] Kohut believed that before a person can *give* love he (she) must have two primal needs satisfied: the "need to be mirrored" and the "need to idealize."[2] To be mirrored means to have one's efforts and creations praised and admired; to idealize is to admire (and to identify with) competent and powerful adults. When these two basic needs are satisfied they set the stage for open sharing and mutual loving, when they are frustrated they set the stage for obsessive, clinging attachments, and irrational hungers.[3]

For many of today's children these needs are not satisfied; the child is insufficiently mirrored by the mother, and the father removes himself emotionally or physically. The failure to be mirrored (acknowledged, praised, admired) and the failure to idealize (to form identifications with powerful or competent adults) stunt the ability to experience compassion and to give one's love; in their place is a web of obsessions which express themselves through irrational cravings to bond.

> When the developing child experiences lack of empathy and non-responsiveness from parents or caregivers, a narcissistic injury takes place. If these breakdowns and injuries are frequent, personality disturbances result. *The individual feels compelled to resort to more desperate measures to maintain a sense of self*, because he or she has not been able to successfully borrow from the resources of available relationships (Wexler, 1991, p. 14).

From narcissistic injury the child experiences a profound disillusionment and takes blame for not being loved; from this blame flows shame and from shame the relentless need to prove oneself worthy of affection.

In what are generally recognized as his two most significant works, *The Analysis of the Self* (1971) and *The Restoration of the Self* (1977), Kohut proposed that the origin of psychopathology is found in the child's failure to integrate the "grandiose self" and the "idealized parental image." As children confront their real shortcomings, so he reasons, their illusion of omnipotence is shattered; when they recognize the idealized powers they have attributed to their parents, they must find a way to overcome their disappointment so as not to fragment.

When the grandiose self is blunted the child fails to develop a sense of being valued; as a consequence, *a pattern of seeking narcissistic recognition is established*. When children are unable to idealize their parents (because of their indifference or rejection) they feel depressed, empty. "Through adulthood they will seek idealized parental surrogates. . . . Since they desperately seek an ideal that is greater than themselves, they are often led to behave in a weak and self-effacing manner, a style that will enable others to overshadow them" (Millon, 1981, p. 164). These individuals, first as adolescents, then as adults, are characterized by low self-esteem and feelings of emptiness.

Mirror-hunger

In Kohut's way of thinking each person has "a basic degree of greatness about oneself, of self-acceptance, a basic minimum or optimum of showing off, of exhibiting oneself, which belongs to mental health" (Elson, 1987, p. 71). This need for a mirror image, an alter-ego, or to use Kohut's phrase, "a twin-like creature," is our way of asking that other people concentrate on us, give us attention, and show us their approval; to applaud us, to call for an encore. In the course of growing up we all learn how to make demands for greater attention, how to direct the spotlight onto ourselves because when we are the centre of loving attention we feel desired, wanted, real. All of these worthy sensations feed the narcissism inherent to our nature.

Parental mirroring is necessary for the child to invest himself (herself) in others.

> If, however, parental mirroring responses are deficient (e.g., due to parental self-preoccupation) or the child's need for parental approval is traumatically frustrated (e.g., by parental rejection), the transformation of the grandiose self fails to occur. The grandiose and exhibitionistic aspects of the self remain in their primitive forms without evolving into effective and mature forms of expression (Stevens, 1984, p. 384).

For mirror-hungry youth the world is a stage where daily performances are acted out before both real and imagined spectators. Unfortunately, the applause they provide does not carry over from day to day or even from event to event; like oxygen, it must be replenished constantly, but the act of replenishment is automatic rather than exhilarating. Which is to say, unfulfilling. Hence, the need for praise which drives these youngsters, no matter how much of it they receive, never completely satisfies.

Parading

The need for recognition and praise, especially during early-adolescence, is often confused with *reactions* from those people whose praise and recognition are sought. Little matter that the reactions are distant, impersonal, or half-hearted. The motives behind parading are basic: to be noticed and to elicit reaction. It is as though the youngster is saying "I may not know for sure who I am, but at least I can make you notice me." Ironically, paraders, despite their constant practice, are usually inept at reading the audience reactions they create. Often they cannot even decode whether the reaction is positive, negative, or neutral. To compensate they present a pose of blank imperviousness to the very responses they so diligently cultivate. When the parader does finally respond to the audience it may amount to little more than strained banter or forced laughter, or some aimless flirtation the purpose of which is simply to manufacture more reaction.

The chirping, giggling, solitary cadence to their speech betrays the fact that they have no interest in communicating anything of substance to the people their parading has attracted; the audience is always secondary to the primary "me."[4]

We expect that adolescents will, in the course of their normal development, learn to distinguish reactions elicited by exhibitionism from reactions triggered by genuine concern. Fortunately, many do. Unfortunately, some youngsters so crave recognition that they do not differentiate one reaction from another, one audience from another. This failure, in no small measure, contributes to their corruptibility.[5]

Ideal-hunger

"Ideal-hungry" youth feel worthwhile only when they can look up to someone greater than themselves; when they affiliate with the power, the beauty, the intelligence of others.[6] Ideal-hungry youth crave someone to admire while mirror-hungry youth crave someone who will admire them. Interestingly, at least as far as the bonding patterns of adolescence are concerned, their opposing needs draw them to each other; each seeks their own balance in the unsatisfied needs of the other.

The craving to attach is as open-ended as ideals themselves; therefore, it may produce a fascination with Einstein, a commitment to Jesus, an emulation of Mother Theresa, an obsession with Hitler, a fixation on Charles Manson, or a glorification of rock musicians, sitcom heroes, etc. For ideal-hungry youth, *the act of attaching* is as important as the object of attachment. It is only with greater experience over a period of time that the young person comes to any kind of objective evaluation of the relationship.

In ideal-hunger the admired person is not the real issue; the real issue is attaining greater esteem and power *through affiliation with* the admired person. Objects of admiration are, for the most part, interchangeable as long as they speak to the needs which ignite the admiration in the first place. Unlike admiration grounded in the qualities of the admired, "ideal-hunger" harbors an element of hostility toward the admired because implicit to the attraction is denial of the admired as an independent person. For this reason youngsters whose admiration is grounded in ideal-hunger may turn against the admired persons when they fail as suppliers. (This, frequently, is the fate of teen "crushes" on teachers: hostile resentment against those who fail to reciprocate). Hence, the pattern of elevating teachers, coaches, counsellors onto a pedestal only to discard them disdainfully. Bondings motivated by ideal-hunger are notoriously subject to sudden rupture when, for whatever reason, one partner becomes disenchanted with the other. In sum, devaluation is the inevitable outcome of idealization borne of deficiency; the greater the idealization the greater the subsequent devaluation.

> archaic modes of idealization are doomed to disappointment. The more an object is idealized, the more radical the devaluation to which it will eventually be subject; the bigger one's illusions are, the harder they fall (McWilliams, 1994, p. 106).

Relationships grounded in ideal-hunger serve an important purpose in teen bondings: they provide an idealized justification for the existence of the relationship; a justification which becomes especially important when the relationship cannot thrive on its own. The deficiencies of one's partner pale when this partner is possessed of heroic, idealized qualities; these great qualities become the antidote to his (her) human frailties.

As one might suspect, ideal-hunger survives into adulthood; the adult, however, may have no more success with its gratification than the adolescent: "As adults, their craving cannot really be satisfied, stemming as it does from early frustrations, and sooner or later each person they admire comes to appear less than perfect. So the search for someone to idealize continues" (Maddi, 1989, p. 303). Nancy McWilliams summarizes the entire cycle tightly: "Some people spend their lives running from one intimate relationship to the next, in recurrent cycles of idealization and disillusionment, trading the current partner in for a new model every time he or she turns out to be a human being" (1994, p. 107).

Alter-ego hunger

Lord Chesterfield once made an observation concerning human friendship which Alfred Adler later made much of in his theory of personality, and which, as well, holds a measure of truth for our inquiry into adolescent relationships. He claimed: "Most people enjoy the inferiority of their best friends."

Before we pursue the substance behind this message it is necessary to remark that many youngsters do not succeed in their attempts to gain flattering mirrors, nor do they attach themselves to an idealized person from whom they extract recognition or purpose. In other words, the strategies employed by ideal-hungry or mirror-hungry youth do not work for them. A third "solution" to bringing peers into one's sphere is finding someone who will submit meekly and totally. Alter-ego hunger produces a personality which experiences itself as most real in the company of those who slavishly conform to its opinions, values, and desires. Youth who are frustrated in satisfying their mirroring needs and who are unsuccessful in satisfying their idealizing needs, and they exist in great numbers, search for companions who will acknowledge them. (This is one dynamic behind the attraction to the narcissistically selfish, discussed in chapter 12).

Youngsters with "alter-ego hunger" cultivate a variety of techniques to bring peers under their spell. The young people they attract are usually themselves so hungry for love, affection, and acknowledgement that they gladly exchange submission for affiliation. For them, any embrace is better than none. These relationships rarely endure very long; the underlying basis for the attraction is simply too deficient. Alter-ego hungry youth are not looking for a friend, but for a slave, and yet their companions are looking for affection, not slavery.[7]

In this brief segment I have introduced the idea that certain (not all) friendships are driven by unmet needs and unacknowledged desires. This idea, of course, is nothing new; it is, in fact, the underlying premise to all psychodynamic theory. I have used, in a loose manner, the ideas of Heinz Kohut to elucidate my own perceptions on this topic. The relevance of these ideas is not so much that they introduce new explanations but that they suggest new insights into teen behavior, especially concerning the needy, impulsive basis to their bondings. And, factoring all of this into the equation, it becomes evident that we need to keep an attentive eye *on relationships grounded in the deficiencies, rather than the virtues, of the partner.*

Coming back to the main trend of our discussion, even if at the risk of being repetitious, it is necessary to remind the reader that in such a deficient grounding many teen relationships live and breathe, which contributes not only to the hit-and-miss quality of their friendships, but also to their vulnerability to peer corruption.

Postscript

In an attempt to better understand hunger bonding we will briefly re-trace paths travelled and take a second look at narcissistic hunger and how it affects the peer world. Narcissistic hunger originates, so it is thought, in the child's failure to receive adequate mirroring from mother (and father), and in the child's failure to identify with competent, loving adults. Three "hungers" predominate: mirror-hunger, ideal-hunger, and alter-ego hunger.

Mirror-hungry youth inflate their sense of smallness by displaying themselves incessantly. The "effectiveness" of paraders and exhibitionists, in the world of teens, depends on their ability to transact these ploys with panache and eroticism. Parading and exhibiting are not for the timid, the shy, or the bashful; when executed without style the parader is merely a show-off, a goofball, a candidate for ridicule. This, unto itself, stifles such behavior in most teens. Required is someone fearless enough, audacious enough, and hungry enough to carry it off; those who can carry it off are an instant allurement to kids who desire recognition and attention but who cannot "walk the walk."

By late-adolescence most youngsters have learned that the vital element in human relationships is not merely to entice just anyone, but rather to attract someone who will share, who will love without being exploitive. This lesson, so vital to the dignity of the adolescent experience, is difficult to learn in the clutch of unsatisfied cravings.

The second hunger is ideal-hunger: a craving for friends to affiliate with for their prestige, their power, their good looks, their intelligence, their moral strength. This hunger is satisfied only when one has found someone to look up to and to emulate; it seeks expression in hero-worship and in over-valuation. It is a dream come true for the teens to whom it is directed. And while true that ideal-hungry youth are motivated by impairments in their own idealization, it is also true that mutual deficiency bonding can be profitable to both partners in the short term; and, in rare instances, such a bond provides the connection, the chemistry which leads to dignified, reciprocal friendship. More typically, however, the attraction erodes because private hunger, not reciprocal caring, is the reason the relationship comes into being in the first place.

The third narcissistic hunger (alter-ego hunger) expresses itself in the craving for friends who slavishly conform to one's opinions, values, and desires. It differs from ideal-hunger in that it is satisfied by domination. Youngsters with alter-ego hunger are trying to fill a void created by insufficient validation in childhood; anyone who will faithfully follow and obey them is cherished and treasured.

Many youngsters willingly accept this invitation; whether they secretly know that the dance really is a march, we can only speculate. What we do know is that these youngsters are echo, mirror, admirer, follower, and lover wrapped in a single package. If they were in short supply alter-ego hungry youth would be in desperate straits, but as every high school counsellor will affirm, there is no shortage of compliant underlings in the teen community. After all, befriending the powerful is a great accomplishment for those who have no power.

Endnotes

[1]   Heinz Kohut died in 1981. For those who want to learn more about him, a brief biography, a clear explanation of his basic ideas, and an overview of his contributions to psychological theory has been written by Susan Quinn, "Oedipus vs. Narcissus," New York Times Magazine, 9 Nov. 1980, p. 120-26, 128-31.

[2]   The key concept here is "to give." Infants and children are programmed to receive love, to take in affection, to be the beneficiary of love bestowed by someone else. *To give* love is more complex and involves a wider range of abilities and attributes. Narcissists, like children, are well constituted to receive love, but, also like children, they must learn how to give it.

[3]   Here is how David Wexler explains mirroring and idealizing:

> The two most vital classes of selfobject functions identified by Kohut are the *mirroring* functions and the *idealizing* functions. . . . The need for *mirroring* is characterized by a desire to feel recognized and affirmed by someone else; through this process of being seen by another, the person develops a cohesive sense of self. This is the child calling out, "Look, Mom, I'm wonderful, I'm flying . . . I know everything. I can do everything. I am perfect in beauty. I am perfect in strength. Everybody loves me . . ." The other person provides an accurate and empathic reflection so that the individual develops self-definition and a belief in his or her own attributes. The selfobject experience involves having one's inner experience or accomplishments recognized and appreciated. This need does not die out later in life; it merely changes in form and intensity (1991, p. 16-17).

[4]   With mirror-hungry youth popularity is valued more highly than friend-ship. Popularity is based mainly on public behavior and does not require much trust or intimacy. Friendship, on the other hand, is more complex, more human; it involves acceptance and trust by each individual. Friend-ship is based on "human" qualities and an understanding of one's own thoughts and feelings; it is subjective, intimate, and loyal, but most of all, it requires the person to put him- or herself on the line with an equal partner.

[5]   One of the most important skills younger adolescents must acquire if they are to weather the squalls of teen culture, is to ascertain the meaning of the reactions they elicit. Which is to say, they must understand *why* their peers are reacting to them as they are.

[6]   During adolescence, idealizing another in order to further glorify oneself, it seems to me, is a basic emotional reflex.

[7]   The clinical origins of the young person's attraction to slave demands are nicely summarized in the following passage.

> In adolescents, impairments in the original idealized selfobject relation-ships often result in total identification with a hero or a group (such as gang involvement). It is often obvious in the form of obsessive romance, as when a boy threatens suicide if the girl he worships becomes unavail-able. *These needs, in moderation, fall in the normal realm of adolescent experience* (Wexler, 1991, p. 17).

Chapter Twelve

the adolescent attraction to the selfish and self-centred

Earlier in this work (chapter seven) I suggested that all youth are characterized by a necessary egoism which allows them to face the challenges of a world far more complex and far more demanding than anything they encountered in childhood. This necessary egoism I call "developmental self-ish-ness." This chapter investigates some of the connections between "normal" youth whose demeanor is characterized by developmental self-ish-ness and those youngsters whose style is dominated by a narcissistic attitude.

To understand the young person's attraction to the narcissist we must first understand the other side of the coin. So, for the moment, we will direct our attention to this issue.[1]

Why are narcissists attracted to individuals younger than themselves?

All narcissists have a need for ego nourishment so powerful that when it is not forthcoming their sense of meaning disappears and their self-esteem plummets. In the absence of constant bolstering they feel depressed, morose, and angry. And while it is true that they use their companions as providers more than as true friends, it is also true that they very much *need* them and, in fact, they are emotionally dependent on them. So, from the beginning it should be made clear that narcissists need friends and companions even though *what they need them for* is different than for the rest of us.

Narcissists crave being treated as if they are heroes. Their hunger is for acknowledgment, not for the acknowledger (as the smoker hungers for tobacco not the vendor). This need for continuous praise and acknowledgment attracts them to younger peers, for it is they who are most likely to serve the role of praiser. It is not a tenure-track position. The role of flatterer, helper, and servant is one which most youngsters tire of in a year or two. As a result, the narcissistically selfish are always recruiting new prospects to fill the roles of which their current providers are slowly, but surely, growing weary. The ideal hunting grounds are among younger comrades whose growing selfhood valorizes individualism, and whose life experience has not as yet made them wise to individuals who are motivated primarily by pervasive selfishness.

As a rule, narcissists form friendships only when doing so advances their personal agenda. They tend not to "fall" into friendship; intimate connections don't "just happen" to them. Their insecurities encase them in a protective cocoon that does not tolerate intruders who might inflict psychic harm. So, from the beginning, they hold a logistical advantage in their human relationships; an advantage which, in the world of teens, goes a long way toward shaping the power hierarchy.

Self-serving youth know that their best connections are not forged with other narcissists. Their ideal partner is someone swamped with the demands of growth, with limited intimacy experiences, with marginal fluency with formal thought (the means by which the pros and cons of any relationship are evaluated); and, finally someone whose hunger for approval is ravenous.

Why are the young attracted to older narcissists?

Early adolescents are consumed with the developmentally necessary task of transforming their child self into an adolescent self. The ideal mentors for this task are older, better travelled peers; or so it seems. The attraction begins on the two-way street they each travel. The narcissistically selfish so desperately need affirming attachments that they are nothing without them; the less experienced, the accepting, the hungry are nothing without affiliation. The merger begins as a symbiotic relationship, but it rarely remains that way for long.

When Anna Freud claimed that teens are "excessively egoistic," and think of themselves "as the centre of the universe" she, quite obviously, over-stated her point; but she was correct in her inference that youngsters *wish* they were the centre of the universe, and that they *crave* to be treated, even fleetingly, as if they were. What she helped us to recognize was the important role which peers play in this process, for it is through them that their egotistic nature blossoms. This vital spirit draws them to peers who exude the aura of grandness. It is an attraction of immense significance in teen society. Millon helps us to better understand it:

> these individuals overvalue their personal worth, and expect that others will not only recognize but cater to the high esteem in which [they] hold themselves. *This form of self-confidence and self-assurance is conducive to success and the evocation of admiration* . . . (1981, p. 158).

By now I hope that it is readily apparent that the assumption that others will cater to them, admire them, cooperate with them in self-serving ventures is by no means groundless. Their "presumption of relevance" is convincing to the inexperienced (one further reason they are attracted to early-adolescents), to the adrift, and ironically, to decent, loving kids who want nothing more than to give, to share, to invest themselves in people they believe are worthy.

All successful narcissists must be able to fascinate, to charm, to entice; otherwise they would not be successful. Their confident persuasion inspires interest from those who have no confidence, real or false. "Having worked so hard at their 'trade,' narcissists are frequently quite well equipped, socially and intellectually, and can be captivating, despite their egocentricity" (DeRosis, 1981, p. 344). However, it is a quality that will eventually pall. "To be with such a person requires a certain subjugation of oneself, for one cannot intrude, complain, or criticize, but must maintain an appreciative and eager receptivity to a beneficent largesse" (DeRosis, p. 345).

To get a better feel for younger teens remember that one of the most important demands of their identity project is to differentiate themselves from all other selves. This demand festers within them an obsession with individualism, with being "my own person," with the importance of being "me." These obsessions they share with every narcissist.

The worst possible fate for narcissists is to think of themselves as being the same as everyone else. Fear of admitting that they resemble the people they loathe causes them to condemn everyone and everything. Such condemnations resonate warmly in the hearts of kids rejected or humiliated by these commoners the narcissist has the courage to hate. The narcissist's contempt bolsters the spirit of his comrades, his Echoes. In return for the distorted superiority the narcissist affords them, they give their loyalty and affection; and even though this may seem unwise, it results in intense devotion to their narcissistic friend.

Finally, we gain some insight into the attraction when we recognize how disdainfully narcissists treat outsiders. Since outsiders serve no emotional function, they are dispensable. Narcissists typically are so insecure about their own achievements that they devalue harshly the achievements of others. All this contempt and scorn for others is music to younger spirits; they are emboldened and aroused by this powerful person who contemptuously denigrates the achievements of others. The continuous deflation of others provides them with a perverse inflation they come to depend upon.

Narcissus and Echo

Earlier I discussed the myth of Narcissus, which Freud, and others, have used to elaborate their views of self-love and self-fascination.

Narcissus, of course, was the personification of self-conceit, his vanity being such that his name is now a synonym for impenetrable vanity. His fascination with himself was so complete that he left in his wake the broken hearts and crushed spirits of those who loved him but received no love in return.

Legend tells us that Echo was a beautiful nymph, fond of the woods and the hills, where she devoted herself to woodland sports. However, she deceived Juno, and when Juno discovered it she passed sentence on Echo in these words: "You shall forfeit the use of that tongue with which you have cheated me, except for that one purpose you are so fond of – reply. You shall have the last word, but no power to speak first."

One day Echo saw beautiful Narcissus as he was hunting in the hills. She immediately loved him and hurriedly followed his footsteps. How she longed to address him in the softest accents, and win him to conversation. But it was not in her power. She, therefore, waited with impatience for him to speak first, and had her answer ready. One day Narcissus, being separated from his companions, shouted aloud, "Who's here?" Echo replied in the only way she could, "Here." Narcissus looked around, but seeing no one called out, "Come." Echo answered, "Come." As no one came Narcissus called again, "Why do you shun me?" Echo then asked the same question. "Let us join one another," said the beautiful youth. Echo answered with all her heart in the same words, and hastened to the spot, ready to throw her arms about his neck. But he turned away in anger and disgust. "Not so," he said; "I will die before I give you power over me." All that Echo could say was, humbly, entreatingly, "I give you power over me," but he was gone. She hid her blushes and her shame in a lonely cave, and never could be comforted. Yet, still her love remained firmly rooted in her heart, and was increased by the pain of having been rejected. Her anxious thoughts kept her awake and made her pitifully thin. They say she has so wasted away with longing that only her voice now is left to her.

My first serious boyfriend was when I was 12. He was 16 years old. There was only two years in schools years. He was very caring to me and, at the time, mature. We went out for four months. He was my first boyfriend. I loved him. He wanted me to sleep with him. When I said that I wouldn't he left me for my best friend. I think it was the smartest choice I ever made. For someone that was tall, dark and handsome, he sure was a slimy creep.
18-year-old describing "first attractions".

So Narcissus went on his cruel way, a scorner of love. But at last one of those he wounded prayed a prayer and it was answered by the gods: "May he who loves not others love himself." The goddess of righteous anger, Nemesis, undertook to bring this about. As Narcissus bent over a clear pool for a drink and saw there his own reflection; on the moment he fell in love with it. And in that instant of mesmerized self-fascination, Narcissus' fate was sealed; and like the narcissists to follow him, he swooned into such a self-obsession that all other people and their concerns ceased to exist.

But here our concern is also with Echo, for it was she who so strongly desired Narcissus, who yearned for him, and pursued him even after he had several times rejected her. All of this she did without even a moment of closeness, without the comfort of touch or caress, and with complete awareness that Narcissus so mistreated everyone who desired to share in his beauty and splendor. Echo's desire for Narcissus remains a mystery (which is part of the myth's allure) but there can be no doubt that, at least by modern standards, Echo's "love" was grounded in an emptiness she foolishly hoped, against all evidence, that Narcissus would fill. Her persistent pursuit confirmed to Narcissus his power over her, while making Echo, because of her desperation, even less desired. Echo "withered away" in the face of her lost love; she starved from a hunger she valorized until the moment of her death. "The story of Narcissus and Echo is one of self-love that precludes the ability to see, hear, or react to the needs of another" (Donaldson-Pressman, 1994, p. 11).

We simplify unfairly if we conclude that Echo was drawn to Narcissus merely by his beauty; her attraction also lived in the illusion that his investment in her would fill her emptiness. The pathos of Narcissus is his inability to invest himself in anything other than himself; the pathos of Echo is her denial that his consuming love for himself precluded him from ever loving her.

> Echo's situation reflects empathy without insight, the opposite of Narcissus' dilemma, (in) sight without compassion. *The lack of meaningful communication between Echo and Narcissus dramatizes the empty nature of narcissistic discourse.* Both Echo and Narcissus suffer from insatiable hunger, despite the abundance surrounding them (Berman, 1990, p. 9).

Narcissus and Echo in the adolescent community

Youngsters with impoverished identities are magnetized to peers with initiative. As Echo was unable to initiate her own speech, these youngsters are unable to initiate their own ideas or their own ambitions. They seek refuge in someone who has a plan, any plan. They so lack direction that, in exchange for affiliation, they willingly allow another to navigate their life course for them.

A similar situation exists among shy youngsters secretive about their feelings, indeed, about the entirety of their inner workings. Many shy youngsters are awkward in interpersonal settings and often behave inappropriately. They are slow to start conversations, and when they do they speak less than non-shy people; they make less eye contact, show fewer emotions, and smile less.

> most shy people strongly desire to get along with others to have friends and lovers, and to experience intimacy, but they are afraid that they will make a bad impression and experience rejection, humiliation, ostracism, and anxiety. They are painfully aware of how they might be perceived by others, and they constantly fear that others might see them in a bad light. They focus on avoiding anything that might produce rejection or embarrassment (Baumeister, 1991, p. 53).

These shy youngsters need to be praised and coddled before they feel safe enough to share themselves; their shyness is their defense against rejection and ridicule. Yet when someone takes the effort to seek them out, to meet them on their ground, and to allay their anxieties, their allegiance and loyalty are freely given. For many youngsters these first moments of glorious sharing occur with a partner who has cultivated them for private gain. Narcissists "open" their friends in order to exalt themselves, but in the shy one the experience often creates a deep gratitude which expresses itself in fidelity, adulation, and with surprising frequency, subservience. For many young people this is the stuff of first friendships.

Youngsters who cannot feel themselves, who have no zest, who are morose and depressed, are drawn to anyone who arouses their passion and invigorates their lost vitality. The allure is in the sizzle, in the heated arousal *of the self experiencing itself*, which, we must never forget, is the foremost narcissistic pleasure.[2] To understand the adolescent we cannot overlook a basic fact of teen phenomenology: the self experiencing itself is its own reward.

Despite the failure of Echo and Narcissus to connect with one another in myth, they do so with remarkable regularity in the real world. Why? Because they each feed off the limitations of the other: "Echo and Narcissus fit together perfectly; neither is able to initiate and sustain dialog. Both are consequences" (Hamilton, 1982, p. 128). Neither recognizes what is required for mutuality; neither understands shared intimacy. Both are hunger-driven, but by opposite hungers. Echo's refusal to see Narcissus for the selfish young man that he is seals her fate. "She offers nothing which might correct Narcissus' ever-expanding delusions of grandeur" (Hamilton, 1982, p. 128). And while no eternal truth dictates that every Narcissus must have an Echo to spurn, or that every Echo must have a Narcissus to pursue, there can be no doubt whatsoever that this drama is played daily in adolescent theatre.

Some further observations

Leo Tolstoy once wrote: "We do not love people so much for the good they have done us, as for the good we have done them." This thoughtful aphorism, like all insights which convey wisdom without explaining it, contains more than a kernel of truth as it applies to the young person's fascination with narcissistic peers.

I think there is much to recommend Tolstoy's claim that attraction blossoms from giving; especially when we focus on ordinary kids endowed with normal social interest. Narcissists are exceptions to this principle: their joy is *only* in receiving; a joy which, ironically, encourages within their friends the natural desire to give. Since narcissists understand giving in utilitarian terms, it is literally impossible for them to respect the giver as a person. Their failure to understand the human connections between giver and receiver blend nicely with their attitudes of entitlement: "Since they feel entitled to get what they wish and have been successful in having others provide them with comforts they have not deserved, narcissists have little reason to discontinue their habitual presumptuousness" (Millon, 1981, p. 172).

Narcissists needs followers to prove the value of their convictions, and their followers need convictions to believe in themselves. In such an exchange each partner receives return for investment. But, essential to understanding the dynamics of the entire operation, the connection works not from reciprocal strength, but from complementary weakness.

> *"If I had the opportunity to date him again, I'm sure that I wouldn't even if I was paid. My standards now are a lot higher than they were then when I was in junior high. Now looks are not on the high list of qualities. I believe that honesty is far more important."*
> 20-year-old describing "first attractions".

The attraction of the selfish to the developmentally immature (and vice-versa) is a vital element in the emotional chemistry of the youth culture. It is the dynamic behind many unequal power relationships, especially the female attraction to older boys.[3] Not to be overlooked in all this is that the selfish know what they want and have a plan to get it; in the teen world this places them in a position of extreme advantage because so many kids have absolutely no plans, no blueprints, no compass. To steer them on to one's own course is not so difficult because they have no course of their own to follow. As I hope is abundantly clear by now, the primary mission of the narcissist (as far as social relationships are concerned) is to steer others onto their course, to have others choose not their own path but the path of the narcissist.

Again, it helps to backtrack to the differences between the self-ish-ness inherent to the adolescent period (developmental self-ish-ness) and the excessive selfishness inherent to narcissism (narcissistic selfishness).

Developmental self-ish-ness is anchored in the natural demands of the developing self, and the identity project; it is an exaggerated, but necessary, self-centredness. On the other hand, in narcissistic selfishness the collective reflexes of narcissism guide behavior. The narcissistically selfish person is "always anxiously concerned with himself, he is never satisfied . . . always driven by the fear of not getting enough, of missing something, of being deprived of something" (Fromm, 1939, p. 521).

Most youngsters don't recognize that even though the narcissistically selfish attain pleasure only in receiving, they do not grow in their admiration for those from whom they receive. (This, we might add, comes as a shock to ordinary kids.) It simply does not occur to giving youngsters that they are mere providers; most foreign of all to their thought is that, as providers, they are completely replaceable. Many youngsters are governed in their human exchanges by what Merleau Ponty called "egocentric sympathy" – the participation in the sentiments of others, living, even if only for a moment, in other people. This willingness to *participate in the sentiments of others* is a necessary precondition for the success of the selfishly motivated. Fortunately for them, many youth are laced with just such a willingness.

Of course, other forces are at work in this complex process. The sense of inferiority (the calling card of all youth) plays an important role in bringing ordinary kids into the sphere of the narcissistically selfish. How? Narcissists presume that they, because of their specialness, should associate only with people who are unique, gifted, "in a class by themselves"; therefore, the people with whom they do associate are granted these qualities (even if only verbally). Because the selfish ones are so heroically special, anyone who flatters their illusions and gives them allegiance automatically becomes greater than the disinterested "others" who do not recognize greatness even when it is paraded before them. The fears and insecurities which gnaw at early- and middle-teens are lessened by the Grand One who, through scorn and contempt, reduces everyone outside their circle to zero. The selfish friend becomes, in effect, the great leveller of social differences; in an insecure world dominated by status and popularity this is no small accomplishment.

Postscript

Let me try to pull together certain ideas hinted at so far.

The relationships between ordinary kids and peers dominated by the narcissistic attitude are not cold and impersonal. Narcissists share a sincere sentimentality with their friends, and give to them support, nurturance and reassurance. The difference between these friendships and friendships where neither partner is consumed by narcissistic attitudes is found in the basis for the initial attraction: "to them a friend is important not as a person, so much as a thing from which to milk support for their self-image . . ." (Polansky, 1991, p. 74). Equally important are the grounds for separation. In essence, the friendship is terminated when the non-narcissistic partner makes demands for increased mutuality, for reciprocity. When the playing field is even the narcissist abandons the game because it no longer holds any advantage.[4]

Narcissists need the loyalty, the allegiance and the commitment of younger peers to handle their own insecurities. The intense anxiety of these fears creates their trademark aura of nervous urgency; but it also makes them willing to vigorously court new clients, to state openly and boldly: "I want you. I need you. I love you." Such overtures are beautiful music to youth who themselves crave companionship; who want to give their allegiance, and to share their private pleasures. What greater way to know that one is worthy than to hear: "I want you. I need you. I love you." If it sounds true, if it feels true, then it *must* be true. Narcissists know better than anyone that he who honors the self becomes magnificent to the one who is honored.

Finally, we need to face up to the fact that much within our adolescent children responds to the lesser side of human nature. Parents, encouraged by psychologists in denial, believe that their children are pure, innocent, harmless; that their children's selfish behavior is caused solely by corrupt institutions, by lack of opportunity, by drugs. An honest look at the adolescent need structure, and even more importantly, at adolescent behavior, does not support such a belief.[5] The vulnerabilities of youth, though shamelessly exploited by the outside world, are not caused by it; their *potential* for corruption resides within their own emotional and intellectual make-up. It would seem a warranted conclusion, then, that it is the responsibility of the adult community to protect and nurture the frailties of youth and to promote, to elevate, to give wings to their abundant abilities and aptitudes. For, at this moment in our culture's evolution, anyone with eyes to see and a heart to feel knows that, without decent intervention, many kids simply cannot make it.

Endnotes

[1] The attraction of the young to narcissists is not the same as the attraction of *adults* to narcissists. Differences in the need structure, in life experience, and in the power of formal thought account for some of the differences.

[2] Whether feeling is positive and affirmative or negative and depressing is not as significant as feeling itself. In adolescence the quest for feeling is so powerful that it can become more important than the content, or the

object, of the feeling. Feeling is an end in-and-of-itself. Hence the allure to that which produces powerful feeling.

[3] The attraction of younger females (approximately from 13-16 years) to older males (approximately 17-20 years) is one of the most significant attractions in the entire adolescent community. The developmental differences between these age groups is so great that they virtually always place the male in a position of power (both intellectually and socially) over the female. The human consequences of this power imbalance are not totally predictable, but they rarely are to the girl's advantage, and they rarely serve her long-term best interests. Perhaps the most significant issue is pregnancy, about which Musick gives us something to think about. She writes:

> "research data indicate that a significant number of adolescent girls are impregnated by males who are at least five years older. Are these pregnancies the result of sexual exploitation or merely of inappropriate dating relationships?" (Musick, 1993, p. 86).

[4] During adolescence the bonds of closeness forged during a two or three month period may take two or three years to untangle. The virtues of decency are too deep in ordinary kids for them to walk away from narcissistic peers who would walk away from them in a minute. Hence, they remain vulnerable to their overtures, to their special requests, to their impassioned pleas for one final, special favor.

[5] The failure to see what is plainly evident is sometimes referred to as a "blind spot." The concept has considerable application here. In physiology, the blind spot is the gap in our field of vision that results from the way the eye is constructed. At the rear of each eyeball is a point where the optic nerve, which runs to the brain, attaches to the retina. This point lacks the cells that line the rest of the retina to register the light that comes through the lens of the eye. As a result, at this one point in vision there is a gap in the information transmitted to the brain. Here the blind spot registers nothing, and the perceiver perceives nothing.

Areas within a person's beliefs, attitudes or perceptions resistant to change also create blind spots. They deny unwanted data, resulting "in an incapacity to bring attention to bear on certain crucial aspects of our reality, leaving a gap in that beam of awareness which defines our world from moment to moment" (Goleman, 1985, p. 15). For many young people this "gap in the beam of awareness" is of monumental significance when it blinds them from seeing the relationship between sexual intercourse and pregnancy, alcohol consumption and automobile accidents. It plays an important role in the young person's attraction to the narcissistically selfish because if the relationship were to be seen clearly and accurately it would not survive.

Concluding Observations on Adolescent Vulnerability

"It is dangerous to show man too often that he is equal to beasts, without showing him his greatness. It is also dangerous to show him too frequently his greatness without his baseness. But, it is very desirable to show him the two together." Blaise Pascal

Here, in the closing chapter of this investigation, I would like to review some of the ideas already brought to your attention. It is my hope that by doing so I will be able to meaningfully tie together the ideas and concepts behind my understanding of adolescent vulnerability.

One theme permeates every chapter: adolescents are extremely vulnerable to self-diminishing behaviors, to deterioration and to corruption. It is my belief that the *source* of many of these vulnerabilities is found within the adolescent; consequently much of our efforts have been expended investigating (a) limitations inherent to the adolescent thought process; (b) predispositions inherent to their emotional make-up; and (c) alliances inherent to their friendship patterns.

This, of course, does not mean that youth are innately, or even inevitably, corrupt; it means only that they are *vulnerable to the corrupting influences* which fill their insulated world; much as the embryo to teratogens.

Summary observations on adolescent vulnerability

[1] When one is vulnerable one is susceptible to injury, open to being wounded. It is of special interest to youth not merely because they are the vulnerable ones, but because its consequences are premature babies and drug addiction, gang wars and incarceration, lost opportunities and broken spirits. Vulnerability is no mere rhetorical concept; to adolescents it is real and so are its outcomes.

It is, of course, unfair to portray young people *only* as vulnerable, for they surely are much more. On the other side of the vulnerability coin is resilience, the ability to spring back, to resume one's original shape, to recover lost strength; to rebound from hardship and to make meaningful sense of what is going on in the outside world. Resilience is the psychological and biological strength required to successfully master change (Flach, 1988).

During the adolescent years vulnerability and resilience go hand in hand; all normal youngsters are vulnerable, but at the same time

225

resilient. One hopes that every youngster will have enough resilience to handle the adversity to which he (she) is vulnerable. As we have seen, this is not always the case. As Anthony and Cohler expressed it in *The Vulnerable Child*: "When the child's most vulnerable area is confronted by severe stress for that area, some degree of breakdown is likely to occur . . ." (1987, p. xi). Vulnerability does not mean that something terrible will happen, it simply increases its probability. "Vulnerability is not necessarily a message of doom, since individuals can bounce back and achieve a significant degree of nonvulnerability" (Anthony and Cohler, 1987).

The resilient individual possesses a collection of skills, abilities, and habits which include the ability to tolerate pain, the capacity for honest insight, the ability to restore self-esteem when it has been temporarily lost, the ability to keep and maintain friends, the ability to function effectively under stress, the capacity to contain within reasonable limits the extent of personal disruption, the ability to negotiate the demands of change, the ability to know when one is in trouble and how to seek help, the ability to give up obsolete or distorted ways of looking at things, a capacity to see clearly what is clear, to not be gullible, and the poise to avoid panic. The resilient individual is characterized by a sense of confidence that life experiences have some order and integration, and by the feeling that he (she) can identify what is happening and activate the necessary resources to manage successfully.

When we talk about vulnerability we are concerned with the opposite of all this: with the inability to tolerate pain, by the reduced capacity for insight, by the inability to restore self-esteem when it has been diminished or temporarily lost, by the inability to maintain friendship, by the inability to function effectively under stress, by the loss of capacity to contain personal disruption, by the inability to negotiate the demands of change, by the inability to know how to seek help, by the inability to give up obsolete or distorted ways of looking at things, by the reduced capacity to see clearly what is clear, by the propensity to be gullible. The vulnerable individual is characterized by a lack of confidence that life experiences have some order and integration, and by the feeling that he (she) cannot identify what is happening and cannot activate the necessary resources to manage successfully. The vulnerabilities of adolescence, like the vulnerabilities of childhood, are grounded in immaturity and inexperience. Of this truism we cannot lose contact.

This book spotlights some of the ways that youth are vulnerable to corrupting influences within their homes, their schools, and their peer groups. In a nutshell, we want to know how the natural limitations of adolescents increase their vulnerability to corruption.

[2] As the 20th century limps to its conclusion our understanding of adolescence remains, from the core out, seriously flawed. Our gravest error is to assume that youth can effectively handle the demands of adolescent life. With a stunning consistency, they cannot. The opportunities for self-diminishing choices are too numerous, too available, and too natural. The price our current generation of teens pay for their youthful mistakes is beyond every standard of fair proportion, especially as they pertain to drug use, to sexual experimentation, and to gang membership. Throughout this book I have tried to support the claim that growing teens desperately need assistance from adults not merely because they lack experience (although this is an important consideration) but, as well, because in the absence of solid guidance and decent direction they are not only vulnerable to, they are *predisposed* to, self-diminishing and self-destructive choices.

Some of the most profound youth tragedies flow from their natural impulses, desires and tendencies; especially from *their impulse* to bond, from *their desire* to give their allegiance, from *their tendency* to honor fables. During adolescence the self is in-process, growing and developing; by definition it is incomplete. And by logical extension, it remains in need of guidance and support; in need of mentors, tutors, coaches, spiritual advisors, and most importantly, of parents who have themselves matured beyond the narcissism of youth.

[3] The moratorium culture in which adolescents live is an artificial world where teens are segregated from the adult community and sealed off from real responsibility, real contribution, and real work. Lack of involvement in the real machinery of society, lack of relevance in their own family, and lack of righteous participation of any kind contributes greatly to their attraction to the trite and trivial, indeed, to their overall vulnerability to deterioration and erosion.

Section One: The Domain of Thought

[4] Before one seeks, one must have a lantern; what one finds is determined not only by one's natural acuity, but also by the power and luminescence of the lantern. To understand how youth seek, and what they are able to find, we must know something of the lantern which guides them. Hence, we have no choice except to investigate both the brightness which illuminates and the dimness which beclouds the adolescent thought process.

[5] Formal thought is the intellectual foundation for philosophical and scientific thought.[1] More intricate, more complex, and more capable of investigating abstract concepts than concrete thought, formal thought may be considered "advanced" and concrete thought "primi-

tive."[2] Aside from physical growth, the onset of formal thought is the most significant developmental event in the entire adolescent period.

[6] The power and efficiency of formal thought, indeed of all thought predicated on objectivity and impartiality, is compromised by *egocentrism*, the preoccupation with one's own needs, desires, and points of view. Egocentrism imbues the thinking process with the power to reject ideas threatening to one's self-esteem and to accept ideas which bolster one's self-esteem. This, unto itself, profoundly reduces thought efficiency during the adolescent years.[3]

[7] Perspective-taking is stepping outside one's own frame to better understand someone else's; during childhood and adolescence it unfolds on a fairly predictable timetable. R. L. Selman's theory was introduced (in chapter two) because of its relationship to egocentrism: as perspective-taking increases egocentrism decreases, and as egocentrism increases perspective-taking decreases. The relationship is a significant one in teen decision-making.

[8] Jean Piaget believed that individuals progress through four stages of egocentrism, three during childhood and one during adolescence. Like all stage theorists, he believed that these stages are sequential and time-bound, and that the ability to successfully negotiate any given stage is dependent on how successfully the previous stages were negotiated. In Piaget's scheme each stage is characterized by a growth advance and by a growth regression. The four stages include:

- *sensorimotor egocentrism*, the egocentrism of infants in which the child acquires the ability to differentiate the self from the outside world;

- *pre-operational egocentrism*, the egocentrism of preschoolers in which thinking about the world always begins from the child's position within it;

- *concrete operational egocentrism*, the egocentrism of middle-years children in which the child acquires the ability to perform elementary syllogistic reasoning and to propose concrete hypotheses; and, finally,

- *formal operational egocentrism*, the egocentrism of adolescents in which formal thought takes hold and the individual acquires the ability to double-check private thoughts, and to comprehensively evaluate the coherence of ideas in general.

[9] As objective reason and impartial analysis strengthen, egocentrism weakens. This decline in the power of egocentrism results in many important behavioral and attitudinal changes; here I provide only a few.

- the adolescent increasingly recognizes that others have a private existence;
- the adolescent begins to perceive adults as separate individuals with their own private individuality;
- the adolescent accepts that it is impossible for another person to *completely* understand what it is like "to be me";
- the adolescent decreasingly demands that others always see things from "my" point of view;
- the fable of one's unique singularity begins to share time with the belief that all people share important commonalities;
- the adolescent is able to join social gatherings without assuming that his (her) arrival carries undue significance.

[10] Embedded within the adolescent thought process are clusters of distortion-creating tendencies. Generally speaking, if the youngster is fortunate enough to live in a supportive household, and has a decent supply of self-esteem, the consequences of these distortions tend to be minimal. For those youngsters with virtually no home support network, for those who associate with emotionally damaged peers, for those who have never cultivated formal thought, these distortions carry profound significance in everyday life. Many of the "at-risk" youth I have interviewed over the past ten years are so contemptuous of cold reason that in many areas of discourse their intellectual *functioning* (not to be confused with their intellectual *potential*) is not much different from ten-year-olds.

[11] In chapter three I discussed some of the irrational tendencies of adolescents, including:

- their tendency to believe they are being closely observed when they are not;
- their tendency to believe that they are so unique that no one can understand them;
- their tendency to try to reform their world so that it better fits their own needs and desires; and
- their tendency to infuse their speech with inappropriate references to their own private feelings and their own immediate concerns.

These tendencies share an ongoing dialog with reason. To claim that all teens are at their mercy is wrong; indeed, many youth handle them quite effectively. But it is also wrong to claim that they carry no weight; indeed, for some kids the weight is crushing.

[12] Throughout this book I have repeatedly referred to the role played by distortional thinking in teen pregnancy. No one has thus far advanced a convincing explanation as to why so many girls become pregnant when they don't want to be pregnant, and when they know how to avoid it. But one thing is crystal clear: teens in their early and middle years do not, perhaps cannot, think clearly and then act upon this clarity when it comes to sexual intercourse. If ever there existed a need for decent, effective intervention in the lives of teens, this is it. Unfortunately, on this topic the thinking of adults is as distorted as the thinking of teens, though for completely different reasons.

[13] At the risk of being repetitious, I want to once again remind the reader that adolescence is a time in the life cycle where the power of thought makes a tremendous forward surge. This surge is not merely one where all mental abilities increase (which, in fact, they do); it also is where the capacity to think in a higher key is born. In other words, teens not only solve problems quicker and more accurately than 10-year-olds, they can solve *kinds* of problems completely beyond the intellectual sphere of the 10-year-old. Formal thought brings to the adolescent an intellectual potential of immense significance.

Formal thought, however, does not operate at peak efficiency all the time. Indeed, there are moments when formal thought doesn't seem to operate at all. These moments can be condemning during adolescence because mistakes carry far greater consequences than correct actions. Because of this unfortunate imbalance, I have tried to bring to light some of the mental habits which contribute to tragic life decisions during adolescence.

[14] There is a difference between the narrow mindedness born of meagre aptitude and narrow mindedness which is self-inflicted; a difference which challenges every student of adolescent psychology because during the teen years it is so difficult to separate one from the other. The student of adolescent behavior is continuously befuddled by whether the narrowness observed in some youngsters results from a lack of maturity, from insufficient instruction, from a lack of experience; or, on the other hand, from fear, from defiance, from self-protection. It always remains something of a mystery as to whether their narrow mindedness could be transcended if they simply rallied their available resources.

[15] Adolescent thinking becomes murky and beclouded under the following conditions:

- when the thinker abandons the system of checks and balances inherent to formal thought and regresses to the more authoritarian concrete thought of children;

- when the thinker rejects cold, objective reasoning in favor of warm, affective logic;
- when the thinker avoids the issue at hand and concentrates solely on how the issue relates to "me."

If these mental habits worked their way into the thought chain only when insignificant or inconsequential topics were being deliberated (as is usually the case in childhood), they would not merit the time and energy devoted to them in this book. However, such is not the case. During adolescence, beclouded thinking may intrude into the thought chain at any time, regardless of the issue being deliberated. For this reason, and for many others already discussed, every adolescent-as-thinker is in need of a co-thinker to serve as an intellectual collaborator, to help with the flow of ideas, and to serve as a brake on the natural propensity to distort ideas to one's favor. The most ideal person for this job is an adult who has the best interests of the young person in his (her) heart. The least ideal person is a peer who serves as nothing more than a flattering mirror. In the real world of teen life, the co-thinker of most teens is the latter; and this, unto itself, heightens teen vulnerability.[4]

Section Two: The Domain of Self

[16] It is my belief that the charge of egocentrism which dominates childhood takes on an even more highly charged glow during adolescence. With the onset of adolescence, egocentrism is infused with an "endocrinologized" emotionality which profoundly alters teen psychology. In chapters 5, 6 & 7 I suggest that these changes carry an intense narcissistic flavor which shapes the entire youth culture.

[17] Two of the most influential thinkers in the literature of narcissism, Sigmund Freud (who is credited with introducing the concept into modern psychological theory) and Karen Horney, who challenged several of Freud's basic premises, were the focus of chapter five and the starting points in our investigation of adolescent narcissism.

[18] Freud claimed that narcissism originates in the infant's turning of love away from the world and inward upon the self, thereby making the self the object of its own love. In his words, "The libido withdrawn from the outer world has been directed on to the ego, giving rise to a state which we may call narcissism" (1914). Freud was convinced that infants begin life in a blissful state of *primary narcissism* where no distinction exists between self and world; hence no unfulfilled desires, no frustration. Primary narcissism is that stage of development where the infant has not as yet established ego boundaries, and thus experiences itself and its environment as one. In Freud's vision of child development primary narcissism is the most primitive of all emotional

states where the infant is bestowed with a grandiose inflation, with feelings of perfection and power. The infant is fused with the mother and the world in wholeness and harmony; a blissful, short-lived state filled with such primal splendor that all of us are driven to recapture its power and its glory.

Primary narcissism, then, is the stage of psychosexual development where the child's pleasures are concentrated within the self and the body. A developmental stage between autoeroticism and object love when distinct autoerotic sensations become fused into one's body, which then, together, become a single, unified love object. This "narcissistic condition" is the libidinal storehouse from which the love of one's self and the love for others emerges. Eventually, much of the child's primary narcissism is abandoned in favor of ego development, and in time, the child replaces self-love with love for others. But the love received from others cannot yield the primal satisfaction of one's original self-love. (This claim is vital to Freud's understanding of narcissism: shared love is less fulfilling than self-love). The belief that other-love comes at the expense of self-love is the defining feature of Freud's narcissism. If you find the idea preposterous, you probably are not much of a narcissist!

[19] Karen Horney viewed the entire process differently and for this break from orthodoxy she was dismissed from the New York Psychoanalytic Society, whereupon she founded the American Institute for Psychoanalysis. Horney emphasized social factors far more than Freud (as did all of the Neo-Freudians), and she held a more encouraging view of human nature. Her theories relied heavily on psychoanalytic concepts, but her differences with Freud were significant, especially her belief that neurosis originated in basic anxiety and disturbed human relationships.

Horney did not support Freud's libido theory, which claimed that self-esteem is a desexualized form of self-love, and that persons tending toward overvaluation must be expressing self-love. She believed narcissism is the identification with the idealized image of the self; in effect, that narcissism is an unjustified self-inflation, an overdone self-absorption. This represents one of her most important contributions to narcissistic theory because it presumes that the self-esteem of the healthy person and the self-inflation of the narcissist are completely different phenomena. (A presumption, by the way, which is of great importance to our understanding of adolescent self-esteem). She viewed healthy self-esteem as genuinely positive feelings of pride and worth. Narcissistic self-inflation, on the other hand, is an attempt to disguise one's lack of self-esteem by pretending to possess what doesn't exist.

Horney also believed that the narcissist is someone whose emotional links to others are brittle, and who, in the effort to protect against further pain, suffers a loss of the capacity to love. Hence, the overvaluation of self is merely a substitute for undermined self-esteem. All narcissists have a critical bias at the core of their perception because they see almost everything through the lens of self-interest. Because of this bias and the loss of objectivity which flows from it, narcissists are, in certain areas of their cognition, learning disabled. As we have seen, this learning disability influences young people in many ways, contributing to their egoism as well as to their vulnerability.

[20] The study of narcissism shares several particulars with adolescent psychology; in chapter six I tried to integrate these two areas of research. From this effort some of the common concerns shared by narcissistic theory and adolescent theory were isolated, including the following.

- Theories of narcissism and theories of adolescent psychology are both concerned with self-experience.

- Theories of narcissism and theories of adolescent psychology are both concerned with how self-other perceptions become distorted.

- Theories of narcissism and theories of adolescent psychology are both concerned with the narrowing of experience, the refusal to experiment with new roles, the fear of failure, indeed, the fear of living.

- Theories of narcissism and theories of adolescent psychology are both concerned with self-esteem, with self-love, and with self-hate.

- Theories of narcissism and theories of adolescent psychology are both concerned with the negative impact a narcissistic culture has on its children.

- Theories of narcissism and theories of adolescent psychology are both concerned with natural self-centredness and its relationship to pathological selfishness.

[21] *Developmental self-ish-ness* is a healthy, necessary phase of adolescent phenomenology. When we think of developmental self-ish-ness our thoughts are directed to the natural demands of a developing self; the term carries no negative connotations. In many ways, it can be understood as a parallel to the egocentrism of childhood.

[22] *Narcissistic selfishness*, on the other hand, is a radically more profound self-centredness. When we think of narcissistic selfishness we think of an infatuation with the self so extreme that the interests of others are ignored. The narcissistically selfish person is always anxiously concerned with himself, is always restless, always fearful of not

getting enough, of being deprived, and filled with a burning envy of anyone who might have more. Furthermore, he (she) is unable to give freely but always anxious to take; the world is viewed from the standpoint of what can be taken from it. The narcissistically selfish lack interest in others, and have little respect for their dignity and integrity. It is an especially corrosive state of mind during adolescence.

[23] Quite understandably, individuals imbued with narcissistic selfishness have extreme difficulty with human relations since they cannot handle normal give and take. Their needs for friendship and intimacy are rarely satisfied because their self-esteem is quagmired in empty, non-productive investments; *they displace their own feelings of unworthiness onto others, even when these others are their friends, their parents, their lovers.*

[24] The belief system of the narcissistically selfish is riddled with egocentric fables and childish presumptions, the most common include:

- the belief that others must always accommodate to my needs;
- the belief that my relevance does not need to be earned or proved;
- the belief that my specialness makes me superior;
- the belief that from my specialness flows a river of entitlements.

[25] *The narcissistic attitude* is a cluster of self-serving beliefs with parallels in both developmental self-ish-ness and in narcissistic selfishness. In subdued instances it more resembles the former, and in chronic instances it more resembles the latter. The narcissistic attitude protects self-esteem by excluding threatening ideas, actions, and experiences from awareness, creating an insulated, censored world akin to a self-contained eco-system in which little enters, and little leaves, the system. The basic ingredients of the narcissistic attitude include:

- excessive entitlement demands;
- deadness to the feelings of others;
- reduced capacity to love;
- diminished moral concerns; and,
- lessened capacity for objective thought.

[26] It is important to understand that the attitude of narcissism is not accompanied by a matter-of-fact, even-keeled awareness within the person in which it lives; which is only to say that the narcissistic individual does not think, in a moment of silent reflection: "Yes, I am a completely selfish person." Or, "I have no interest in anything except as it pertains to me." Or, "I scorn that which moves the focus away from

me." On the contrary. Youngsters embroiled in the narcissistic attitude are taken by total surprise when they are accused of being selfish. The accusation leaves them genuinely confused. Why? Because the "felt-experience" of the narcissistic attitude is not one of clear insight, or even an honest recognition of one's behavior and beliefs; rather, the emotional state of the narcissistic attitude is primarily one of remoteness and imperviousness. The attitude makes one indifferent to the needs and feelings of others, and this indifference is behind their lethargic disinterest in either the good or the bad which happens to their friends, their family, their teachers. This is why we hear from them "What's all the fuss about?" when someone has been injured in a car accident; or "Why is everyone so excited?" upon hearing sad news about the failing health of a relative.

[27] By narrowing the range of shared emotional investments, by reducing the circumference of intellectual concerns, and by egocentrifying morality, the narcissistic attitude diminishes the adolescent as a person, and collectively, it reduces the entire adolescent experience.

[28] If we have learned anything about the basic need structure of the adolescent, it is that their good health depends on getting outside themselves, on participating in constructive projects, on sharing their real feelings, on being useful, on making meaningful contributions to their family, on real work, on believing in something greater than themselves, on volunteering, on giving their muscle and energy to those who need it. The unsolved mystery is *how* do youngsters learn to get outside themselves, to grow beyond their narcissistic bubble. *How* do they learn to venture out to meet the world on its terms?

Section Three: The domain of relationships

[29] It is hard to imagine a network of human relationships more diverse than those found in virtually every high school in North America. A remarkable spectrum of connections exists in these communities, ranging from deep love to shallow attachments, from selfless devotion to jealous backbiting, from intimate sexuality to distant hostility. It's all there. So, how does one summarize the essence of adolescent friendship? One doesn't, for the simple reason that there is no single essence to adolescent friendships. However, important trends and themes are to be found, and taking into account the biases I bring to this topic, I presented some of them to you for your evaluation.[5]

[30] In tackling the question of adolescent friendship we do well to keep in mind that they are sometimes molded from necessity, sometimes from desperation, sometimes from emotional hunger, and sometimes from the dignified core of a beautiful, sharing self. But, most

typically, from a little of each. My investigation of adolescent friendship starts from the premise that all youngsters need friendship, intimacy, and love. However, these core needs for human contact are frustrated by an elementary fact: teens *tend* to be too little concerned with the needs of their partner and too much concerned with their own. Although they very much want to experience meaningful relationships with friends and lovers, their expectations about giving and receiving often lead to their partners' dissatisfaction.

[31] While we can never solve the mystery of teen attachments, we can dispose of certain misconceptions; the first of which is that the teen world is some idyllic utopia where kids play harmless games with each other, and harbor harmless grudges which any perceptive adult can defuse. That is not what it is like and it never has been. The adolescent community is described by teens themselves as one in which the all too human failings of betrayal, gossip, and slander are facts of daily life, and facts which must be dealt with in a practical, straightforward way.

Because their social world is tough, sometimes cruel, adolescents are attracted to companions who perceive them in a favorable light, and who are willing to overlook their limitations and shortcomings. Such attractions result in a profound desire to be in each other's presence since it is only in each other's company that defects become virtues, weaknesses strengths, and personal failings the failings of others. These bonds are strengthened by "synchronized self-deception" where partners agree not to bring up the shortcomings or the limitations in their friend. Such friends may draft solemn agreements to do nothing which will hurt or embarrass the other.

[32] Adolescent relationships are, in part, designed to help young people to "learn the ropes" of their social system; hence, friendships are both intimate and instrumental. During adolescence friends are bonded by many forces other than the human qualities of the partner.

[33] More than is generally recognized by romanticizers of the adolescent experience, adolescent relationships can be darkened by the tendency to pretend to be what one is not, by the tendency to pretend *not* to be what one is, and by the tendency to humiliate their peers. Hypocrisy is merely the portrayal of one's defects as less than they are and of one's virtues as greater than they are; the art of self-promotion. Most teens have learned a vital lesson by grade 8: if they don't promote themselves few others will.

[34] Adolescent friendships sometimes require each partner to give approval in exchange for it being returned. Convincing a friend that his or her defects are really virtues in exchange for the friend doing the same is what I call "reciprocal rationalization." Reciprocal rational-

ization is not the pillar which supports all teen friendships, but it certainly is a buttress without which many would collapse.

[35] Adolescents (especially early- and middle-adolescents) are weak at reading the private motives of others, a weakness which dims their insight into the unspoken agenda of their friends, and ultimately increases their vulnerability to manipulation and exploitation.

[36] Let us again consider, for a moment, the fact that adolescents want to be noticed, to be accepted, and to be loved. From this it follows that approval is necessary for their social and emotional well-being, and that to desire it and to pursue it are consequences of natural appetites. Adolescent approval is about becoming someone. In the teen community it is impossible to be someone without approval from others. In sum, the need for approval is natural, the desire for it is healthy, and the pursuit of it is necessary.

[37] In chapter nine I advanced two hypotheses: the first was that a self unsure of itself cannot validate itself; the second was that a self unsure of itself tries to validate itself by gaining the approval of others. I also suggested that young people who do not believe in their self-evaluations have no choice except to rely upon the evaluations of others. They come to feel that the source of all good is outside of themselves and that the only way to obtain the "desirable" is from outside sources.

[38] In the past two decades the most significant transformation in the social world of teens has been their march into the work force. Most assuredly, it was not a forced march. Both teens and parents agreed that work-for-pay was a solid idea, although for quite different reasons. Teens wanted the money and the esteem it buys. Parents were motivated by a cluster of well-meaning, but essentially false, beliefs. Notably:

- the belief that work-for-pay is good for youngsters and that it helps them "to get their feet wet in the real world";
- the belief that work helps kids to assume responsibility;
- the belief that working youth contribute to the financial welfare of their household;
- the belief that income permits young people to "pay their own way";
- the belief that learning about work smooths the transition to the harsher, less personal world of adult work.

[39] The research findings do not support the hopeful expectations of either parents or teens. Most distressing are the findings which indicate that youth employment:

- undermines the quality of education;

- leads to increased spending on luxury items;

- leads to increased consumption of junk food;

- promotes certain kinds of illegal behavior, especially alcohol and marijuana use;

- fosters cynicism toward "lower-level" work; and,

- encourages a self-esteem network based on the acquisition, and display, of goods.

Findings such as these have led researchers to conclude that the benefits of adolescent work-for-pay are overestimated while its costs are underestimated.[5]

[40] Intimacy is the deepest, the most profound, and the most complex of the adolescent bonding connections. Some youth experts assume that intimacy does not blossom until both partners have attained a certain maturity of identity. Erik Erikson expressed it this way: "It is only when identity formation is well on its way that true intimacy ... is possible" (1968, p. 135). Dignified intimacy requires *mutuality* and *reciprocity* and a deep and abiding concern for the partner. Sullivan claimed that intimacy requires: "a clearly formulated adjustment of one's behavior *to the expressed needs of the other person* in the pursuit of increasingly identical – that is *more and more nearly mutual – satisfactions*" (1953, p. 246).

[41] If their interactions with peers are an indication, and if their testimony can be believed, then it appears that adolescent loyalties are shaped by a *predisposition* to faithfulness, and by an inherent *desire* to give one's allegiance to someone or something. I am of the impression that this predisposition (which I call *fidelity*) is a powerful force in adolescent intimacy yearnings, and in their tendency to periodically bond with partners who, except for the bond, bring nothing beneficial to the relationship.

In the clearest possible language: youth harbor a predisposition to give their allegiance and their dedication to someone or to some cause. This predisposition to share oneself is such a vital force in adolescent bondings that, in my estimation, their friendships and love relationships cannot be understood except in relation to it.

[42] Adolescent bondings are further shaped by the predisposition to believe that the person with whom an experience is shared is the *cause* of that experience. This is what I call *particularization*. Rather than attribute the experience to their own inner feelings, their warmth, or their sexuality, the experience is attributed to the partner. In this way the partner attains a splendor (and a power) beyond what is known in ordinary friendships. Particularization is encouraged by the fact that

many young people are attached to the idea that the best within them cannot surface on its own; that it can be elicited only by a special, wonderful, heroic person.

[43] Adolescent love is not blind, as is so often reported, rather it is dazzled by its own fire, ignited by its own intensity, and inflamed by its own urges. Love glows within but illuminates outward. The blindness is not in love, but in the failure to see honestly what has been illuminated by the glow of love. In a very real sense, the power of adolescent love rises not only from romantic and erotic passion, but from the failure to properly distinguish love's object from love's source.

[44] Most everything in our society geared to teens caters to the lesser within their nature, to the weaker among their abilities, to the stimulation of their desires and to the deadening of their perspective, so it is not surprising that it is hard for them to know the difference between a person of substance and an impersonator of substance. This limitation is a great advantage to every narcissist, for their success depends on friends who do not know, or do not care about, this difference.

The attraction of the developmentally immature to the narcissistically selfish (and vice-versa) catalyzes the emotional chemistry of the youth culture. This attraction brokers many of the unequal power relationships in the teen community, especially the female attraction to older boys. Not to be overlooked in all this is that the selfish know what they want and have a plan to get it; in the teen world this places them at an extreme advantage because so many kids have no plans, no blueprints, no compass. To steer them on to one's own course is not difficult because they have no course of their own to follow.

[45] The narcissist has no willingness to invest himself beyond the circumference of his own vanity. This refusal is both his strength and his weakness: the first by allowing him to rally all of his energy and protective defenses to his own concerns; the second by making it impossible for him to form genuine alliances, to gain strength from the honest participation in the bounty of others, to grow from giving not merely from receiving.

The allure this selfish self-focus has for young people is found in the way in which it is perceived. Intense self-involvement is seen by them as proof that the selfish one is rightfully engrossed, as confirmation that he truly is substantive and worthwhile. How else could he possibly have such sustained interest in himself?

This perceptual (and conceptual) error is most commonly observed among those youngsters who themselves have no real idea of what self-worth means, who possess no legitimate self-esteem, who confuse shadow with substance, who see in bravado strength, in defiance will, in negation affirmation, in crudity charm, in fear courage. In sum, their lack of self-importance makes nearly impossible their understanding of importance, and their lack of self-worth prevents their understanding of worth.

[46] The mission of every adolescent is to attain greater sharing and greater loving than their narcissism permits. This is done not by suppressing their natural narcissism, but by acquiring strategies through which respect and appreciation for others can grow. Everything worthwhile in the adolescent socialization process is but a means to this reconciliation. And, as straightforward as it sounds, the failure to reconcile the narcissism of youth with the needs of society is at the heart of today's youth predicament. The failure is given momentum by a failure on the part of adults to recognize a truism of human development: one learns to extend beyond oneself through constructive work and through the giving of oneself over to a cause greater than oneself.

Endnotes

[1]   See chapter one for an overview of formal thought.

[2]   See chapter one for an overview of concrete thought.

[3]   See chapter two for an overview of egocentrism.

[4]   See chapter eight for a discussion of "flattering mirror."

[5]   Few assignments are more difficult than to formulate a coherent appraisal of the adolescent experience in North America. The reasons are many; here I will provide a short list to which readers can easily add further entries of their own.

  •   Adolescents represent an extremely diverse population, hence accurate generalizations about them are hard to come by.

  •   The term "adolescent" usually spans ages 13-19; therefore, changes within the same person during the course of adolescence are remarkable. One can make the case (as I did in *The Nature of Adolescence*) that late adolescents are so fundamentally different from early adolescents that they represent two different developmental stages rather than the extremes of one.

  •   The most serious youth problem in every moratorium culture is pregnancy; a fact which makes females inherently more vulnerable to dropping out of school, to unemployment, to protracted stay on welfare roles, to minimum-wage employment.

Despite these differences, adolescents are connected by a cluster of developmental similarities which stamp them with characteristics found during no other period in the life cycle, including:

  •   the physical transformations of puberty;

  •   the intellectual transformations of formal thought;

- the emotional transformations induced by endocrinological changes;
- the *onset* of sexual arousal and sexual attraction; and,
- the departure from childhood.

[6]   As an aside: to my knowledge no researchers have as yet investigated the ideological consequences of pouring 16-year-olds into futureless jobs. I suspect that it has gone a long way to further their entrenchment in a consumerist mentality where gloss and glitz rule the hour. Youth with "shop till you drop" stickers on their purses now patrol school corridors previously cluttered with "ban the bomb" graffiti.

Bibliography

Adams, G.R. & Adams, C.M. (1985). Developmental issues, in *Recent developments in adolescent psychiatry*. Hsu, L.K. & Herson, M., eds. New York: John Wiley & Sons.

Adams, G.R. & Archer, S. (1994). Identity: A precursor to intimacy, in *Interventions for adolescent identity development*. Archer, S.L., ed. Thousand Oaks, CA: Sage.

Adams, G., Adams-Taylor, S. & Pittman, K. (1989). "Adolescent pregnancy and parenthood: A review of the problem, solutions and resources." *Family Relations, 38,* 223-229.

Adelson, J. (1972). The political imagination of the young adolescent, in 12 to 16: Early Adolescence, Kagan, J. & Coles, R., eds. New York: Norton Publishing Co.

Adler, A. (1939). *Social interest*. New York: Putnam.

Alford, F.C. (1988). *Narcissism*. New Haven: Yale University Press.

Allan, G. (1989). *Friendship*. London: Harvester-Wheatsheaf.

American Psychiatric Association. (1994). Diagnostic and statistical manual of mental disorders (4th ed.). DSM-IV. Washington, D.C.: American Psychiatric Association.

Anthony, E.J. & Cohler, B.J. (1987). *The invulnerable child*. New York: The Guilford Press.

Apter, M.J. (1983). Negativism and the sense of identity, in *Threatened identities*, Breakwell, G., ed. New York: John Wiley & Sons.

Arnett, J. (1992). "Reckless behavior in adolescence." *Developmental Review, 12.*

Atwater, E. (1988). *Adolescence*, 2nd ed. Englewood Cliffs, NJ: Prentice Hall.

Ayers, L.K. (1994). *Teenage girls*. New York: Crossroad Publishing Company.

Baker, M. (1985). *"What will tomorrow bring?".* . . *A study of the aspirations of adolescent women*. Ottawa, ON: Canadian Advisory Council on the Status of Women.

Bandura, A. (1986). *Social foundations of thought and action: A social cognitive theory*. Englewood Cliffs, NJ: Prentice-Hall.

Barrett, H. (1991). *Rhetoric and civility*. Albany, NY: State University Press of New York.

Baumeister, R.F. (1986). *Identity: Cultural change and the struggle for self*. New York: Oxford University Press.

Baumeister, R.F. (1991). *Escaping the self*. New York: Basic Books.

Bellah, R. (1985). *Habits of the heart*. New York: Harper & Row.

Benditt, T.M. (1982). *Rights*. Totowa, NJ: Rowan & Littlefield.

Berman, J. (1990). *Narcissism and the novel*. New York: New York University Press.

Bishop, J.H. (1989). "Why the apathy in American high schools?" *Educational Researcher, 18* (1), 6-10.

Blasi, A. & Oresick, R.J. (1987). Self-inconsistency and the development of the self, in *The book of the self*, Young-Eisendrath, P. & Hall, J.A., eds. New York: New York University Press.

Bloom, A. (1993). *Love and friendship*. New York: Simon & Schuster.

Blos, P. (1962). *On adolescence*. New York: Free Press.

Boyer, E.L. (1983). *High school: A report on secondary education in America*. New York: Harper & Row.

Branden, N. (1973). *The disowned self*. New York: Bantam Books.

Branden, N. (1983). *Honoring the self*. Los Angeles, CA: J.P. Tarcher, Inc.

Brooks-Gunn, J. & Furstenberg, F.F. Jr. (1986). "The children of adolescent mothers: Physical, academic and psychological outcomes." *Developmental Review, 6,* 224-251.

Brown, B.B., Mory, M.S. & Kinney, D. (1994). Casting adolescent crowds in a relational context: Caricature, channel, and context, in *Personal relationships during adolescence*, Montmeyer, R., ed. Thousand Oaks, CA: Sage.

Bruner, J. (1986). *Actual minds, possible worlds*. Cambridge: Harvard University Press.

Burns, D.D. (1986). The perfectionist's script for self-defeat, in *The pleasure of psychology*, Goleman, D. & Heller, D., eds. New York: New American Library.

Bursten, B. (1977). The narcissistic course, in *The narcissistic condition*, Nelson, M.C., ed. New York: Human Science Press.

Bursten, B. (1986). Some narcissistic personality types, in *Essential papers on narcissism*, Morrison, A.P., ed. New York: New York University Press.

Campbell, S.F. (1976). *Piaget sampler*. New York: John Wiley & Sons.

Carnegie Council on Adolescent Development. (1989). *Turning points: Preparing American youth for the 21st century*. Washington, D.C.

Catterall, J.S. (1987). "On the social costs of dropping out of school." *The High School Journal, 71*(1), 19-30.

Centre for Educational Research and Innovation. (1983). *Education and work: The views of the young*. France: Organization for Economic Co-operation and Development.

Chandler, M. & Ball, L. (1990). Continuity and commitment: A developmental analysis of the identity formation process, in *Coping and self-concept in adolescence*, Bosma, H., ed. Berlin: Springer-Verlag.

Chomsky, N. (1989). *Necessary illusions*. Boston: South End Press.

Cobb, N.J. (1992). *Adolescence*. Toronto, ON: Mayfield.

Cole, M. & Cole, S. (1989). The development of children. New York: Scientific American Books.

Coleman, J.S. (1975). *Youth: Transition to adulthood*. Chicago: University of Chicago Press.

Collins, W.A. & Repinski, D.J. (1994). Relationships during adolescence: Continuity and change in interpersonal behavior, in *Personal relationships during adolescence*, Montmeyer, R., ed. Thousand Oaks, CA: Sage.

Conger, J.J. & Peterson, A.C. (1984). *Adolescence and youth*, 3rd ed. New York: Harper & Row.

Conrad, D. & Hedin, D. (1987). *Youth service: A guide for student reflection in youth participation programs*. Washington, D.C.: Independent Sector.

Cooper, A.M. (1986). Narcissism, in *Essential papers on narcissism*, Morrison, A.P., ed. New York: New York University Press.

Corson, D., ed. (1988). *Education for work: Background to policy and curriculum*. New Zealand: The Dunmore Press.

Cousins, N. (1986). *Human options*. New York: Berkley Books.

Crain, W. (1992). *Theories of development*. Englewood Cliffs, NJ: Prentice-Hall.

Csikszentmihalyi, M. & Larson, R. (1984). *Being adolescent*. New York: Basic Books, Inc.

Danzig, R. & Szanton, P. (1987). *National Service: What would it mean?* New York: D.C. Heath & Co.

Davis, R.A. (1989). "Teenage pregnancy: A theoretical analysis of a social problem." *Adolescence, 24*, 19-27.

Dept. of International Economic and Social Affairs. (1986). *The situation of youth in the 1980s and prospects and challenges for the year 2000*. United Nations.

DeRosis, L.E. (1981). "Horney's theory and narcissism." *American Journal of Psychoanalysis, 41*(4).

DeVaron, T. (1972). Growing up, in *12-16: Early adolescence*, Kagan, J. & Coles, R., eds. New York: W.W. Norton.

Donaldson, M. (1978). *Children's minds*. Glasgow: Fontana.

Donaldson-Pressman, S. (1994). *The narcissistic family*. New York: Lexington Books.

Driscoll, M.P. (1994). *Psychology of learning*. Boston: Allyn & Bacon.

Dusek, J.B. (1991). *Adolescent development and behavior*. Englewood Cliffs, NJ: Prentice Hall.

Dyfoos, J.G. (1990). *Adolescents at risk*. New York: Oxford University Press.

Dyfoos, J.G. (1993). Common components of successful interventions with high-risk youth, in *Adolescent risk taking*, Bell, N.J., ed. Newbury Park, CA: Sage.

Eagle, M. (1988). Psychoanalysis and self-deception, in *Self-deception: An adaptive mechanism?* Lockard, J.S. & Paulhus, D.L., eds. Englewood Cliffs, NJ: Prentice-Hall.

Egan, K. (1990). *Romantic understanding.* New York: Routledge.

Egner, R.E. & Denonn, L.E., eds. (1961). *The basic writings of Bertrand Russell.* New York: Simon and Schuster.

Ekman, P. (1988). Self-deception and detection of misinformation, in *Self-deception: An adaptive mechanism?* Lockard, J.S. & Paulhus, D.L., eds. Englewood Cliffs, NJ: Prentice-Hall.

Elkind, D. (1967). "Egocentrism in adolescence." *Child Development, 38,* 1025-1034.

Elkind, D. (1974). *Children and adolescents.* New York: Oxford University Press.

Elkind, D. (1978). "Understanding the young adolescent." *Adolescence, 13* (49), 127-141.

Elkind, D. (1985). "Egocentrism redux." *Developmental Review, 5,* 218-226.

Elkind, D. (1987). "The child yesterday, today and tomorrow." *Young Children,* 42(4), 6-11.

Ellis, H. (1898). "Auto-erotism, a psychological study." St. Louis *Alienist and Neurologist,* vol. 19.

Elson, M. (1987). *The Kohut Seminars.* New York: W.W. Norton.

Enright, R.D., Lapsley, D.K. & Shulka, D.G. "Adolescent egocentrism in early and late adolescence." *Adolescence,* 14(56), 687-696.

Enright, R.D., Levy Jr., V.M., Harris, D. & Lapsley, D.K. (1987). "Do economic conditions influence how theorists view adolescents?" *Journal of Youth and Adolescence,* 16(6), 541-559.

Erikson, E.H. (1946). Ego development and historical change, in *The psychoanalytic study of the child,* Vol. II. Eissler, R., ed. New York: International Universities Press.

Erikson, E.H. (1956). "The problem of ego identity." *Journal of American Psychiatric Association, 4,* 56-121.

Erikson, E.H. (1959). *Identity and the life cycle: Selected papers.* New York: International Universities Press.

Erikson, E.H. (1960). "Youth and the life cycle." *Children, 7,* March/April, 43-49.

Erikson, E.H. (1968). *Identity, youth and crisis.* New York: W.W. Norton & Co. Inc.

Etzioni, A. (1993). *The spirit of community.* New York: Crown Publishers.

Evans, R. (1967). *Dialogues with Erik Erikson.* New York: Harper & Row.

Feldman, R.S. & Custrini, R.J. (1988). Learning to lie and self-deceive: Children's nonverbal communication of deception, in *Self-deception: An adaptive mechanism?* Lockard, J.S. & Paulhus, D.L., eds. Englewood Cliffs, NJ: Prentice-Hall.

Fenichel, O. (1945). *The psychoanalytic theory of neurosis*. New York: Norton.

Fine, R. (1986). *Narcissism, the self and society*. New York: Columbia University Press.

Flach, F. (1988). *Resilience*. New York: Fawcett Columbine

Flaste, R. (1988). "The myth about teenagers." *The New York Times Magazine*, Oct. 9.

Flavell, J.H. (1963). *The developmental psychology of Jean Piaget*. New York: Van Nostrand.

Frank, D. (1983). *Deep blue funk and other stories: Portraits of teenage parents*. New York: Ounce of Prevention Fund.

Freud, A. (1966). The ego and the mechanisms of defense, in *The writings of Anna Freud*. Vol. 2. New York: International Universities Press.

Freud, S. (1914). On narcissism, in *On Metapsychology*. Harmondsworth: Penguin, (1984).

Freud, S. (1932). *The ego and the id*. Vol. 19 of *The standard edition*. London: Hogarth.

Friedenberg, E. (1959). *The vanishing adolescent*. New York: Dell.

Friedman, M.I. & Willis, J.L. (1981). *Human nature and predictability*. New York. Lexington Books.

Fromm, E. (1955). *The sane society*. New York: Holt, Rinehart & Winston.

Fromm, E. (1964). The heart of man. New York: Harper & Row.

Fromm, E. (1939). "Selfishness and self-love." *Psychiatry*, 507-523.

Fromm, E. (1973). *The anatomy of human destructiveness*. New York: Holt, Rinehart & Winston.

Frosh, S. (1991). *Identity crisis: Modernity, psychoanalysis and the self*. London: Routledge.

Furnham, A. & Stacey, B. (1991). *Young people's understanding of society*. London: Routledge.

Fuhrmann, B.S. (1990). *Adolescence, adolescents*, 2nd ed. Glenview, IL: Scott, Foresman/Little Brown Higher Education.

Furman, W. & Werner, E.A. (1994). Romantic views: Toward a theory of adolescent romantic relationships, in *Personal relationships during adolescence*, Montmeyer, R., ed. Thousand Oaks, CA: Sage.

Gallatin, J.E. (1975). *Adolescence and individuality*. New York: Harper and Row.

Gardner, H. (1983). *Frames of mind*. New York: Basic Books.

Gardner, W. (1993). A life-span rational-choice theory of risk taking, in *Adolescent risk taking*, Bell, N.J., ed. Newbury Park: Sage.

Garrod, A., Smulyan, L., Powers, S. I. & Kilkenny, R. (1992). *Adolescent portraits: Identity relationships, and challenges*. Boston: Allyn and Bacon.

Gendlin, E.T. (1987). A philosophical critique of narcissism, in *Pathologies of the modern self*, Levin, D.M., ed. New York: New York University Press.

247

Gilligan, C. (1982). *In a different voice.* Cambridge: Harvard University Press.

Ginsburg, G. & Opper, S. (1979). *Piaget's theory of intellectual development.* Englewood Cliffs, NJ: Prentice-Hall.

Ginzberg, E., Berliner, H.S. & Ostow, M. (1988). *Young people at risk: Is prevention possible?* London: Westview Press.

Glass, D. (1968). Theories of consistency and the study of personality, in *Handbook of personality theory and research,* Borgatta, E.F. & Lambert, W.W., eds. Chicago: Rand McNally.

Goffman, E. (1959). *The presentation of self in everyday life.* New York: Doubleday.

Goldberg, C. (1980). *In defense of narcissism.* New York: Gardner Press.

Goldman, R. (1965). *Religious thinking from childhood to adolescence.* New York: Seabury Press.

Goleman, D. (1985). *Vital lies, simple truths.* New York: Simon & Schuster.

Goleman, D. (1986). Insights into self-deception, in *The pleasures of psychology.* New York: New American Library.

Greenberger, E. & Steinberg, L. (1986). *When teenagers work: The psychological and social costs of adolescent employment.* New York: Basic Books, Inc.

Grice, H.P. (1975). Logic and conversation, in *Syntax and semantics: Vol. 3. Speech acts,* Cole, P. & Morgan, J.L., eds. New York: Academic Press.

Grovetant, H.D. (1993). The integrative nature of identity, in *Discussions on ego identity,* Kroger, J., ed. Hillsdale, NJ: Lawrence Erlbaum.

Gurwitsch, A. (1985). *Marginal consciousness.* Athens, OH: Ohio University Press.

Habermas, J. (1973). *Legitimation crisis.* Boston: Beacon Press.

Hahn, A. (1987). "Reaching out to America's dropouts: What to do?" *Phi Delta Kappa, 69,* 256-263.

Hall, C. (1979). *A primer of Freudian psychology.* New York: New American Library.

Hamburg, D.A. (1992). Today's children: Creating a future for a generation in crisis. New York: TimesBooks.

Hamburg, D.A. & Takanishi, R. (1989). "Preparing for life: The critical transition of adolescence." *American psychologist, 44*(5), 825-827.

Hamilton, V. (1982). *Narcissus and Oedipus: The children of psychoanalysis.* London: Routledge & Kegan Paul.

Hartup, W.W. & Overhauser, S. (1991). "Friendships." *Encyclopedia of Adolescence.* New York: Garland.

Heath, D.H. (1977). *Maturity and competence.* New York: Gardner Press.

Henninger, M.G. (1989). "The adolescent's making of meaning: The pedagogy of Augustine's confessions." *Journal of Moral Education, 18*(1), 32-44.

Hewitt, J.P. (1989). *Dilemmas of the American self.* Philadelphia: Temple University Press.

Hoffer, E. (1951). *The True Believer*. New York: Harper & Brothers.

Holmes, J. & Silverman, E.L. (1992). *We're here, listen to us*. Ottawa: Canadian Advisory Council on the Status of Women.

Horney, K. (1937). *The neurotic personality of our time*. New York: W.W. Norton.

Horney, K. (1939). *New ways in psychoanalysis*. New York: W.W. Norton.

Horney, K. (1942). *Self-analysis*. New York: W.W. Norton.

Horney, K. (1945). *Our inner conflicts*. New York: W.W. Norton.

Horney, K. (1950). *Neurosis and human growth*. New York: W.W. Norton.

Ingersoll, Gary M. (1989). *Adolescents*, 2nd ed. Englewood Cliffs, NJ: Prentice-Hall, Inc.

Inhelder, B. & Piaget, J. (1958). *The growth of logical thinking*. New York: Basic Books.

Irwin, C.E. (1993). Adolescence and risk taking: How are they related?, in *Adolescent risk taking*, Bell, N.J., ed. Newbury Park: Sage.

Jackson, A.W. & Hornbeck, D.W. (1989). "Educating young adolescents: Why we must restructure middle grade schools." *American Psychologist, 44*(5), 831-836.

Jacoby, M. (1990). *Individuation and narcissism*. New York: Routledge.

Johnson, S.M. (1985). *Characterological transformation*. New York: W.W. Norton.

Jones, E.E. & Pittman, T.S. (1982). Toward a general theory of self-presentation, in *Psychological perspectives on the self*, Vol. 1. Suls, J., ed. Hillsdale, NJ: Lawrence Erlbaum Associates.

Josselson, R.L. (1987). *Finding herself: Pathways to identity development in women*. San Francisco: Jossey-Bass.

Kaplan, L. (1984). *Adolescence: The farewell to childhood*. New York: Touchstone Books.

Kernberg, O. (1970). Factors in the psychoanalytic treatment of narcissistic personalities, in *Essential papers on narcissism*, Morrison, A., ed. New York: New York University Press.

Kernberg, O. (1978). "Why some people can't love." *Psychology Today, 12*(1), 54-59.

Kiell, N. (1964). *The universal experience of adolescence*. London: University of London Press.

Kimmel, D.C. & Weiner, I.B. (1985). *Adolescence: A developmental transition*. Hillsdale, NJ: Lawrence Erlbaum Associates.

Kohut, H. (1971). *The analysis of the self*. New York: International Universities Press.

Kohut, H. (1977). *The restoration of the self*. New York: International Universities Press.

Kostash, M. (1989). *No kidding*. Toronto, ON: McClelland & Stewart.

Kroger, J. (1989). *Identity in adolescence*. London: Routledge.

Kubey, R. & Csikszentmihalyi, M. (1990). *Television and the quality of life.* Hillsdale, NJ: Lawrence Erlbaum Associates.

Lage, G. & Nathan, H.K. (1991). *Psychotherapy, adolescents, and self-psychology.* Madison: International Universities Press.

Lapsley, D.K., Enright, R.D. & Serlin, R.C. (1985). "Toward a theoretical perspective on the legislation of adolescence." *Journal of Adolescence, 5*(4), 441-466.

Lapsley, D.K. & Power, F.C. (1988). *Self, ego and identity: Integrative approaches.* New York: Springer-Verlag.

Lasch, C. (1978). *The culture of narcissism.* New York: W.W. Norton.

Lasch, C. (1984). *The minimal self.* New York: W.W. Norton.

Lees, S. (1986). *Losing out: Sexuality and adolescent girls.* London: Hutchinson.

Levine, S. (1987). *Tell me it's only a phase.* Scarborough, ON: Prentice-Hall.

Lewis, H.B. (1987). Shame and the narcissistic personality, in *The many faces of shame*, Nathanson, D.L., ed. New York: The Guilford Press.

Lipsitz, J. (1984). *Successful schools for young adolescents.* New Brunswick, NJ: Transaction Books.

Lloyd, M.A. (1985). *Adolescence.* New York: Harper & Row.

Lockard, J.S. & Paulhus, D.L. (1988). *Self-deception: An adaptive mechanism?* Englewood Cliffs, NJ: Prentice-Hall.

Looft, W.R. (1972). "Egocentrism and social interaction across the lifespan." *Psychological Bulletin, 78*, 73-92.

Lowen, A. (1983). *Narcissism: Denial of the true self.* New York: Macmillan Publishing Co.

Maddi, S. (1989). *Personality theories: A comparative analysis.* Chicago: Dorsey Press.

Madison, P. (1969). *Personality and development in college.* Reading, MA: Addison-Wesley.

Manaster, G.J. (1989). *Adolescent development.* Itasca, IL: F.E. Peacock Publishers, Inc.

Marcia, J. (1987). The identity status approach to the study of ego identity development, in *Self and identity*, Honess, T. & Yardley, K., eds. London: Routledge and Kegan Paul.

Martin, M.W. (1985). *Self-deception and self-understanding.* Lawrence: University Press of Kansas.

May, R. (1961). *Existential psychology.* New York: Random House.

May, R. (1975). *The courage to create.* Toronto, ON: Bantam Books.

McAdams, D.P. (1990). *The person.* San Diego: Harcourt Brace Jovanovich, Publishers.

McGuire, P. (1983). *It won't happen to me: Teenagers talk about pregnancy.* New York: Delacorte.

McWilliams, N. (1994). *Psychoanalytic diagnosis*. New York: Guilford Press.

Mead, L.M. (1986). *Beyond entitlement*. New York: The Free Press.

Miller, A. (1979). Depression and grandiosity as related forms of narcissistic disturbances, in *Essential papers on narcissism*, Morrison, A., ed. New York: New York University Press.

Miller, P. (1989). *Theories of developmental psychology*. New York: W.H. Freeman.

Millon, T. (1981). Narcissistic personality: The egotistic pattern, in *Disorders of personality DSM-III: Axis II*. New York: John Wiley & Sons.

Millstein, S.G. (1989). "Adolescent health: Challenges for behavioral scientists." *American Psychologist, 44*(5), 837-842.

Mitchell, J.J. (1971). *Adolescence: Some critical issues*. Toronto, ON: Holt, Rinehart & Winston.

Mitchell, J.J. (1972). *Human nature: Theories, conjectures and descriptions*. Metuchen, NJ: Scarecrow Press.

Mitchell, J.J. (1973). *Human life: The first ten years*. Toronto, ON: Holt, Rinehart & Winston.

Mitchell, J.J. (1974). *Human life: The early adolescent years*. Toronto, ON: Holt, Rinehart & Winston.

Mitchell, J.J. (1975). *The adolescent predicament*. Toronto, ON: Holt, Rinehart & Winston.

Mitchell, J.J. (1978). *Adolescent psychology*. Toronto, ON: Holt, Rinehart & Winston.

Mitchell, J.J. (1980). *Child development*. Toronto, ON: Holt, Rinehart & Winston.

Mitchell, J.J. (1985). *The nature of adolescence*. Calgary, AB: Detselig Enterprises.

Mitchell, J.J. (1989). *Human growth and development: The childhood years*. Calgary, AB: Detselig Enterprises.

Montagu, A. (1966). *On being human*. New York: Hawthorn Books.

Monte, C.F. (1991). *Beneath the mask*. Fort Worth: Holt, Rinehart & Winston.

Montmeyer, R. (1994). *Personal relationships during adolescence*. Thousand Oaks, CA: Sage.

Moore, K.A. (1982). *Private crisis, public cost: Policy perspectives on teenage child-bearing*. Washington, D.C.: Urban Institute Press.

Moore, S. & Rosenthal, D. (1993). *Sexuality in adolescence*. London: Routledge.

Moriarty, A.E. & Toussieng, P.W. (1976). *Adolescent coping*. New York: Grune & Stratton.

Morrison, A.P. (1986). Shame, ideal self and narcissism, in *Essential papers on narcissism*, New York: New York University Press.

Moschis, G.P. (1978). *Acquisition of the consumer role by adolescents*. Atlanta: University of Georgia.

Muller, H.J. (1960). *Issues of freedom*. New York: Harper & Row.

Musgrove, F. (1964). *Youth and the social order.* Bloomington: Indiana University Press.

Musick, J.S. (1993). *Young, poor, and pregnant: The psychology of teenage motherhood.* New Haven: Yale University Press.

Muuss, R.E., ed. (1990). *Adolescent behavior and society,* 4th ed. New York: McGraw Hill, Inc.

Muuss, R.E. (1982). "Social cognition: David Elkind's theory of adolescent egocentrism." *Adolescence, 17(66).*

Muuss, R.E. (1988). *Theories of adolescence,* 5th ed. New York: Random House, Inc.

Nietzsche, F. (1968). *The will to power.* Kaufmann, W., ed. New York: Vintage.

Nelson, M.C., ed. (1977). *The narcissistic condition.* New York: Human Sciences Press.

Newcomb, M.D. & Bentler, P.M. (1988). "Impact of adolescent drug use and social support on problems of young adults: A longitudinal study." *Journal of Abnormal Psychology, 97(1),* 64-75.

Newman, P.R. & Newman, B.M. (1988). "Differences between childhood and adulthood: The identity watershed." *Adolescence, 23(91),* 551-557.

Nickerson, R.S. (1991). Some observations on the teaching of thinking, in *Enhancing learning and thinking,* Mulcahy, R., ed. New York: Praeger.

Oakes, J. (1985). *Keeping track: How schools structure inequality.* New Haven: Yale University Press.

Ornstein, R. (1992). *The roots of the self.* New York: W.W. Norton.

Ortman, P.E. (1988). "Adolescents' perceptions of and feelings about control and responsibility in their lives." *Adolescence, 23(92),* 913-924.

Otto, L.B. (1988). "America's youth: A changing profile." *Family Relations, 37,* 385-391.

Overton, R. (1991). Formal thought, in *Encyclopaedia of adolescence.* New York: Garland.

Paget, K.D. (1988). "Adolescent pregnancy: Implications for prevention strategies in educational settings." *School Psychological Review, 17(4),* 570-580.

Pagliaro, A.M. & Pagliaro, L.A. (1993). "Knowledge, behaviors, and risk perceptions of intravenous drug users in relation to HIV infection and AIDS." *Advances in Medical Psychotherapy, 6,* 1-28.

Paul, R.W. (1986). Critical thinking in the strong sense and the role of argumentation in everyday life, in *Argumentation: Across the lines of discipline. Proceedings of the conference of argumentation,* van Eemeren, F.H., Grootendorst, R., Blair, A. & Willard, C.A., eds. Dordrecht, The Netherlands: Foris Publications.

Peck, R.F. & Havighurst, R.J. (1960). *The psychology of character development.* New York: John Wiley & Sons.

Peel, E.A. (1971). *The nature of adolescent judgment*. New York: Wiley-Interscience.

Peterson, A.C. (1988). "Adolescent development." *Annual Review of Psychology, 39*, 583-607.

Phoenix, A. (1991). *Young mothers*. Cambridge: Polity Press.

Piaget, J. (1928). *Judgment and reasoning in the child*. New York: Harcourt Brace Jovanovich.

Piaget, J. (1967). The mental development of the child, in *Six psychological studies by Piaget*, Elkind, D., ed. New York: Random House.

Piaget, J. & Inhelder, B. (1958). *The growth of logical thinking*. New York: Basic Books.

Poirier, R. (1971). *The performing self*. New York: Oxford University Press.

Polansky, N.A. (1991). *Integrated ego psychology*. New York: Aldine de Gruyter.

Postman, N. (1986). *Amusing ourselves to death*. New York: Penguin.

Pulver, S.E. (1986). Narcissism: The term and the concept, in *Essential papers on narcissism*, Morrison, A.P., ed. New York: New York University Press.

Putney, S. & Putney, G. (1964). *Normal neurosis*. New York: Harper & Row Publishers.

Quadrel, M.J., Fischoff, B. & Davis, W. (1993). "Adolescent (In)Vulnerability." *American Psychologist, 48*, No. 2.

Raskin, R.N. & Shaw, R. (1988). "Narcissism and the use of personal pronouns." *Journal of Personality, 56*, 393-404.

Roth, P. (1974). *My life as a man*. New York: Bantam.

Rothstein, A. (1984). *The narcissistic pursuit of perfection*. New York: International Universities Press.

Sabini, J. (1995). *Social psychology*. New York: W.W. Norton.

Santrock, J.W. (1990). *Adolescence*. Dubuque, IO: Wm. C. Brown Publisher.

Satinover, J. (1987). Science and the fragile self: The rise of narcissism, the decline of God, in *Pathologies of the modern self*, Levin, D.M., ed. New York: New York University Press.

Schmookler, A.B. (1988). *Out of weakness*. Toronto, ON: Bantam.

Sebald, H. (1984). *Adolescence: A social psychological analysis*, 3rd ed. Englewood Cliffs, NJ: Prentice-Hall, Inc.

Seifert, K.L. & Hoffnung, R.J. (1994). *Child and adolescent development*, 3rd ed. Toronto, ON: Houghton Mifflin Company.

Selman, R.H. (1980). *The growth of interpersonal understanding: Development and clinical analysis*. New York: Academic Press.

Siegler, R.S. (1986). *Children's thinking*. Englewood Cliffs, NJ: Prentice-Hall.

Sigel, E.I. & Cocking, R.R. (1977). *Cognitive development from childhood to adolescence*. New York: Holt, Rinehart & Winston.

Simon, R.W., Eder, D. & Evans, C. (1992). "The development of feeling norms underlying romantic love among adolescent females." *Social Psychology Quarterly*, 55(1), 29-46.

Slovic, P. (1986). Risky assumptions, in *The pleasures of psychology*. New York: New American Library.

Stern, D. (1985). *The interpersonal world of the infant*. New York: Basic Books.

Steinberg, L. (1989). *Adolescence*, 2nd ed. New York: Alfred A. Knopf.

Stiffman, A.R., Earls, F., Robins, L.N., Jung, K.G. & Kulbok, P. (1987). "Adolescent sexual activity and pregnancy: Socioenvironmental problems, physical health and mental health." *Journal of Youth and Adolescence*, 16(5), 497-509.

Stolorow, R.D. (1986). Toward a functional definition of narcissism, in *Essential papers on narcissism*, Morrison, A.P., ed. New York: New York University Press.

Strauss, A. (1959). *Mirrors and masks*. Glencoe, IL: Free Press of Glencoe.

Sullivan, H.S. (1953). *The interpersonal theory of psychiatry*. New York: W.W. Norton.

Thornburg, H.D. (1982). *Development in adolescence*. Monterey, CA: Brooks/Cole.

Tice, C.H. (1989). "Youth opportunity: A private sector investment in prevention." *Children Today*, 18(2), 20-23.

Toulmin, S.E. (1977). Self-knowledge and knowledge of the self, in *The self*, Mischel, T., ed. Oxford: Basil Blackwell.

Wadsworth, B.J. (1989). *Piaget's theory of cognitive and affective development*. New York: Longman.

Wallach, M. & Wallach, L. (1985). "How psychology sanctions the cult of the self." *The Washington Monthly*, Feb., 46-54.

Walliman, I. (1981). *Estrangement*. London: Greenwood Press.

Webber, M. (1991). *Street kids*. Toronto, ON: University of Toronto Press.

Wegner, D.M. & Vallacher, R.R. (1980). *The self in social psychology*. New York: Oxford University Press.

Weiss, E. (1950). *Principles of psychodynamics*. New York: Grune & Stratton.

Weiss, P. (1980). *You, I, and the others*. Carbondale: Southern Illinois University Press.

Wexler, D.B. (1991). *The adolescent self*. New York: W.W. Norton.

Whitbourne, S.K. (1991). "Intimacy." *Encyclopedia of Adolescence*, 19. New York: Garland.

William T. Grant Foundation, Commission on Work, Family and Citizenship. (1988). *The forgotten half: Non-college youth in America*. Washington, D.C.